THE WIRE-CUTTERS

the Wire-Cutters

BY MOLLIE E. MOORE DAVIS

with an introduction by Lou Halsell Rodenberger

TEXAS A&M UNIVERSITY PRESS
COLLEGE STATION

First Texas A&M University Press edition, 1997
Manufactured in the United States of America
All rights reserved
04 03 02 01 00 99 98 97   5 4 3 2 1

Originally published in 1899 by Houghton, Mifflin and
Company, Boston and New York

The paper used in this book meets the minimum requirements
of the American National Standard for Permanence
of Paper for Printed Library Materials, Z39.48-1984.
Binding materials have been chosen for durability.

Library of Congress Cataloging-in-Publication Data

Davis, M. E. M. (Mollie Evelyn Moore), 1852–1909.
    The wire-cutters / by Mollie E. Moore Davis ; with an
introduction by Lou Halsell Rodenberger. — 1st Texas A&M
University Press ed.
        p.   cm.
    ISBN 0-89096-796-2
    1. Frontier and pioneer life—Texas—Fiction.   2. Ranch
life—Texas—Fiction.   3. Cowboys—Texas Fiction.   I. Title.
PS1516.D25W57   1997   97-33380
813' .4—dc21   CIP

To
T. E. D.

CONTENTS

INTRODUCTION

BY LOU HALSELL RODENBERGER

Contrary to the perception of most literary historians interested in fiction of the West, it was a Texas woman writer who produced the first serious Western novel. In introductions to reprints of *The Virginian,* critics frequently refer to the author, Owen Wister, as a myth-maker who established permanent criteria for the fictional cowboy hero. A Harvard graduate who spent the summer of 1885 in Wyoming recovering from mental depression, Wister is lionized as the creator of the classic Western. More emphatically, he is credited with establishing authentic patterns of characterization and action for cowboy novelists who followed. *The Virginian* was published in 1902.

A year later, Andy Adams, who had come to Texas from Indiana in 1882, explored cowboy life in Texas and on the trail in *The Log of a Cowboy.* J. Frank Dobie designates this narrative "the classic of the occupation," although he admits it is "a novel without a plot, a woman, character development, or sustained dramatic incidents." Both novels are entertaining and admittedly pacesetting, but Mollie E. Moore Davis, who grew up in Texas, beat both writers to the draw.

The Wire-Cutters, although not recognized as a bench-mark for future Westerns by critics, contains most of the fictive elements of the genre. The novel was published in 1899, three years before Wister's work appeared. Unlike Andy Adams' narrative, Davis structures *The Wire-Cutters* with all of the imaginative character-istics that Dobie perceives is missing from Adams' tale. The novelist tells an engaging story, creates realistic characterizations of both women and men, and develops dramatic subplots, which include a violent mur-der, a gun battle, a search for a lost child, and an arson arrested in progress, all common to popular percep-tions of frontier experiences.

In this work, Mollie Davis depicts life on the Texas ranch frontier in the 1880s with both humor and obvi-ous understanding of Texas' early settlers, often called "briar-breakers." In her characterization of the novel's protagonist, Roy Hilliard, Davis introduces a young South Carolinian who has come to Texas to be a suc-cessful cattleman. Davis's hero embodies all of the traits that later became the stereotyped characteristics of the fictional cowboy. According to critic W. H. Hutchinson, the Western hero possesses "self-reliance, individual-ism, acceptance of danger, disdain for class distinctions, pride in country, and a self-imposed obligation to aid those in distress" (p. 517). The failures and successes of Davis's would-be cattleman, who subsequently finds himself reluctantly involved in the infamous Texas Fence Cutting War, provide material for development of both an admirable hero and an intricate plot. The author's own observations of the Texas frontiersman's capacity for both neighborliness and mindless violence informed the timely theme of this narrative.

It is true that before *The Wire-Cutters* appeared, Thomas Pilgrim, who wrote under the pseudonym of Arthur Morecamp, created "the live boys," Charlie and Nasho. In his fiction, Morecamp relates the adventures of two boys, a Texan and a Mexican, as they go up the cattle trail to the Indian Territory in Kansas. Although *The Live Boys; or, Charlie and Nasho in Texas,* published in 1878, and Morecamp's second juvenile, *The Live Boys in the Black Hills* (1880), introduce the idea of the trail drive as setting and episodic, rowdy adventures as plotmakers for Western fiction, other writers of the period seemed unimpressed. If they wrote Westerns, they were of the dime novel variety or fashioned with pulp markets in mind. No novelist before Mollie E. Moore Davis had experienced the realities of frontier ranch life as personally as she. Moreover, her understanding of motivation behind frontiersmen's actions adds a dimension no other writer of literary Westerns would explore until Dorothy Scarborough wrote *The Wind* in 1925.

Inspired by local skirmishes in the Fence Cutting War, which Davis is sure to have followed during one of her annual summer visits to her brother Tom's home in Comanche County, Texas, the novelist creates in the newcomer Roy Hilliard a believable hero who sees both sides of the conflict. During the drought of 1883, deliberate nightly raids destroyed ranchers' fences, which increased animosity between free-range advocates and legitimate landowners. The raids also provided enter-

tainment for countless footloose young men who suc-
cumbed to the leadership of charismatic outlaws act-
ing on private agendas. Controversies over land and
water rights would later become an overused motif in
Western novels, but Davis was the first to recognize
the human drama in this conflict and its possibilities
for fictional re-creation. Furthermore, Davis knew from
personal experience that eager visionaries who came
to Texas to find the good life were often in for the disappointment that the enthusiastic Hilliard soon faces.
Her father, John Moore, was cursed with "itchy feet,"
as old-timers designated the urge of restless family men
always searching for their main chance. Moore moved
his family from failure to failure in Texas all of Davis's
early life.

Born on April 12, 1844, Mary Evelyn, who changed her
name to Mollie when she began publishing poetry as a
teenager, arrived in Texas from Talladega, Alabama, with
her parents and brothers a few weeks before her twelfth
birthday. After crop failures at Manchaca in Travis
County in 1856 and on a farm near the origin of the
San Marcos River the next year, John Moore, a country
doctor and failed businessman, resettled his family near
Tyler, Texas, in the fall of 1857. Here, despite continued poverty, Mollie's parents were able to send her to
school for a few brief months. By age sixteen, Mollie
was teaching school and publishing her poetry regularly in Texas newspapers.

In 1861, Mollie, at seventeen, was beginning to gain
statewide attention for both her poetry and her short

stories. E. H. Cushing, who owned the *Houston Weekly Telegraph,* recognized her talents, undeveloped as they were. He and his wife invited her to come to Houston for an extended visit with his family. Her difficult trip alone by stagecoach proved worth it for Mollie.

At the Cushing's elegant home, which had an extensive library, she acquired social know-how and satisfied her eager appetite for knowledge. Although Mollie returned home regularly to assist her ailing mother with family responsibilities, she spent much time with the Cushings for the next five years. Her visits to Houston gave her the opportunity to become friends with a number of young women who, like Mollie, loved books and aspired to be writers. Among them was Aurelia Hadley Mohl, already contributing critical articles on prominent poets of the time to the *Telegraph.* Three decades later, in 1893, Mohl would become chief organizer of the Texas Women's Press Association, which would provide much needed support for Texas women writers and contact with professional women who were publishing regularly.

With the encouragement of this Houston network of young women writers and the sponsorship of the Cushings, Mollie's work began to gain attention across the South. When her family moved in 1866 to Galveston, where her mother died, Mollie assumed responsibility for the younger children in the family until she met Major Thomas E. Davis, a graduate of the University of Virginia and a former officer in the Confederate army. They were married in October, 1874. A year later, Major Davis's tobacco business failed, and the couple moved to Houston, where Major Davis went to work at the *Telegraph*. In 1887, Thomas Davis was appointed editor-in-chief of the newly established Houston *Telegram*.

By 1879 the Davises had settled in New Orleans, where their home would be for the rest of their lives. Major Davis had accepted the job of editorial writer for the *New Orleans Times* and was soon appointed editor-in-chief, a position he held for the next twenty-five years. Mollie's reputation as a poet was already established when they arrived. In 1869, a three-page biographical critical study of her work was included in *Living Writers of the South,* where she was praised for lack of sentimentality and judged to be both Southern and Western in her style and subject matter.

Such a judgment so early in her career is significant. Despite her early life in Alabama, Mollie Davis had become a thorough Texan before her marriage. However, after she arrived in New Orleans, she discovered that the often snobbish Creole society of the city was unaccepting of Texans fresh off the frontier. Davis soon saw that it was best to let stand the impression among her acquaintances that she grew up on a Southern plantation in East Texas. Soon, the young matron was opening her French Quarter home to prominent writers, actors, and artists and became famous for her February Friday receptions where Southern literati gathered during the Mardi Gras season. By 1899, when *The Wire-Cutters* was published, Davis was a popular Southern writer, already author of three collections of poems, a play, a collection of short stories, and *Under the Man-*

Fig (1895), a well-received novel set on the Brazos River in Texas. One volume of her work, designated as "semi-autobiography," which she titled *In War Times at La Rose Blanche* (1888), reinforced the notion that Davis was of genteel background, a product of Southern plantation life.

Like Katherine Anne Porter later, she said nothing to change the impression that she was of aristocratic birth, even among her biographers. Nevertheless, the hard-scrabble life she had led as a child and her frequent visits to her brother Tom's home at Proctor in Comanche County, Texas, provided a tough reality that, providentially, influenced both the content and the style of her best fiction. Davis suffered from lung problems most of her adult life. New Orleans' summer humidity and heat increased her discomfort. Traveling by train to Waco and from Waco to Comanche County by freight wagon was difficult, but spending summer months in the higher and drier area led to better health for the writer. This region was considered to be the western ranch frontier in the 1880s. It is more accurately described today as the western edge of Central Texas.

As arduous as the trip to west Central Texas was, Davis felt rewarded when she arrived at her brother's home, although, obviously, she was not there for a rest cure. In an extant fragment from her journal, Davis reports:

> Got up early and went deer hunting with Tom. Rode about nine miles 'thro' brush and brake' but saw very little game—no deer at all. We brought home

some squirrels and partridges. The ride, thro' the
fresh, dewy morning hours! Oh, that was worth
something! Everything looked as if it were 'made
over.' The sky had that wonderful blueness I have
never seen anywhere but in San Antonio; the hill-
sides were green with the tender green of spring
and there was a perfect blaze of flowers everywhere.

In this journal, which the author's niece Mollie Moore
Godbold transcribed and gave to a descendant of Mollie
Davis at Christmas in 1955, Davis continues with de-
tailed descriptions of the flowers she saw and adds that
"Tommy kept me amused with his hunting stories and
his tales of the adventures and happenings of frontier
life."

Clearly, in West Texas Mollie felt right at home. Her
journal reveals both her strong sense of place in descriptions of this landscape she obviously loves, and
her keen writer's eye in her careful, witty portrayals of
people and events she observed. One afternoon, she
reports that she spent "an hour or so" listening to the
tales of Old Ned, a veteran of both the Texas Revolu-
tion and the Mexican War. Later, Old Ned was in
Comanche feeling "just a little mellow and holding forth
to a lot of men on the public square concerning his visit
with me." One can see Mollie Davis smiling, pleased,
as she continues:

He said that, by George, he had known Henry
Clay and Calhoun and Webster and heard'em all
speak, but he had never heard anybody as *eloquint*

as Mollie Moore. He said, furthermore, that if he was twenty-five and had a million dollars, and Mollie Moore for a wife, by George, he would just start out and conquer the whole world!

Such careful attention to character and speech as well as her understanding of human motivation, as revealed in this journal, provided the essentials for Davis's realistic portrayal of a South Carolina native, educated to be a Southern gentleman, who heads to West Texas to make a life with "a fortune into the bargain," he believes. *The Wire-Cutters,* a sentimental romance so long as the setting is the South becomes, after the first sixty pages, a realistic reflection of life as it really was for young men visionaries on that frontier.

In all probability, Davis was familiar with the battle with fence cutters that a gutsy woman had fought in 1883 to save her ranch in nearby Coleman County. Mabel Doss Day, a young widow, owned the largest fenced ranch in Texas when the Fence Cutting War started. Trampled to death in a cattle stampede, Day's husband left her with a 78,000-acre ranch to manage and a $117,000 debt to pay. When she formed a corporation and brought in money from investors in Kentucky, where she had gone to school, the Coleman County free-range supporters saw her fences as representative of what bringing in "Northern capitalism" could mean for the Texas cattleman.

Day hired a gunman to ride her fences, confronted the raiders as they lounged in Coleman City bars, and wrote scathing letters to newspaper editors. Her lobbying along with that of other ranchers suffering the same fate finally persuaded Texas governor John Ireland to call a special session of the legislature in January, 1884. Fence cutting was declared a felony and punishable by one to five years in prison. After four disastrous months in which ranchers endured at least $20,000,000 in losses of fences and cattle, the Fence Cutting War ceased.

In an essay on his grandmother's life which appeared in the West Texas Historical Association *Year Book* in 1950, James T. Padgitt, grandson of Mabel Day, quotes an unattributed newspaper clipping which he found among Day's letters. Without a doubt, the events in this story provided Mollie Davis with inspiration for the plot of her novel. The article declares that the men "who destroyed Mrs. Day's fence were outlaws in the fullest sense of the word." It continues:

> The chief fence cutter in this country was considered as the 'boss' and seemed to be running everything pretty well his own way until he stole McCreight's cotton and skipped the country. He was said to have been the leader and since his flight from the country, we have heard of no more fence cutting in that section. His conduct caused those thoughtless boys, who were following his leadership, to stop and think about what they were doing—and there could be but little doubt but what much fence cutting has been done by thoughtless boys, who have followed the leadership of older heads. (p. 58)

Mollie Davis's novel develops this theory in her explo-
ration of the charismatic Deerfield's ability to lead most
of the young men in Crouch's Settlement into outlawry.
As a villain, Deerfield excels in shrewd knowledge of
human psychology. Davis's development of the events
that lead to Deerfield's downfall and the subsequent
shame exhibited by his pliable young followers reveals
her own intelligent understanding of human behavior.

Davis introduces all of the elements of the classical
Western in the rivalry that develops between the out-
sider Deerfield and Hilliard. As in real life, some of the
ranchers who fenced their land ignore small landowners who had acquired land bordered on all sides by the
rancher's acres. Country roads are blocked by fences.
Hilliard takes up the cause of the wronged landowners, as a true cattleman must, and faces down the fence
builders' foreman. But he rides out during the daytime.
He condemns the night raids, refusing to participate,
declaring that most of the fencing is legitimate enclo-
sure of purchased land. Finally, he loses face among
all of the young men who once had been his admirers.
Hilliard's decency prevails despite the young outlaws'
willful destruction of his property and his loss of most
of the male population's good will.

Although the events of the fence cutting debacle
provide much of the major action in the novel's plot,
the strength of the work lies in Davis's creation of the
Western hero. In addition, the novel demonstrates the
author's command of technique in her witty characterizations of community eccentrics, her inclusion of epi-

sodes reflecting the folk culture of the region, and her obvious understanding of the difficulties of women's lives on the frontier.

Proof of Davis's ability to create believable, entertaining characters are her portrayals of the good-hearted Amen Bagley, the bickering Parsons brothers, Red and Green, the community outcast grave digger Abner Croft, and the diminutive Reverend David French, who proves heroic despite his size and furthers the cause of the 'Piscopals at Peleg Church. Faithfully recreating the vernacular and idioms of West Texans of her time, Davis integrates into the main plot narratives of the search for the lost child, the baptizing in No-Bottom Hole, and the annual measuring of a country road. Davis describes folk methods of searching for water, raising a submerged body, building a water tank dam, and "cutting-out" eligible girls after church services.

Most revealing of Davis's realism in her fictional portrayals of Western life are her empathy with women on the Texas frontier and her understanding of their life. She portrays the women in this novel as hard-working and uncomplaining. They often demonstrate a redemptive sense of humor. Davis's most graphic description of the contrast between men and women's lives in Crouch's Settlement reflects her observations of the life her sister-in-law Sallie led. Thomas Moore, Davis's brother, was the community postmaster, distributing mail at his home. Mollie Davis describes her response to men fence sitters who daily invaded her sister-in-law's home expecting a meal:

Sallie, my sister, has become a very sedate and a very sweet and patient woman. Indeed I wonder at her. The house is never emptied of visitors—men mostly—that stay for dinner and supper and breakfast—that tramp over her clean floor and wake her baby . . . She herself says this is a kind of paradise for men (who work for three months of a year and amuse themselves the rest of the time) but a hard country for women. . . . Sallie, like all the rest, does her own milking, scrubbing, washing, ironing, sewing, etc., besides having a baby every three years!

In several other entries, Davis wonders at Sallie's fortitude.

In the novel, these observations are reflected in Davis's assessment of Mrs. Crouch's life, which is dictated by the garrulous hospitality of husband Billy who welcomes all comers to his table. On the day that the settlement loungers arrive to hash over the fence cutting news, Davis describes Mrs. Crouch as "making no pretense of farm-work." Instead she and her daughters spend the day in the kitchen as Billy greets the idlers and draws water for their horses. The novelist adds, "It may be remarked that Billy never dreamed of drawing water for Mrs. Crouch."

Flawed though *The Wire-Cutters* is by its improbable, romantic beginning and conclusion, Davis, after the first sixty pages set in the South, switches to dramatic realism when her hero arrives in the West and creates an admirable prototype of the Western hero before Wister had set pen to paper. A realistic portrayal of the tragedies associated with the Texas Fence Cutting War, a gripping murder story, and a witty revelation of the daily life of West Texas settlers, *The Wire-Cutters* deserves recognition as the first serious Western, which established for the first time the criterion for the Western hero.

NOTE

The author gratefully acknowledges the generosity of John B. Meadows, a direct descendant of Mollie Moore Davis's brother, Thomas Moore, and chairman of the board of the Texas Historical Foundation, who provided a copy of Davis's journal and Clyde Winfield Wilkinson's 1947 dissertation, "The Broadening Stream: The Life and Literary Career of Mary Evelyn Moore Davis," which includes an accurate biography of the novelist. To Margaret Waring, director of the Comanche Public Library, goes the author's sincere appreciation for her enthusiastic sharing of her knowledge of Mollie Davis.

FOR FURTHER READING:

Brady, Patricia. "Mollie Moore Davis: A Literary Life." In *Louisiana Women Writers,* edited by Dorothy H. Brown and Barbara C. Ewell, pp. 99–118. Baton Rouge: Louisiana State Univ. Press, 1992.

Gard, Wayne. "Fence Cutting." In *The New Handbook of Texas,* vol. 2, pp. 976–77. Austin: Texas State Historical Association, 1996.

Hutchison, W. H. "The Cowboy in Short Fiction." In *A Literary History of the American West,* edited by J. Golden Taylor et al., pp. 515–22. Fort Worth: TCU Press, 1987.

Padgitt, James T. "Mrs. Mabel Day and the Fence Cutters." *Year Book,* pp. 51–67. West Texas Historical Association, 1950.

Rodenberger, Lou. "The Novel of the Cowboy." In *A Literary History of the American West,* edited by J. Golden Taylor et al., pp. 523–34. Fort Worth: TCU Press, 1987.

THE WIRE-CUTTERS

THE WIRE-CUTTERS

I

THE PORTRAIT

Mrs. Hilliard met the messenger at her front gate.

She had seen him from an upper window, coming along the plantation road, his open buggy almost overtopped by the tall cane on either side. She felt sure that the coatless person in blue linen trousers and panama hat, who approached in a leisurely fashion warranted by the heat of the September afternoon, was the bearer of the long-expected decision. She turned, trembling, from the window, seized by an almost irresistible impulse to rush into an inner room, close and lock the door, and so at least postpone the inevitable revelation. The next moment she had caught up a garden hat and was descending the broad stairway, pale but composed, at least in outward appearance. She waved back the negro lad who had started on a run to open the gate, and passed swiftly along the shaded carriage-drive.

Lilla Hilliard, thus advancing to meet the de-

cree which, according to proper calculation, should
restore her to freedom, but which, on the other
hand, might condemn her to a lifetime of mortification and wretchedness, was an extremely beautiful young woman. A little past two and twenty
years of age, she was tall and erect, with a slight
yet well-rounded figure, which swayed, as she
walked, like a lily on its stem. Her head was
crowned with a luxurious mass of blond hair rippling away from a somewhat narrow but very white
forehead. The delicate lines of her eyebrows, distinctly darker than her hair, arched above eyes of
a clear, almost startling blue. The perfect oval
of her face was unmarred by seam or dimple. Her
mouth and chin alone arrested unsatisfactory attention. These suggested something indefinable — a
something which meant firmness or hardness, according to the more or less lenient judgment of the
observer.

Her black gown trailed on the shelled drive,
making no noise, but her light footsteps echoed
loudly in her own ears, and her heart beat audibly
as she drew near the tall iron gates. The buggy
had come to a halt in the road outside. A moment earlier the driver, a sallow young man with
shrewd black eyes, a sharp nose, and a wide, expressive mouth, had loosed his tongue for a halloo
and a ready curse on the tardy negro gate-opéner.
But at sight of the mistress of Eastwood he
jerked on his coat and leaped to the ground.

"Good-day, Mrs. Hilliard," he said respectfully,

taking off his hat as he approached. His face betrayed, in spite of himself, his intimate acquaintance with her affairs.

He lifted the heavy bar, and one of the gates swung slowly outward.

"How do you do, Mr. Milgrove," she returned, with haughty resentment of his knowledge. "You come, I presume, from Mr. Ralston?"

Milgrove drew back the hand which he had instinctively put out. "I left Mr. Ralston this morning," he said, a slight flush rising to his thin cheeks. He turned to the buggy and took some papers from a small leather bag lying on the seat. "Mr. Ralston wished you to have these as soon as possible, Mrs. Hilliard, and I volunteered to bring them over." This time his face was impassive, showing no familiarity with the contents of the official-looking envelope which he handed to Mr. Ralston's client, or of the suit whose result it announced, and whose details were far better known to the lawyer's clerk than to the principals themselves.

"Thank you." Mrs. Hilliard spoke calmly, but Milgrove's keen eyes noted the vise-like grasp of her slim fingers around the envelope which fluttered visibly against her bosom.

He was chagrined at seeing her turn away, without a second glance at himself. He looked after her as she moved obliquely across the well-kept lawn and passed up the steps into the house. His face darkened; he recalled his eagerness in offer-

ing to take the hot twenty-mile drive from St.
Denis, where the court had been sitting, to Eastwood plantation; he remembered the airy visions
which had beguiled that drive! He had foreseen
himself called into the stately library at Eastwood
to read and explain to its beautiful chatelaine the
important document of which he was the bearer,
— perhaps to give legal advice, or even counsel of
a personal and more intimate character; he had
basked in advance in the sunshine of her lovely
eyes! He smiled, grimly humorous, at a reality
which left him standing — a forgotten lackey —
without the gates. "Oh, very well, Lady Lilla,"
he muttered. "Our account may stand over."

"Mis' Lilla say please come in, Mist' Milgrove.
Yo' dinner gwine to be served in de co'se o' present'y; an' yo' nag fed an' fresh-up, befo' you
drives back to town."

Samp, the negro lad, threw open the gates as he
spoke; and Milgrove stepped into his buggy and
drove up the circular carriage-way to the house.

It was not until she had reached the library and
closed the door behind her, that Mrs. Hilliard
broke the seal of the bulky envelope. There was
a letter within, in the lawyer's well-known handwriting, and a copy of the final decree issued by
the court in the case entitled: *Lilla Hilliard vs.
Leroy Hilliard. Petition for Absolute Divorce.*
Her lips whitened as she glanced over the page.
Its technical phrases made but a confused impression on her agitated senses. But the conclusion

was unmistakably clear. The plea was granted, unconditionally. She was free, and privileged to resume her maiden name.

She dropped the paper, sobbing hysterically, and covered her face with her hands. But almost instantly her sobs ceased. She arose and walked deliberately to her own writing-desk placed in the sunny curve of a bay-window, and drawing a sheet of paper toward her, she wrote her new name, — that name she had renounced three years before to assume the one she now so gladly discarded. It had an oddly familiar look, — *Armstead, Lilla Armstead*. She wrote it several times in the slender, delicate characters then in vogue, and continued to gaze at it with fascinated eyes, while Ralston's personal letter slipped from her lap and lay on the floor at her feet.

. . . .

Lilla Armstead was barely eighteen when Leroy Hilliard came from his home in South Carolina on a prolonged visit to Eastwood Plantation. His father and her own had been friends and class-mates at college, and it was not without a secret intention on the part of Henry Armstead that the young people were thus familiarly thrown together. He watched the first meeting between his mother-less girl, and only child, and the son of his old friend, hardly able to repress his delight upon seeing how exactly the superb young pair seemed mated. Lilla's blond beauty and fragile grace had never indeed showed to such advantage as

when contrasted with the dark comeliness and
massive strength of the young Carolinian.

Hilliard was rather below the medium height,
but the perfect proportion of his powerful sinewy
body almost invariably made him seem taller than
the men around him.   His features, though open
and engaging, were strongly marked; the square
chin showed great firmness, — perhaps obstinacy;
the perpendicular furrow on the broad forehead
was an open warning of a hot temper.   But the
head, with its close-cropped bronze curls, was a
fine one, nobly poised upon the supple neck, and
the tawny brown eyes had a singular look of softness beneath the black brows and lashes, — like
the unexpected gleam of a mountain tarn beneath
wild and rugged cliffs.

An ardent hunter, an excellent horseman, graceful in the dance as in the *salle d'escrime*, gay,
daring, responsive, and masterful, small wonder
was it that this well-born, wealthy, and cultivated
stranger should have caught, almost from the moment of his arrival, the fancy of beautiful Lilla
Armstead, — the spoiled and petted queen of Eastwood.   The attraction was mutual; the wooing
short and impetuous.   The June roses were blooming when Hilliard first came riding, like a knight
of romance, along the levee-road to the great old-
time plantation-house on the Mississippi River.
In September, after a brief return to his paternal
home in Carolina, he came again to claim his promised bride.   The wedding was celebrated with

unusual pomp and ceremony at Eastwood. The
stately mansion, famous for its hospitality, threw
wide its doors for this occasion to a brilliant array
of guests from the city and from the surrounding
parishes. The humbler folk of the neighborhood
were feasted during two whole days in ample tents
on the lawn; the Eastwood negroes entertained in
their own quarters the coachmen, body-servants,
maids, hostlers, and other retainers who swelled
the wedding-train. When the newly married pair
— walking on roses — descended the veranda steps
to the carriage which conveyed them to the boat-
landing on the river, there was among all these
guests and dependents but one opinion: here at
last was that rare and wonderful happening, a
suitable match!

Mr. Armstead, who was already in failing health,
lived long enough to see his son-in-law display extraordinary ability in the management of the vast
sugar-plantation. This completed his own satisfaction and self-gratulation. He died, having but
one longing left ungratified, — the desire to hold
in his arms, before he looked his last on fair Eastwood, an heir to its broad acres.

The heir did not come, either before or after
Henry Armstead's death. But in its place was
born something which soon waxed lusty enough
and terrible enough to drive Hilliard into long
absences from home, and change his wife into a
pale shadow of her former self. His scowling face
startled more than one belated traveler hurrying

along the country roads at midnight; his voice, grown harsh and defiant, echoed in disreputable squabbles over card-tables and across rude bars in the little town of St. Denis, twenty miles from Eastwood; he made frequent trips down the river to the city, and came back wearing each time a more dare-devil expression on his dark, handsome face. Meantime, Lilla, white and reserved, sat alone in her pew in the small neighborhood church, drove alone in her carriage, flitted alone — a sad-eyed ghost — about the silent rose-garden at East-wood.

What was the trouble? Whence or whose the influence which wrought these monstrous effects? No one could divine. But that there was serious discord between this apparently perfectly mated pair was only too evident. People at first were too amazed to say "I told you so." But it presently began to be remembered that Leroy Hilliard had been known to flash into inexplicable rage over some commonplace trifle; and that at such times he was not a pleasant person to deal with. His losses at the gaming-table were reported, and exaggerated, — a man surely does not become a gambler in a day! He had been seen reeling, under the influence of liquor, across the gang-plank of the river-packet to the landing, — it takes time to make a drunkard! The case became plain enough to friend and gossip. Hilliard was a game-ster, an unfaithful husband, a sot, a wife-beater. Lilla, whose fine reticence concerning her troubles excited general admiration, was surely an unselfish martyr!

After two and a half years of such married life, this abhorred husband disappeared altogether, leaving his horses in the Eastwood stables, his other personal and private belongings in the Eastwood mansion, his reputation to any tongue that chose to wag, and the bitter secret of their difference in the breast of the woman whom he had called his wife.

Mrs. Hilliard followed for some months the dreary routine to which she had accustomed herself; seeing no one, rarely stirring abroad, companioned only by Miss Bolton, the old maiden aunt who had, after her mother's death, assumed nominal care of her. At the end of six months she took a step.which fairly electrified the community, — it may almost be said, the entire State. She made application for a divorce.

At that time, some forty-five years ago, the very word *divorce* was spoken, if spoken at all, with bated breath; the thing itself carried with it all manner of ignominy and disgrace. It seemed incredible that a member — a woman! — of a proud old family like the Armsteads should so scandalize public opinion! But Mrs. Hilliard, consulting no one but Edmund Ralston, her father's trusted lawyer, held quietly on her way in the matter. The most rigid moralist, indeed, could hardly blame the young creature, who for more than two years had suffered every indignity which a cruel and dissipated husband could heap upon her. The affair, which was most delicately managed, brought her in the long run almost universal compassion, — a compassion which was tinged with a certain awe of her courage.

The charges against Hilliard, it was understood, were ill-treatment and abandonment. The case dragged a little; everything, even the courts of justice in those leisurely days, moved with dignified slowness. Hilliard filed no answer to the charges against him. He maintained an obstinate silence, and failed to put in an appearance when the case was called. And now, after some eight months of waiting, the injured wife held in her hand the order of the court granting her absolute freedom.

She read Ralston's letter. It was filled with formal advice and stately congratulations.

"With a stroke of the pen, my dear Lilla," he said, "the past has been set at naught." But had it? "And you may now order your life as may best suit you. I trust you will do this wisely. I will come to Eastwood within the week," he concluded, "and there confer with you in person on all matters further pertaining to this and other business."

She seized her pen again and wrote a few lines in reply, then leaned idly back in her chair, flushed and happy. A hummingbird circled above her head, and darted out again through an open window. She followed its flashing flight with her eyes;

then with a sudden impulse, she rose, pushed open
a blind, stepped out upon the veranda, and walked
rapidly down the steps into the rose-garden at its
farther end.

When she reëntered the house, she wore on her
fair hair a wreath of crimson rosebuds. A fanci-
ful girdle of the same flowers, intertwined with
feathery sprays of the cypress-vine, encircled her
slender hips; the heavy, half-blown buds emitted
a warm perfume and glowed like molten embers
against the dead black of her gown. She looked
suddenly barbaric and splendid.

"Why, Lilla!" exclaimed Miss Bolton, who
encountered her unexpectedly in the hall. Miss
Bolton was a small, dark-skinned, black-haired,
shriveled-looking old body, with humped shoulders
and timid dark eyes. She stood in great awe of
her dead sister's child, — the tall, fair, imperious
Lilla, who "took after" her father's people.

"Yes, Aunt Pauline," Lilla said, smiling and
stooping to drop a careless kiss upon the dark
cheek, "I have gone out of mourning! I am
celebrating the happiest moment of my life. I
am Lilla Armstead once more; and I am *free —
free — free!* "

She passed on, humming the refrain lightly.
Miss Bolton hurried on to the storeroom whither
she was bound, her bunch of housekeeping keys
jingling at her waist. She wiped her eyes furtively, terrified at the thought of Lilla seeing the
tears which she could not repress; for whatever

the rest of the world thought of Leroy Hilliard,
Aunt Pauline loved him. To her he had been
invariably gentle and chivalrous. He was the only
human being, the little old creature told herself
passionately, who now seemed to remember her
existence. And Lilla — But here she stopped.
Even to herself she dared not formulate the
thought!

Aunt Pauline, strange to say, was not entirely
alone in her kindly judgment of the absent. Here
and there about the parish there were men — and
women — who had a genuine liking for the black
sheep, in spite of his admitted faults and mad
follies. There were children who cherished him
fondly in their solemn little souls; one, at least,
wailed herself sick when told that he had gone
away, for ever and ever. The negroes at Eastwood
without exception adored him. His occasional
outbursts of violence seemed but to deepen their
awesome affection for him. On one occasion, a
powerful black giant, named Jerry, — the leader
of the field-gang, — received for some misdemeanor
a chastisement at his hands, almost brutal in its
severity. Such occurrences were rare, a master
in those times seldom coming in direct contact
with his slaves; the report of it flew abroad, and
the same night a negro from a neighboring plantation condoled loudly with the supposed sufferer,
coupling his sympathy with a curse on the master.
In an instant, Jerry's sledge-hammer fist had
felled the unfortunate visitor to the ground.

"Name o' Gawd, Jerry," growled the discomfited sympathizer, scrambling to his feet, "what mek you do dat?"

"Shet yo' big mouf, nigger!" roared Jerry, hot with wrath. "Marse Roy kin lay de lash on my back whenever an' however it suit him. You heah me? An' ef you don't clar yo'se'f out'n dis quarter, I gwine ter brek ever' bone in yo' fool body!"

The house-servants had discussed among themselves the unaccountable absence of the master. They had been for months vaguely aware that something inimical to him was in progress in "de co'te," and resented the fact fiercely. When, therefore, Mrs. Hilliard entered the dining-room where Samp was respectfully attending Hannibal the butler, who was rather superciliously attending the lawyer's clerk, two keen pairs of eyes besides Milgrove's own instantly remarked the change in her manner and appearance.

She stopped near the table where Milgrove was sitting, with a bottle of wine before him. He arose and stood in a waiting attitude. "I have a letter for Mr. Ralston," she began; "will you" —

"I am at your service, Mrs. Armstead," he interrupted, with a significant pause on the last word.

Samp pricked up his ears and tipped a wink to the butler, who on the entrance of his mistress had become abnormally dignified and polite. He glided into the pantry and thence made a bee-line for the kitchen, bursting with news.

Lilla smiled and blushed. The smile went far toward dissipating the poison which had gathered in Milgrove's soul. The infinitesimal drop which remained had entirely evaporated in the aura which surrounds a beautiful woman, by the cool of the evening when he stepped once more into his buggy and started on his return drive to St. Denis.

His hostess watched him pass down the brown dusty road, between the fields of rustling blue-green cane; then she went back to the library. The rosebuds on her head and about her waist had opened wide their velvet petals, and showed their golden hearts. She looked at herself in a pier-glass with a smile of satisfaction. Surely she had never been more beautiful! She was young, and she was free! At the thought, a face hitherto resolutely banished from her mind seemed to flash out and shine, exultant, beside her own in the mirror. Life stretched out in an enchanting vista before her.

She turned and swept her eyes triumphantly around the room, as if calling even the inanimate objects around her to witness her happiness. She started back with a sharp cry. A yellow glow from the sunset sky fell almost weirdly upon a portrait of Leroy Hilliard, which stood on an easel in an obscure corner. His dark face looked out at her from within the gilt frame. She tried to turn away, but his eyes — those deep, meaning eyes — held her spellbound; the unfathomable

smile on his lips terrified her into silence. She
stood for many minutes, like one paralyzed, face
to face with him and with their mutual past.
Scene after scene crowded upon her memory, — a
series of hideous nightmares, confused but vivid,
which jostled against each other, clamoring for
notice; snatches of words, wooing, passionate,
scornful; looks tender, reproachful, withering;
delirious kisses; echoes of bitter laughter; velvet
touches of caressing fingers; the hot clinch of a
stern hand on her wrist! She crouched at length
to the floor, bowing her head to her knees, unable
longer to bear his wrathful, questioning gaze.

Suddenly a quiver passed along her inert limbs;
she threw up her arms, shaking her clenched fists
in a sort of frenzy, and uttering inarticulate spas-
modic sounds. She sprang up and bounded to a
cabinet, wrenched open the locked door, and seized
a Sicilian knife, a silver-hilted dagger which
formed a part of Hilliard's own collection of for-
eign weapons. Turning again to the portrait, she
paused a moment. Her livid face expressed the
cunning fury of a wild beast; her eyes blazed with
a green light; her breath came and went in short
labored gasps. "You — dare — ah " — The disjointed words choked her. She slashed the keen
blade furiously across the pictured face. The
heavy frame lunged forward under the blow and
fell with a crash, dragging the easel with it.

Miss Bolton, startled by the sound and by the
shriek which echoed through the silent house,

rushed into the room. She found her niece stretched, unconscious, on the floor, with the dagger clutched in her hand, her brow death-white beneath its crown of fading roses.

A deep cut across the cheek gave a curiously sinister look to Hilliard's face. Lilla Armstead, recovering consciousness, shuddered as she looked at it. The mutilated portrait, by her order, was carried to the garret, and there left to the companionship of other discarded and forgotten things.

II

THE CHILD

When, a little more than a year after her legal separation from Hilliard, Lilla Armstead married again, there was a universal note of disapprobation. It was one thing for a woman to sever the tie which bound her to a brute; it was quite another for her to defy world-old prejudice by venturing her neck a second time under the yoke. True — the unseemliness of the proceeding aside — it was difficult not to admit that here was a match still more "suitable" than the former one. Francis Deerford was not a stranger, but a prosperous young planter whose handsome estate was separated from Eastwood by the yellow flood of the Mississippi. He had known his fair neighbor from his and her own childhood; he had wooed her with a gallant persistence which, though fruitless, certainly merited success; and at the time of her marriage with Hilliard he had gone abroad, making no secret of his disappointed hopes. His second and successful wooing, indeed, — though frowned upon on principle, — excited covert admiration. It was even said as time passed on, and Mr. and Mrs. Deerford continued to live in harmony at Eastwood, that Lilla's first marriage had been an arbitrary arrangement of her father's, and that in her inmost heart she had never loved Hilliard; or that her feeling for him at most was that of the moth under the baleful glamour of the lamp, or of the charmed bird for the rattlesnake.

Deerford was tall, slender, and blond like his wife; he was openly vain of his good looks, and narrow in idea, with certain petty traits of character which made his mild rule at Eastwood as odious as Hilliard's stormy one had been popular. For the rest, he was good-tempered, agreeable, and courteous; a lover of books, moderately fond of sport, hospitable, — an ideal country gentleman, in short, and nearly everything which poor Leroy Hilliard had contrived not to be, — or at least to appear!

Deerford's fondness for his wife was excessive. Her own naturally cold nature responded to this warmth with an ardor which surprised herself. They were, perhaps, as nearly absolutely happy as it is given to mortals in the uncertain estate of matrimony to be. Deerford's business management of Eastwood, which now included his own inherited acres, was as admirable as had been that of his predecessor; the plantation flourished; only an heir to its wide fields and outlying woodlands was wanting. This was a source of keen regret both to husband and wife, — the one flaw in the clear crystal of their wedded lives. But even this did not disturb the tranquil years which drifted over fair Eastwood mansion, where, except by insignificant little Miss Bolton, Leroy Hilliard was as utterly forgotten as his own mutilated portrait in the dust-strewn garret.

One day in late April Mrs. Deerford was lying on a low lounge drawn into the bay window of the library at Eastwood. She had been three years the wife of Francis Deerford; these years had but given an added grace to her beauty; their unbroken sunshine seemed to have brightened the glory of her hair and ripened the red of her perfect lips. At the moment, however, she was slightly pale, and an unusual languor pervaded the graceful white-clad form nestling amid the embroidered cushions. The window-blinds were drawn, for the noon sun was hot, but the sash was open, and the perfume of damask roses mingled with honeysuckle floated in on the river breeze, which stirred the muslin curtains. The lounger reached out a slender hand and turned the slats of the jalousied blind.

"The smell of the honeysuckle makes me ill," she said a little fretfully, moving her head nervously from side to side.

Aunt Pauline, darker and more withered and shrunken than ever, looked up from her tambour-frame. "I like the smell of honeysuckle, myself," she said absently. "Your mother and I used to wear it in our hair " — she stopped suddenly, aware of having expressed an individual opinion.

"I — I mean — I heard a boat whistle at the boat-landing about an hour ago, Lilla," she added, irrelevantly.

"So did I," returned Mrs. Deerford. "It screeched like a demon. I believe that is what gave me this splitting headache."

"Poor darling! Can I do anything for you, Lilla?" asked Miss Bolton timidly.

"No." The monosyllable was decisive and unmistakably cross. Aunt Pauline bent her head again over the woolen roses she was stitching into canvas. Her niece clasped her hands above her head and stared up at the ceiling with wide-open eyes; their blue was intensified by heavy purple half-moons beneath them; there was a drawn look about the corners of her mouth.

"She is really ill," thought Miss Bolton, glancing furtively at her. "I never saw her ill before. What shall I do? Oh, what shall I do!"

Her alarmed meditations were interrupted by a sound which sent an unaccountable shock through her own small body. The sound in itself was ordinary enough, — the galloping beat of a horse's hoofs on the hard road which led past the lawn gates. These hoof-beats echoed loudly on the still air; then, growing fainter in the distance, died at length into silence.

Mrs. Deerford sat up, pressing her hand to her heart, her ear straining toward the closed window, her startled eyes fixed upon her aunt, who stared wildly back at her.

"It sounded like — I thought it was" — stammered the older woman, after a long pause, trembling still from some inner excitement.

Mrs. Deerford sank wearily back among her cushions. "How perfectly ridiculous you are with your fancies, Aunt Pauline," she said, closing her eyes to prevent further conversation.

Deerford at the same time was riding about his fields, — his regular morning occupation, — inspecting work, overlooking improvements, directing important operations. He had grown somewhat stouter, and sat his easy-going, well-groomed horse with the careless slouch of a man who lives much in the saddle, but does no hard riding. The growing cane, rustling in the breeze, allowed a far-reaching view of the level fields with the dividing ditches, where the springing weeds marked the symmetrical squares with a fringe of darker green. Gangs of laborers were at work among the cane-rows; the dark blue blouses of the men and the gaudy turbans of the women made bright spots of color in the landscape. The roof of the plantation-house, with its great dormer windows, and a glimpse of the pillared galleries below, showed in the distance amid sheltering trees. The planter's eyes roved over the scene with satisfaction, fixing themselves at length on the tall sugar-house chimneys under the horizon, red and massive against the noon sky. "I must send over to the landing for that new boiler. I heard the boat whistle some time ago," he mused, touching his horse's

flank lightly with his spur. A grove of pecan-
trees jutting out from a bit of uncleared woodland
made a sharp curve in the road before him. As
he turned the curve he came face to face with
Leroy Hilliard.

Hilliard, who had been called out from Carolina
on important business, which related solely to
his own affairs, had calculated the possibility of
encountering Deerford, when, in order to save
valuable time, he had taken the short cut across
Eastwood plantation, from the boat-landing to
St. Denis. He was therefore prepared for the
momentary meeting. His face preserved its impassiveness as he thundered past on a huge black
horse which was glistening with foam. A single
glance, an almost imperceptible inclination of the
head, — the instinctive courtesy of the well-bred
man, — and he had swept out of sight.

Deerford reined back his horse with a grip
which threw the animal on his haunches. When
Hilliard had disappeared, he sat for a moment
with his hands resting on the high pommel of his
saddle like one suddenly turned to stone. Then
recovering himself with an effort, he rode on to
the house. Had his wife been quite well, she
could not but have remarked his unwonted agitation. He found her lying on the lounge in the
library, alone; for, at his approach, Miss Bolton
had fled to her own room. There, kneeling by
her bed, she was weeping the gentle tears of age,
and praying for the welfare of him whose image

had arisen mysteriously, but with startling vividness, on her mind.

Deerford did not mention Hilliard's reappear-
ance. And neither then, nor at any time of her
life, did his wife know that the incarnation of her
wretched past had galloped in bodily form before
her gates.

Hilliard indeed remained but a few hours in the
vicinity. He returned by a more circuitous route
to the landing, and left the same afternoon for the
city.

"He come like a comic, Marse Roy did," black
Jerry afterward remarked wistfully, "an' he went
like a comic. But he is jes' de same! He ain'
tu'n a hair."

Even Deerford had had time in their brief meeting to note that the hated face was unchanged; or
rather that the slight lines of care had vanished;
and the cheeks, awhile back swollen by dissipation,
had regained their healthy glow.

In January of the following year there was
extraordinary rejoicing in the stately home so long
echoless of childish voices. An heir was born, —
a sturdy, strong-limbed boy, whose first cry pierced
the stillness of the house like a shrill trumpet-call.

Mr. Deerford's overseer, by the master's order,
proclaimed a general holiday for the plantation
negroes; and Mr. Deerford himself, standing on
the veranda, announced the name of his first-born
to the throng of house-servants and field-hands

assembled in the yard below, — *Francis Armstead Deerford*. A distribution of small gifts and generous drinks at the quarters further commemorated the joyous event.

Within the house, Mrs. Deerford was gazing eagerly at the small head lying for the first time in the hollow of her arm. The light from a blazing wood fire in the fireplace played over her own fair locks, deepening their sheen, and touched the curiously thick curls on the new-born infant's head.

"Why, he has black hair!" she suddenly exclaimed, with a movement of distaste.

"So he has," said Aunt Pauline, hovering over him. "So he has. He will take after your mother's family. We are all black-haired. At least, my dear," she added quickly, seeing that she had managed as usual to say the wrong thing, "I mean — his hair is black now, but it will change, of course. A baby's hair is always black. But it will be blond. Oh, of course."

"Do you think it will? Are you sure?" appealed Lilla, with unusual gentleness in her voice.

Some days later, she called her nurse. "Look, Maum Dicy," she said, "what is this?" She traced with her slender forefinger the thin red mark across the boy's soft cheek.

"Dat?" sniffed the experienced nurse. "Dat ain't no more 'n a wrinkle, Mis' Lilla. Don't you be frettin' 'bout dat. It 'll smoove out, by time lil Marse Francis is got his eyes fair open."

But the child's hair did not change its color, and the thin scarlet line on the left cheek did not smooth out. The dark curls grew darker, as the tender skin whitened and the baby features lost their first look of vacuity. The small jaw squared itself; the brow broadened; a pair of soft brown eyes looked out from beneath long black curling lashes. And, slantwise across the left cheek, the slender line showed itself like a lightning streak, when Francis Armstead Deerford became angry. And angry he often was, though for the most part a lovable, cooing, dimpled bit of humanity.

No one noticed it for a time, or no one seemed to notice it, — the strange likeness of the young heir of Eastwood to Leroy Hilliard. Doubtless the servants — those lynx-eyed despots whose presence we ignore, and who hold us in the hollow of their hands — saw it earlier, and seeing it, discussed it among themselves.

But the boy was wearing his first short frock, and standing by a chair alone, with his mother hovering near, with anxious outspread arms, the day Mrs. Deerford first remarked her son's startling resemblance to the man so long banished from her life. The thing came upon her without warning, and like a lightning-shock. They were all assembled in the library. Deerford leaned against a corner of the mantel, his eyes fixed with a brooding gaze upon his wife's laughing face. Miss Bolton sat on the edge of a sofa watching the child and trembling with suppressed joy. The September sunlight, streaming in at the open windows, enveloped his rosy little body with warm radiance. A hummingbird darting in through the lattice-work of honeysuckle vines circled on iridescent wing above him. He threw back his head, open-ing wide his tawny eyes, and laughed, — a low, musical laugh which sounded like a far-away echo of the laughter which had once filled the room.

Mrs. Deerford started and turned instinctively to her husband. A flash of sudden and painful recognition leaped from one pair of blue eyes to the other. Deerford flushed, turned on his heel, and left the room without a word. Miss Bolton sprang forward and caught Francis, who had loosed his grasp on the chair and was tottering uncer-tainly on his sturdy little legs. And seeing the mother absorbed in thought and apparently obliv-ious for once of the child's presence, she bore her treasure away to her own room, for there was a strange, almost pathetic tie between lonely Aunt Pauline and the dark-haired boy of Eastwood. He rewarded her furtively displayed adoration with a defiant challenging affection, which amused stran-gers, but hitherto had secretly irritated his mother; he rarely showed in her presence those bursts of anger which touched into color the birth-mark on his cheek. His first attempt at speech had been her name. He clung to her now, patting her with-ered neck and cooing softly: "Pau-yeen! Pau-yeen!"

Meantime, Mrs. Deerford remained as if rooted

to the spot where she had stood when the revelation came to her. Her pale lips framed silently and over and over the question "What does it mean? What can it mean?"

She asked herself the question so often during the next two years that she sometimes felt as if she were mad. She watched the growing child with a sort of terror; the brown yellow-glinted eyes and the masterful streaked face fascinated and repulsed her. The mother-love within her wrestled with something almost akin to hatred for this monstrous alien who had stolen unawares into her life. At times, when the boy was out of her sight, she persuaded herself that the hideous likeness existed only in her excited imagination; but with his presence the conviction returned, each time with more telling force. She studied her husband furtively and incessantly; and she could not long blind herself to the fact that he had ceased to show either love for the son or pride in the heir so eagerly welcomed. She found herself breathlessly planning and contriving to keep the child out of his father's sight, as if the little creature were some accursed thing.

Deerford's affection for herself, however, showed no diminution; and when, a year after the birth of young Francis, a second son came to them, he lavished upon the blond babe — a blended image of himself and Lilla — a wealth of tenderness well nigh delirious in its intensity.

One day the two boys were at play in the nur-

sery. Francis was then about three years and a
half old, — a beautiful, bold, and defiant little
being, already aware by some subtle instinct that
his brother Allan was preferred before him. He
looked up at his mother, who was watching them,
from under drawn, sullen brows. The look made
her shudder; she *remembered* it so well! "Am I
torturing myself needlessly," she exclaimed inwardly, "or is the likeness really there!" Even
as the thought flashed through her brain Francis
stooped, and in pure wantonness set his white teeth
savagely in Allan's bare shoulder. Mrs. Deerford
snatched the screaming child to her breast with
a cry; and in a transport of rage struck the ag-
gressor furiously upon the mouth. Then ashamed
and terrified, she fled from his uplifted silent questioning face, leaving the brothers together.

An hour later, she paused in her long monotonous walk up and down the front veranda; she
stood a moment in uncertain thought, then she
mounted the stairs again to the nursery. The
nurse was sewing by the window; Allan lay sleeping quietly in his crib bed, his yellow curls flowing
over the pillow. Francis sat on the floor playing
with some tin soldiers. He looked up as his mo·
ther entered. The scarlet line on his cheek had
faded to its normal dull pink color; his large eyes
were soft and tranquil.

"Come, Francis," Mrs. Deerford ordered author-
itatively, holding out her hand.

He regarded her in grave silence, but did not
move.

"Come with mother, Francis," she continued in a coaxing tone. He got up instantly and placed his small brown fist in her white palm.

She led him down the long hall and opened a closed door near the end. She hesitated a moment before the short flight of steps within; then ascended rapidly, drawing the child after her. He toiled up, planting first one foot and then the other upon each step. "Don't yun so fas', muzzer," he cried at length, frowning up at her. She looked down at him with unseeing eyes and hastened on.

The garret at the head of the stairway was one long room, whose low unceiled roof almost touched the intruder's head. It contained a heterogeneous mass of rubbish, — the accumulated un-throw-awayable stuff of several generations of Armsteads. It took Mrs. Deerford some time — stepping about in the dust unmindful of her trailing gown — to find what she wanted. Francis seized upon an ancient rocking-horse, shouting with delight as he dragged it about.

Finally, Lilla came upon the portrait; it was lying face downward upon a huge packing-box. She lifted it and set it upon the floor, leaning it against the wall where the light from the low attic window fell full upon it. The gilt frame was tarnished, the pictured face was obscured by dust and cobwebs. She brushed these off carefully with her handkerchief, then sank on her knees in front of it.

"Francis!" She turned to beckon the boy to her, but he had already approached quietly and was standing unbidden at her elbow. She drew him with her arm and gazed long and searchingly from Leroy's dark visage, with the disfiguring cut across it, made by her own hand, to the blooming young face, marred only by its birth-mark, resting against her shoulder.

"Pitty man! Pitty man!" lisped the boy, touching the portrait with the tips of his fingers.

"It is true! Oh, it is cruelly true! God help me!" moaned the kneeling woman, with a sob in her throat.

The unconscious pressure of her arm hurt and angered the child. He faced her, scowling, the red line leaping, as it were, into vividness on his cheek.

At that moment a slight noise disturbed the stillness of the room. Mrs. Deerford looked up. Her husband was standing in the doorway.

"Lilla?" There was an agonized question in his voice as he came slowly forward.

"Oh, I hated him, Francis! I loathed him!" she cried, answering the unspoken question. "I loathe his memory! But — oh — you see!" she sobbed hysterically with her face on his breast, "the child — the child!"

"Yes, I see. I have known from the first — almost," he replied gravely. He seemed about to say more, but checked himself, and drew her away with soothing words and tender caresses. They passed arm in arm down the stair, leaving the child alone and forgotten in the dusty garret. An hour later Aunt Pauline found him there. He was sitting before Hilliard's portrait, babbling to it with the innocent confidence of babyhood.

III

CAST OUT OF THE NEST

WITHIN the next six months, Deerford effected the sale of Eastwood and all its belongings, including the negroes, with the exception of a few of the house-servants. This unexpected transaction caused considerable comment, but Deerford was known to be a shrewd business man, and many of his friends afterward gave him credit for a discernment which he did not possess. In reality, he noted no more than the planters around him the gathering clouds which preceded the storm of the Civil War. He was actuated solely by a dread — shared by his wife, though in secret, for the matter was never openly discussed between them — lest his older son's extraordinary resemblance to Leroy Hilliard should, in the course of time, become a subject of comment. So far, the nursery walls had effectually barred neighborhood gossip. But when nursery days should be over, what then? "I dare not risk it," Deerford concluded, appalled at the thought.

He left Eastwood with his family as soon as possible after the transaction was concluded which gave the old Armstead plantation a new owner.

The birth of a daughter — a miniature copy of
the still beautiful mother — celebrated their in-
stallment into their newly purchased home, — a
handsome house with ample grounds, situated near
a rural town in the State of Kentucky.

The sense of restraint which had long oppressed
the husband and wife passed suddenly. Even
the black-haired alien seemed to have lost the
power to disturb the tranquil atmosphere of the
new home. Unloved, rarely noticed, except by
Aunt Pauline, he was at least no longer a menace;
and his presence in the household was suffered, his
physical needs, as always, scrupulously supplied.

The tempest was over; the skies so long over-
shadowed were once more clear and sunny!

Deerford occupied himself with the final settlement of his affairs and the investment of his
money, finding himself a very rich man, and gave
as yet a rather careless attention to the rapid
course of events which were hurrying on the inevitable conflict between the States.

The summer of '61 had set in. The fall of
Fort Sumter and the excitement which followed
had sent a thrill of excitement through the little
town near which the Deerfords had settled. Deerford himself drove or rode in daily to hear the
latest news concerning the gathering armies. One
afternoon he returned home, bringing with him a
guest, — a Mr. Richard Allington, an elderly man
who had known Lilla's father, and who had visited
Eastwood both before and after her marriage with

Hilliard. He had, it appeared, been living for some years in England, but had hurried over to look after some property, unsafe, perhaps, in the event of war. He was genial and talkative; the early country dinner was prolonged far beyond the usual sitting; the red slanting rays of a setting sun flooded the great gallery as he came out with his hosts, all in unwontedly joyous mood, and stood looking about him.

"Fine children, Mrs. Deerford," he observed heartily. "Uncommonly fine children." He glanced at the group assembled on the lawn in front of the steps. Mabel, the baby girl, sat on the nurse's knee; Francis, with his arm about her and his black locks touching her blond curls, had his eyes fixed in an ecstasy of childish admiration upon his younger brother Allan. Little Allan, clad in a single light garment that left his arms and his rosy little legs bare, was dancing to the music of a mouth-harp played by a negro boy. A wreath of blood-red roses crowned his fair hair. He swayed to and fro, throwing out his small hands and tossing his head with the grace and abandon of a young fawn.

"A beautiful child," said Mr. Allington, watching him, "and very like his mother. Your older son, madam," continued the old gentleman amiably, "resembles his father remarkably, re-markably. I knew Hilliard quite well. Fine fellow he was, too. Pity he died," he added reflectively and quite unconsciously.

Mrs. Deerford flushed painfully. Deerford made a casual remark, which changed the current of his guest's rambling talk.

It is but fair to record that Mr. Richard Allington, learning later the facts of the case, was so shocked at his own indiscretion that he took to his bed and came near dying.

"Lilla," said Deerford, entering his wife's dressing-room a week later. Something in his tone caused her to look up hastily. He held an open letter in his hand. He did not glance at her as he proceeded. "I have here a letter from my cousin Mary, Mrs. Wright. You will no doubt remember that she has lived for some years in New York city. She has no children of her own. She is now a widow, and she has consented " — he paused a second to clear his throat and went on hurriedly — "consented to take Francis for — for a while. I wrote her that the boy was high-tempered and unmanageable, and that I — we — wished to remove him for a time from association with my — with the other children. You will understand, my dear," his hard voice softened a little, but immediately hardened again, "that this is only a temporary arrangement, and that you can see the — the child at any time you may desire. I shall take him myself to New York. I will start to-morrow, if you will have him ready. It is for the best," he concluded, looking his wife full in the face for the first time.

"Yes — it — is — for — the — best," she gasped. She watched him go out and close the door behind him. Then she arose and walked about the small room, the prey to feelings so intermingled that she could not herself understand or analyze them. She was conscious of a deep pang of self-reproach as a small face rose before her inner vision, and a pair of soft eyes looked wistfully at her. She was at the same time horribly conscious of a wave of relief, immense, inexpressible, which surged over her.

The next day, when the carriage which bore her first-born into exile left the gates, she wept bitterly. She leaned from an upper window and watched it as long as she could see it whirling along the turnpike road. But when it was quite out of sight, she looked down at Allan and Mabel playing on the shaded lawn below, and drew a long breath. She felt, in spite of herself, as if a chain which had bound her chest had snapped asunder, leaving her heart liberty to beat. Then she cowered to the floor and lay there prone, like a guilty thing.

It was Aunt Pauline, bewildered by this inexplicable step, and who, strange to say, had been blind to the boy's mysterious resemblance to Hilliard, who truly mourned and truly wept.

Deerford, in the railway coach, saw to the boy's wants, but otherwise paid as little attention to him as possible; he sat in a corner of the seat brooding gloomily, and hardly glancing out of

the window at the signs of excitement everywhere
visible.

Tents were gleaming white, here and there,
under the horizon; a strange flag was flying from
buildings in the towns; raw recruits were crowding
the platforms at the stations; soldierly-looking men
got off and on the train; boys, passing along the
aisles of the coaches, were selling newspapers with
startling head-lines; the battle of Bull Run had
just been fought.

Deerford looked at last with feverish eyes at a
paper he held in his hand. "When I am free,"
he muttered; he looked at the little boy, who was
kneeling upon the seat opposite, staring with all
his might out of the window, "when this weight
is off my mind, I will have time to think. The
burden of the last ten days has been more than
I could bear." He groaned aloud.

Suddenly his form straightened as if by an inner
spring. A paragraph in the column of dispatches
had arrested his attention. It was dated at Rich-
mond, Virginia, and read thus: —

"Captain Leroy Hilliard has received his com-
mission as Colonel of the ——th Regiment of South
Carolina Volunteers. Colonel Hilliard, who has
raised and equipped this regiment largely at his
own personal expense, is at present at B——, his
old home, near which his men are encamped. He
expects to receive marching orders within the
week."

Deerford dropped the paper and remained for

some time lost in deep thought. He roused himself with a sigh to examine a railway guide. Later, he had a consultation with the conductor, and some time during the same night he quitted the train, carrying the sleeping child in his arms.

IV

FACE TO FACE

COLONEL LEROY HILLIARD'S office, pending the enlistment and organization of his regiment, was in a small room, formerly sacred to the women-folk in the old Hilliard mansion at B——. Certain tokens of femininity still lingered there, but the pile of official documents on the small desk, the maps unrolled upon the table, the silk flag tossed carelessly over the back of a chair, the sword and sash which Hilliard himself had just taken off and placed on the low mantel, — all this gave a look of business — and disorder — to the ancient boudoir, of which the originals of the portraits on the walls (slim ladies with short waists and looped-up curls) would certainly have disapproved. But there was no woman at hand to resent the disarray or question the intrusion of business into her territory. Hilliard dwelt alone, with his retinue of servants, in the old house. His mother had long been dead, and his only sister was married and lived in another part of the town.

The summer night was warm, and the master of the house opened the window-blinds to the faint breeze, before taking his seat. The only other

occupant of the room, a tall gray-haired old man
with a benignant face and keen deep-sunken eyes,
who sat on a lounge, smoking, looked at the
newly appointed colonel with frank admiration.
Hilliard was now in the prime of manhood. His
thick hair and drooping mustaches were slightly
powdered with gray, the furrow on his forehead
had deepened, there were lines about his mouth
which gave it a look of sternness. But his figure
was lithe and erect in his close-fitting gray uniform, a youthful color came and went in his cheeks,
his brown eyes retained their winning softness.

"You are a good-looking young dog, Roy," said
Doctor Greaves earnestly, taking his pipe from
his mouth.

"A dog, and good-looking, I grant you, Doctor," returned Hilliard, laughing, "but, alas, no
longer young!"

"Oh, to an old fellow like me" — the doctor
shrugged his shoulders and leaned back among the
cushions, leaving the sentence unfinished. Hilliard drew up a chair and sat down.

"When do you leave?" the older man asked,
with a quick return to seriousness.

"I am expecting orders from the War Depart-
ment at any moment. Impatiently, I confess.
The regiment is fully equipped and in fine condition, but the men are growing restless under their
enforced inactivity. They — I may say we — are
anxious to get into the thick of things."

"They will not 'hanker' so ardently by this

time next year." Doctor Greaves smiled as he made this prophecy.

"This time next year!" echoed Hilliard. "You confounded old croaker! we shall have wiped the Yankees out of existence and got back to our plough-handles inside of six months."

Doctor Greaves shook his head.

"But look at Bull Run, Doc," argued his companion excitedly. "And it stands to reason, with such a beginning when our troops are raw and inexperienced, that when they are fairly drilled and disciplined we shall be able to make quick work of bringing the weak-kneed North to terms."

The old man's heart stirred at the ring of boyish enthusiasm in the speaker's voice.

"My dear Roy," he said, laying his hand impressively on the gray-clad shoulder, "never undervalue your foe, and particularly in this instance. You are fighting, God save us! against men of your own race, your own blood, your own temper — your very brothers! Does it stand to reason, as you say, that an imaginary line drawn across this great country from east to west will leave all the brave men on the one side of it, and all the cowards on the other? No, no! The common ancestry who gave to the one section tough fibre and hot blood has been no less liberal to the other, you may depend upon it. Prepare yourself for a stubborn and bloody conflict. I see, with the eyes of age, dim as they are, many things which are hidden from yours by the dancing of

banners and the glitter of bare blades; I hear
ominous cries which for your ears are drowned in
the beat of the drum and the loud call of the
trumpet."

Hilliard listened respectfully. That he was not
convinced was evident from the remonstrant tone
in which he began, after a short pause: "But the
cause for which the South has taken up arms " —

He was interrupted by a low knock on the closed
door. His body-servant, a staid, middle - aged
negro man, presented himself in response to his
master's ringing "Come in."

"A gentleman to see you, Marse Roy," he said;
"a gentleman with a " —

"Very well, Robert. Show him into the library." Robert bowed respectfully and withdrew.
"Doubtless a courier from the camp. I will not
have him brought in here to interfere with what
may be our last evening together for a long time,
Doc; but I must see him at once."

He rose as he spoke, and had taken a single
step forward, when the door was thrown violently
open again, and Francis Deerford appeared on the
threshold. He carried the little boy Francis in
his arms; both father and son were travel-stained
and weary-looking. Deerford, usually so elegant
in his dress, was unkempt and unshaven. His
face was pale and distorted, his eyes were blood-
shot. He stepped across the room and set the child
on the floor at Hilliard's feet. Then he stood back
and regarded him for a moment in silence.

"I have brought you your child, Leroy Hilliard," he said, in a thick, muffled voice.

Hilliard stared at him, speechless with amazement. "What do you mean?" he demanded at length, with a questioning frown.

"I have brought you your child, Leroy Hilliard," Deerford repeated. "Look at him! Look at him, and deny him if you dare!"

Hilliard turned mechanically and gazed down at the small face lifted wonderingly to his own. But he literally saw nothing. A mist of rising wrath blinded his eyes.

"I desire you distinctly to understand," Deerford went on, and something in his tone and manner compelled Hilliard to listen, "I desire to impress upon you above everything that I hold my wife absolutely blameless " —

"Your wife!" echoed Hilliard, puzzled beyond expression.

"I know my wife to be as spotlessly pure in thought, as white and unsullied in soul, as if this child — your child and hers! had never been born. If she surrendered herself to your hellish passion during my absence " —

"Good God, Deerford!" exclaimed Hilliard, recoiling as from a blow, "are you mad!"

" — she submitted to brute force alone. Of that I am as sure as that I stand here in the presence of a brute, and she remains as innocent in my eyes as if her stainless body — oh, my God, my God! — had never been cursed with the weight of this

miserable image of yourself.   God knows how she
has suffered.   God knows the torture I have endured for the past four years.   Now, it is your
turn.   I cannot make your heart bleed drop by
drop in agony, as hers has done.   I cannot place
you upon the rack where I have lain, but I have
brought you your child, Leroy Hilliard, that you
may at least understand why you die the death of
a dog and a ravisher."

His voice had risen to a hoarse shriek, his lips
foamed as the torrent of words poured from them.
As he concluded, he thrust his hand into his bosom
and leaped forward; Hilliard, with a quick movement, caught his wrist; a pistol-shot rang sharply
on the air, and a ball, hurtling upward, buried
itself in the ceiling.

Hilliard's grasp on the white wrist tightened;
with the other hand twisted in the madman's collar,
he forced him backward upon his knees.   There
was a gurgling sound in the throat against his
powerful knuckles.

"*Leroy!*"   The doctor's warning grasp and
authoritative voice penetrated his frenzied senses
just in time.   He loosed his hold; the kneeling
man rolled heavily to the floor, where he lay for
a second, gasping painfully.   Then he got upon
his feet slowly, and stood looking about him with
dazed eyes.

"Go," said Hilliard sternly.   "Go while you
may."

Deerford did not move.   His pale lips parted,

and a few incoherent words escaped them. His
hands wandered, trembling, over his breast, trying
mechanically to smooth his disordered garments.
There was a strange, almost pitiful droop in his
shoulders. Doctor Greaves laid a hand on his
arm, and drew him quietly from the room, and
out of the house into the front garden. There,
as if seized by some sudden impulse, he shook
himself free, and rushed precipitately into the
street, muttering as he went.

Hilliard had dropped upon a chair, utterly unnerved by Deerford's monstrous accusation and
the fierceness of his assault.

Little Francis had remained standing in the
middle of the room, where his father had placed
him on entering. He had cowered at the report
of the pistol, and his eyes had widened in terror
during the short struggle which followed between
the two men. But he had stood quite still, and
silent. A short sob escaped him now, as Doctor
Greaves, coming back into the room, lifted him in
his arms and placed him on the lounge.

"You mustn't cry, little man! Are you hungry?" The old doctor placed his palm under the
small square jaw and lifted the tear-stained face.

"No." Francis choked back his sobs bravely
and shook his head. Seeing a pleasant pair of
eyes so near his own, he smiled brightly, showing
his jagged white teeth.

"Thirsty, then, eh? sleepy? tired?"

"No, no, no; was so'gers on ee twain wif but-

tons an' guns, an' shiny sings," he added confid-
ingly. Poor little man! It was the first time for
three days that he had looked into a kindly face.
"I *yike* so'gers."

"Do you? So do I "—

"An' guns, an' shiny sings. I *wish* I had
some shiny sings to play wif, an' guns!" The
small head was turned on one side, and a smile,
intended to be deeply cunning, parted the red lips;
the brown eyes were fixed hungrily on the sheathed
sword, with its glittering hilt, lying upon the
mantel.

Doctor Greaves chuckled understandingly. He
took the sword and laid it across the little boy's
knees. "Here's your plaything, Mr. General,"
he said. "Doesn't it shine, though! And look
at the tassel! Now, mind you, keep quiet, sir,
while I talk to the soldier yonder. Understand?"

Francis received the sword with a cry of delight.
He hugged it to his bosom and nodded a grave
acquiescence to the old man's admonition.

Doctor Greaves seated himself opposite Hilliard,
and regarded him for a time in silence.

"Leroy," he began finally, and there was a hint
of stern reproof in his voice, "is this boy yours?"

Hilliard lifted his head and looked proudly into
the face of his dead father's friend. "Doctor,"
he said solemnly, "I swear to you by the memory
of my mother, that I have never even seen Lilla
— Deerford's wife, since the day I left her, nearly
two years before she was married to another man."

"I believe you, my boy," returned the old man quietly, "fully and unreservedly. But tell me of her," he continued, divining that the young man, who was as a son to his own childless age, was feeling — unconsciously to himself, perhaps — the need of open speech. "You have told me so little of your — of that episode in your life. Did you love her?"

Hilliard's laugh was a bitter one. "Love her?" he echoed. "Yes. At least I thought I did. She was young and beautiful; what more does a boy of twenty-two ask in a wife! Yes," he went on in a gentler tone, "I loved her, and I thought she loved me. Why else should she, so sought after, so courted and caressed, why else should she have married me? But we were no sooner man and wife than her love — or whatever the feeling was which she had for me — seemed to turn to hatred — a bitter, vindictive hatred, which made my very presence loathsome to her. She could not hide her horror of me, — indeed, she did not try to do so. I will do her the justice to say that I believe this feeling was uncontrollable. I think I must have been, in some subtle and un-reasoning way, physically and spiritually antipa-thetic to her. And certainly she roused in me my worst self, — tastes and passions which hitherto had not seemed to exist! If I had lived with her ten years, I should doubtless have been the demon she gave me out to be.

"She showed to all about her — to her father

who idolized her, and to the aunt who had been a second mother to her — a sort of careless cruelty. But it may have been contact with me which awakened this, together with her furious and shuddering aversion for myself. Perhaps if she had married some one else — perhaps Deerford even, narrow and shallow as he is, may have made her — different." He paused and sighed heavily. "Well, within a short time, life became unbearable to us both. The death of Mr. Armstead removed all restraint. . . . I am not fond of remembering myself as I was during those two wretched years, Doc! But I am sorry for myself when I do think of them! I am sorry for her! I was sorry for her then, much as I hated her. God, how I hated her! . . . You know how it all ended, — nine years ago. I have never seen her since. And except for a hurried business trip, something over four years ago, I have never even set foot in the State where she lives. At that time, I had a single passing glimpse of Deerford. He seemed prosperous and happy, riding about his fields at Eastwood plantation. As for the child, no one but a madman " —

He broke off abruptly, his gaze fixed upon the little boy, whom he now really saw for the first time. He flushed and then grew deadly pale. A look of wild terror flashed into his eyes.

"God Almighty, Doctor," he whispered hoarsely. "What does it mean? Am I dreaming? Am I mad? Is he — God! the boy is my image."

"Yes," returned the doctor in a low voice. "He is marvelously like you; but listen, Roy, listen, man," — for Hilliard's excitement was becoming painful. "It is a well-known fact," he continued impressively, "and remember, I speak professionally, — it is an established fact that the children of a second marriage sometimes resemble the first husband, — particularly if the woman at the time of the first union was young. I have myself known of one such instance before, though far less pronounced than this. In this case, it may be explained by the powerful impression you undoubtedly made upon the mind of your wife. That you were repulsive to her would seem only to have intensified the result."

" Can this be true?" murmured Hilliard, rising and walking about the room, deeply agitated. "It must be. It is the only possible, the only conceivable solution. Poor Deerford, how he must have suffered!"

"How his wife must have suffered, if she saw the resemblance. And if she realized his suspicions."

Hilliard shrugged his shoulders. "Perhaps," he admitted. "Poor Deerford, poor devil! I wish he could know," he said, pausing in his restless walk and looking at the small Deerford, busy with the hilt of the sword.

"He would not believe it — in his present condition of mind, at least. He is as nearly insane as a man well can be who has not actually crossed

over the invisible border into the debatable land.
And you must be careful, Roy. I think he may
again try to do you bodily harm."

"Oh, I am not afraid of him," the younger man
returned, with his eyes still on the boy.

"Shall you return the child to his mother? I
think it would hardly be safe to trust him in the
hands of yonder madman now. Or shall you keep
him yourself, for the present? But don't answer
me. Think it out for yourself, Roy. Only remember that I am at your service, in this as in all
other matters, life and death."

"Thank you, Doctor," returned Hilliard, grasping the outstretched hand closely. "I do not
know. I shall probably send him back to her at
Eastwood. In any case, I will ask you not to
speak of what has occurred here to-night."

"Certainly not," replied the doctor, turning ;
but he lingered. There was a wistful look in his
eyes, which his companion interpreted and answered gravely. "Don't be afraid, Doc. The
chap is safe enough with me. Poor little outcast!"

Upon this, with another affectionate handshake,
Doctor Greaves withdrew.

Hilliard re-seated himself. The room had become very quiet. The occasional tramp of passing
feet on the street outside had ceased. The bugle
in the distant camp had sounded taps more than
an hour before, — the clear call winding shrilly
out on the night air. The night-blooming jessa-

mine in the garden sent its heavy, sickening perfume through the uncurtained windows; it reminded the man sitting, with his head bowed to his breast, of those long-ago summer nights at Eastwood; he moved his head angrily.

Little Francis, wearied at last of his coveted plaything, had been sitting bolt upright on the sofa, with his feet dangling over the edge, listening soberly to the talk between the two men. He was used to being unnoticed; he was not surprised when Doctor Greaves passed out of the room without remarking his outstretched arms, or responding to his whispered appeal. He waited a very long time, or so it seemed to him. Then he slipped from his perch and pattered across the bare floor to where the officer sat, brave with brass buttons, and slipped his small hand into the large one, lying palm upward on the arm of the chair.

"Is you my fa-zer, *now?*" he demanded with infinite solemnity.

"No," said Hilliard roughly, shaking off the rose-leaf touch. Francis turned away without a word, too used to harsh treatment to insist. He went back to the sofa, his shoe-lace dragging on the floor as he went. He was beginning to be sleepy in spite of the long afternoon nap in the railway-car, and hungry in spite of a hearty supper. And he was very tired. He climbed up among the cushions again. Great tears rolled down his cheeks, making furrows in the grime and dust there. He was a forlorn little figure in

his soiled and crumpled kilts, with his head drooping, and his tousled black locks falling over his
forehead. His shoulders shook convulsively, but
he made no sound.

A wave of pity surged over Hilliard. It was
followed by a sudden resolution. "Leroy Hilliard," he called peremptorily, "come here."

Francis looked at him with a puzzled air; but
his face brightened; his sobs ceased instantly; he
clambered down and came once more to Hilliard's
knee.

"I name Fwancis," he volunteered, looking up.

"Your name is Leroy Hilliard," said Hilliard
sternly, "and I am your father — now."

"I name ' Lewoy Hi'yar,' " repeated the child,
"an' you my fa-zer — now."

A formal handshake, as between man and man,
ratified this compact. Hilliard lifted the other
contracting party to his knee.

"I love my fa-zer — now." The murmur was
scarcely audible; the tumbled head fell against
his arm, the weary eyelids closed, and the long
regular breathing announced the sound sleep of
childhood.

"Poor little mite," mused the self-adopted father with an involuntary groan. "By some wild
and unaccountable freak of nature you have inherited my outer semblance. To whose soul are
you heir? To Lilla's, — selfish, vain, and cruel?
Deerford's, — narrow, suspicious, and crafty? To
mine? God help you in any case, my little lad!"

He reached out a hand and touched the bell upon the table. Robert answered the call. "Send Martha to me," ordered the master briefly. In a few moments the man reappeared, accompanied by his wife, a negro woman, quiet and staid like her husband, and with a pleasant motherly face. She courtesied quietly, and stood in a waiting attitude, showing no surprise, however much she may have felt.

"Martha," her master said, with an attempt at a smile, "this young gentleman is Leroy Hilliard, Junior. You will give up your other duties and look after him — after my son — from this time on."

"Yes, sir," said Martha.

"I will probably send him to my sister's to-morrow, as I shall be leaving here very soon. He will stay there during my absence. You will accompany him and remain with him. Put him to bed now. The poor little fellow has traveled a long way. He is worn out."

He laid the sleeping child in Martha's welcoming arms.

"Lawd, *ain't* he a sugar-man! An' de very spit o' you, Marse Roy!" she exclaimed.

"His — his mother was my wife," Hilliard said hastily. His face reddened. He stooped and kissed the boy's moist pouting lips, and an inexplicable lump rose to his throat.

Left alone at last, he turned with characteristic energy to his official reports. An hour passed, broken only by the scratching of his pen over the paper. Suddenly he lifted his head. His keen ear had caught the sound of a footstep on the graveled walk which led across the wide old garden to the house. He rose, bracing himself for another — perhaps a fatal encounter with Deerford. Happily he was mistaken. The late-comer, for the hands on the clock pointed to twelve, proved to be a courier bringing the long-expected marching orders.

He wrote a hasty note to his sister, confiding his adopted son to her care, and gave concise but explicit instructions to his servants respecting the management of his house during his absence.

He then threw himself upon the horse already saddled and at the gate, and galloped out to where his regiment was encamped half a mile away, followed by his body-servant.

There, his orderly having preceded him, everything was in disciplined confusion; the tents were already down, wagons were rumbling into the open road, the men were falling into line, and one hour later, by the light of the summer stars, the ——th South Carolina Volunteers marched with their colonel toward the front.

V

COLONEL HILLIARD saw his adopted son but twice after that July night when the child had been so unceremoniously thrust into his life. The rapid and exciting progress of the Civil War left him little time for private affairs, and his two visits to B—— were made at long intervals; they were also very brief, but they served to fix him forever in the boy's mind, — a splendid image, which neither time nor distance could dim, nor death efface.

All recollection of his past, however, people, places, and things, gradually faded from the consciousness of the little transplanted Deerford child. Aunt Pauline, with her dark, sad, loving eyes, lingered longest of all; and with her a swaying rose-vine full of blood-red roses that seemed to climb up to the sky on a beautiful white fluted column. This last was doubtless a fragment of his once-unquestioned patrimony clinging to the memory of the once-unquestioned heir of Eastwood. Finally these also passed, and Leroy Hilliard, Junior, as he was named from the moment of his new life's beginning, grew and thrived in the quaint Hilliard mansion set in the midst of its century old garden. For Mrs. Blackmore, Colonel Hilliard's only sister, widowed early in the struggle between the States, had returned to the home of her childhood. She drew an arm of love around the cast-out Deerford, as around her own numerous brood. Tears often filled her motherly eyes, in the earlier days, when she saw the wondering look on the uplifted face of the young stranger, and the slow, incredulous curl of the baby lips at some proffered mark of affection, — a smile of invitation, an approving word, a tender caress.

"He ain't been use' to Hilliard treatments, certain an' sho', Mis' Mandy," old Martha once observed to her mistress, with a wise shake of her turbaned head. "Look like he everlastin' feared somebody goin' to slap him."

With more unrestrained candor, she said to her husband, "I ain't sayin' a blessed thing ag'ins' the dead, Robert, but Marse Leroy's wife must ha' been a limb o' Satan! The chile fair shrivels up when you ax him about his ma!"

The warping, fortunately, had not gone deep enough for ruin. The atmosphere of love and confidence soon did its work. In it the little creature expanded like a flower; he ceased to shrink before an outstretched hand; he grew less wayward, day by day; the line on his cheek rarely deepened to scarlet, — sign of anger or impatience; he became, in short, a normal, healthy human being.

"Your little Roy is a charming child," Mrs. Blackmore wrote to her brother. "He lords it over his cousins, my children, like a true Hilliard. But since they are *only girls*, like a true Hilliard still, he coddles them, and protects them, and stands between them and danger (of the gander in the kitchen-yard, and marvelous, imagined monsters in the rose-garden)! Of course they all worship him, as most women, big and little, are fated to worship every (male) Hilliard who dawns on their horizon. Jesting aside, my dear Roy, he is a fine boy, and a great comfort to me already. Pray God he may prove so to you. It is touching to note his admiration and adoration of you. He will stand for hours with his chubby elbows resting on the table, staring at your photograph; the merest mention of your name brings him running to my knee; his choicest plaything is one of your old belts. The only time that inexplicable mark has reddened his face for months was a day or two since, when he found one of his playmates — a visitor — buckling this belt around him!"

This letter, written soon after Hilliard's second visit to his old home, and just before the close of the great internecine struggle, was perhaps the last he ever read. He had served a losing cause with distinction, twice receiving promotion on the battlefield, and he wore the uniform of a general when, leading a charge in one of the last skirmishes of the war, he dropped from his horse, mortally wounded by a flying shell. He was car-

ried to a farmhouse near by, and there died, after
some hours of intense agony. His sister's letter
was found, stained with his life-blood, in his
breast-pocket. It was carried back to her by his
faithful body-servant.

The gallant young general was buried in the
garden of the farmhouse. The remnant of his
brigade, grim and powder-blackened and silent,
followed the body to the grave; a detachment from
the ——th, his own old regiment, fired the last
volley above it.

A sudden plunge from affluence into poverty, so
painful in most cases to middle or old age, has no
terrors for childhood. That happy-go-lucky age
cares little — so its stomach be decently lined
(and even on this point it is not over particular!)
— whether its raiment be linen or gunny-sack; its
sleep is as sound on a pallet as in a four-posted
bed with high-piled mattress and silken hangings.
To the Blackmore girls and Roy Hilliard the
Second there seemed no change worth noting. A
world had tumbled in pieces; the crash in the
ears of their elders was appalling. But the old
house stood firm, though in course of time the
plastering dropped and the paint scaled. The
same portraits of past-and-gone chatelaines looked
down from the walls, though the stately array of
servants that did their bidding had dwindled to
old Martha alone in the kitchen, and old Robert
alone with his dead master's decrepit war-horse in

the stable. The garden, with imaginary griffins, or black-bearded giants lurking behind lilac and syringa bushes, was there; it became indeed more fascinating as the unpruned vines hid the doors of the summer-houses, and the grass waved knee-deep over the flower-beds; the carriage-house remained, with the great family carriage, and master's stan-hope and Ole Mis' buggy, — all, perforce, fallen into disuse, but the noblest of hiding-places; stable-loft, greenhouses, tool-house, had lost even the memory of their times of riotous living, but what unparalleled playhouses!

"Don't fret, Amanda. Poverty will not hurt them," Doctor Greaves said half mockingly one day just before he died. He was sitting on the broad front gallery with Mrs. Blackmore. The sturdy boy and the five ruddy-faced bareheaded girls were playing a round game in a corner of the rose-garden. The refrain of the catch they were singing came into the gallery, intermingled with bursts of boisterous laughter: —

> " What care I for gold and silver ?
> What care I for house and land ? "

"It is true," continued the old man earnestly. "They do not care. Why should they? They, who have so much! Poverty will not hurt them, I tell you. It is good for them. It will strengthen them, and it will teach them the value of many things."

"Perhaps," returned the despoiled chatelaine with a wistful sigh.

She held fast to the old house through thick and thin, and by dint of patient and anxious managing she gave her daughters what education the town afforded — unsettled and distracted as it was by the after-effects of the war. But with the old-fashioned distinction between the needs of the sexes, she sent Leroy to college. He graduated with an average record as a student and an enviable reputation among his fellows for loyalty, pluck, and manliness.

The next day after his return to the only home he could remember, he followed Mrs. Blackmore into her small morning-room. It was the room which had been from time immemorial sacred to the Hilliard women-folk; the room which, for a few weeks in war-time, Colonel Hilliard had used as his private office, and where an abandoned child had found a second father. "Aunt Amanda," he said, dropping on the rug at her feet, and folding his arms across her lap, — his favorite attitude, "did my father ever express to you any especial wish as to what I should be, or do, in life?"

"No," said Mrs. Blackmore, passing her hand affectionately through the dark curls clustered thick over the white brow. "No, dear. He could not, of course, foresee all the changes which have come to pass. He probably looked forward to sending you abroad for a year or two, as he himself was sent, as his father before him was sent, to see something of the great world outside; and

afterward he would have made you his successor
in the management of the plantations he owned;
or, if he had chosen a profession for you, it would,
I am sure, have been the law. My father, although a planter, was a lawyer also."

"Yes," assented the lad eagerly; "I know what
an eminent lawyer my grandfather Hilliard was.
I am sure this would have been my father's choice.
I shall make the law my profession, later; but
first of all, Aunt Amanda, I am going to work,
for anybody, and at anything which will pay me
decent wages. Do you think I do not realize —
now, — I have been blind enough all these years,
but the scales of selfishness have fallen from my
eyes! Do you imagine that I do not know what
sacrifices you and the girls have made for me?
But now, please God — oh, you need not try to put
your hand over my mouth, Aunt Amanda! I am a
man, you know, and a Hilliard, and I will have my
way!" He drew the dear face, seamed and lined
by care, down to his own, and kissed the thin
cheek. "Now," he continued, leaping lightly to
his feet, "I am going to try and prove myself
worthy of the grand old name I bear, — worthy
of my father who left it to me as my noblest heri-
tage;" his voice dropped to a reverential tone with
the last words. He seemed to see before him once
more the martial figure in gray uniform, the grave
kindly face with the wonderful eyes, which he remembered so well. "I cannot fail," he murmured
to himself, "for *he* will be my inspiration."

The feeling of young Leroy Hilliard for the man whose son he believed himself to be almost amounted to idolatry; Hilliard's lightest word, his most careless glance, remained graven on his memory, as if written with steel in his very being, — like his own birth-mark! He rarely spoke of his dead father outside of his family circle, and he heard with pained astonishment the light and careless remarks made by other young men about their fathers. "It is not because I am different from other sons," he often thought; "it must be because he was — is — so different from other fathers! And I shall succeed because he will be watching over me."

But success does not always go hand in hand with enthusiasm. Leroy Hilliard the Second found many and bitter disappointments in his brave and tireless struggle to gain a firm foothold in the petty business world immediately around him; and at length, nearly two years after his return from college, and the day upon which a well-to-do classmate of his own married Mary Blackmore, the oldest of his adopted sisters, he sought Mrs. Blackmore again in her morning-room.

"No, I am not downhearted," he said, smiling up at her with his arms crossed on her lap, "for that is what your blessed blue eyes are saying, whatever your lips may say; but now that you have Howard to take my place" —

"No one can ever take your place," interrupted

Mrs. Blackmore, with something of her brother's occasional sternness.

"Yes, I know;" a lump rose unexpectedly in his throat; "and I know that there is a crust for me on the table, and a corner for me in the old house, as long as the crusts hold out, and the old house stands on its foundation, God bless its rafters! But you must let me go away now, Aunt Amanda. There is surely a place for me — and a fortune into the bargain! — somewhere in the world. And I think that I have at least found the place. Look here."

He drew some papers from his breast-pocket. "In West Texas " — he continued.

Mrs. Blackmore gasped and paled; it was as much as if he had said the Fiji Islands, or Siberia, or the Moon! But she listened patiently to the scheme which in truth sounded vain and boyish to her sober ears.

There was, it appeared, a tract of rich bottomland, with some fine prairie pasturage, to be had on easy terms along a certain Mesquit Creek in Western Texas. The place had been under cultivation, was fenced and partly stocked with farming implements. There was a roomy and comfortable dwelling, with stables, outhouses, etc., a well, and a good orchard. The opportunity for getting rich by farming and stock-raising lay under the very feet of any young man who had the pluck and the brains to stoop and pick it up; the agent wrote with an enthusiasm which was catching to an inexperienced youngster.

"I can get all the money I need for a start, and I shall make a fortune on that Texas ranch for you and the girls, Aunt Amanda," he cried playfully, — and in his secret heart believing more than he said, — folding up the letter. "I shall call it the Amanda ranch! And while I am amassing that fortune the agent writes so glibly about, I shall complete my law studies. Who knows but you may see me a fat pursy old chief justice, yet!"

But it was not until after much and grave family discussion, and much weeping and wailing on the part of his foster sisters, that Hilliard finally prevailed.

He stopped at Crouch's Well one day late in October, and in company with Amen Bagley, who good-naturedly volunteered to show him the way thither, he proceeded to his ranch on Mesquit Creek, some six miles distant. His heart fell as they drew rein at length beside a broken rail-fence; and he surveyed the roomy "and comfortable dwelling" described in the agent's letter. It was a one-roomed log-cabin, with a porch in front, and a shed in the rear. The top of the rock chimney had tumbled in, the doors and the shutter of the single window see-sawed on broken hinges, the weather-boarding was mildewed and rotting, weeds grew breast-high through the cracks in the porch floor, and completely hid the rickety steps. There were no outhouses; in one corner of what may once have been the stable-lot, a confused pile of scantlings and shingles remained to tell of a

stable, or cow-shed, or a cotton-pen, — perhaps in
its day all three! The orchard, except for one
forlorn peach-tree, whose leafless branches whipped
the corner of the house, existed only in the agent's
imagination. The fields had long been turned out
to grass; the fences were down. A plentiful crop
of sunflower-stalks and kurkle-burrs, indeed, gave
token of rich soil, but Hilliard was not farmer
enough to understand this.

A keen norther was blowing; it whistled through
the pecan-trees and the naked cottonwood-trees on
the banks of the creek which skirted the fields;
crows were screaming in the topmost branches of
the trees, bushy-tailed squirrels whisked up and
down the trunks, a few razor-back hogs nosed the
dry rustling leaves below, squealing and eying the
two human intruders viciously.

Not a word passed between Hilliard and his
companion for some moments. The former kept
his face set steadily toward the dilapidated cabin;
he was still young enough to have a lump incon-
veniently ready to mount to his throat. Bagley
cast a side glance at him, but delicately refrained
from speech. Finally, he gathered up his bridle-
reins. "There's one comfort, Mr. Hilliard," he
drawled. "You can wollop Benson, the agent.
He lives down the creek. If you need a hand,
call on me."

This speech somehow loosened Hilliard's tense
nerves. He threw back his head and burst into a
roar of gay boyish laughter.

"Amen!" laughed Bagley; and he reached out a hand and slapped the newcomer heartily on the back.

The next day Mr. Bagley reported at Crouch's: "The boy is young, and he's as green as a cymlin, of course. But he'll do. He's gritty. He talked all the way over about his ' ranch,' and his dwellin'-house and stables. I thought I'd bust, but I didn't let on. I waited to see what sort o' spunk he'd show when he saw Bill Kinchley's rotten old shanty. I'll be d—d if he didn't take it like a briar-breaker! I saw him swaller pretty hard once or twice, and that squeenchy mark on his face looked like a blaze o' lightnin'. And then he set his jaw, and then he laughed, and I knowed he was game. And I hope to God he'll whack the life out of Benson."

There were many times during the next year when Hilliard would gladly have turned tail and fled; many times when he longed to cross his arms on Aunt Amanda's lap and sob out his ups and downs like a child; many more times when he swore he would wollop Benson without anybody's help. But he did none of these things. He kept his troubles to himself, and thanks to Amen Bagley's timely remark, which tickled the fountain of healthful laughter, he never again experienced the utterly helpless and dismal dismay which threatened to swamp him that October afternoon.

By the end of the third year, his hard and systematic labor showed results nothing short of marvelous in the eyes of his easy-going neighbors. The repaired cabin had become a snug and habitable abode, albeit showing in a certain picturesque disorder within unmistakable signs of a bachelor proprietor. The fields, outlined with good fences, were white, in crop-time, with bursting cotton-bolls, the rough cribs were piled with corn and fodder, hogs were fattening in the creek-bottom, a small bunch of cattle grazed on the open prairie-land, there were a couple of mules and a saddle-horse in the stable. A vigorous young orchard flanked the cabin on one side, and a vegetable garden, with homely flowers bordering its squares, the other. Hilliard himself worked all day beside his two hired Mexicans, Juan and Manuel; he wagoned his own cotton and pecan crops to W——, a hundred miles away; he did his own housework.

"Your questions are searching, not to say impertinent, young women," he wrote gayly to his foster sisters in Carolina. "But I do not mind telling you that I have a valet — a remarkably fine fellow — for a valet! who makes my bed and my coffee. The same useful individual saddles my horse and polishes my boots on a Sunday (I scorn shoes!). He even shaves me and curls my hyacinthine locks with a curling iron. His name? Oh, it is Leroy Hilliard."

In a more serious strain he wrote to Mrs. Blackmore: "The ranch, which, by the way, is not a ranch at all, but only an insignificant farm, grows more and more homelike. Next year, remember, you are to come out and visit me. I shall come after you, as soon as my cotton is laid by. I am hoping that you will consent — now that the girls are all married — to stay with me altogether. I throw up my hat at the thought! Meantime, the place and all its belongings are paid for, and you cannot, in justice to me, persist in your refusal to let me help take care of you. Dear Aunt Amanda, you wish to make me jealous of your new sons-in-law!"

VI

A BAPTIZING

SUNDAY afternoon, early in the June of eighteen hundred and eighty-three.

The new-fangled religious service with its amazing down-sittings and uprisings, the short but soul-swelling sermon, the "sandy" little preacher in his robe, the texture and shape of the robe itself — all these weighty matters had been gravely discussed over the abundant basket-dinner spread out on the grass in the pecan grove behind the church.

There remained time — before the baptizing — for a little neighborhood gossip. To this end, the congregation had broken up into groups, which were scattered over the unfenced grounds, the more forehanded choosing their places on or near the banks of the creek.

Peleg Church stood on the brow of a long slope which dipped gently down to Mesquit Creek. A dozen sturdy pecan-trees sheltered its rear from the north winds, a single enormous live-oak shaded its wide, low, front doorway from the summer sun. A number of mesquit trees studded the slope, giving it the appearance of an abandoned peach

orchard; the soft mesquit grass made a carpet
under foot, green or brown, according to the season of the year.

The lonely church, for the nearest habitation
was several miles away, was a weather-stained log-
house, with a rock chimney bulging out from one
end, a door opening to the east and facing the
creek, and a single heavy-shuttered sashless window on each side.   Within, there was an ample
fireplace, and a cramped box-pulpit, before which
stood several ranges of split-log benches innocent
of backs.   The building had been raised (on
ground donated by himself) by Uncle Joe Wyatt,
with the assistance of his neighbors.   Uncle Joe
had also selected the name under which the church
had now been famous for the better part of ten
years.   The day upon which the last hewn shingle
had been nailed into place, and the great wooden
latch mounted on the door, Mr. Wyatt, Bible in
hand, ascended the horseblock set up for the ac-
commodation of the women-folk. "Fellow-citizens,
an' bretheren in the Lord," he said in a loud
oracular voice to the assembled multitude, "I have
been app'inted to pick out a name for this here
church-house.   An' considerin' of the fac' that
the congregation to set under the droppin's of its
pul*pit* repersents all sorts o' *dee*-nominations,—
Babtisses, Methodisses, Presber*tee*rians, *an'* Soul-
Sleepers, — I p'opose callin' it Peleg Church,
Peleg bein' a Bible-name, the meanin' of which is
divided : ' And they called him *Peleg*, for in his

day the earth was divided.' Genesis 10th chapter,
21st verse. This church-house, gentle*men*, bein',
as it were, divided 'mongs' the aforesaid *dee*-nomi-
nations, Babtis, Methodis, Presber*tee*rian, *an'*
Soul-Sleepers, shell be hencefo'th an' forever, if
no objections is offered, Peleg Church."

The name was adopted with enthusiasm, and for
ten years the four Sundays of each month had
been parceled out according to Mr. Wyatt's calculation, leaving an occasional fifth for a protracted
meeting, or a combined religious debate, at which
all hands assisted.

"You did n't count on Episcopalians, Uncle
Joe?" said Amen Bagley, lounging with young
Joe Wyatt up to the horseblock, where some of
the older men were still discussing the sermon.

"No, I did n't," returned Mr. Wyatt shortly.
He was a large, ruddy-faced old man. His small
twinkling gray eyes were set in a network of wrin-
kles, which radiated away from them like the
spokes of a wheel; his cheeks and chin were lost
in a forest of stiff red beard. He walked wide-
legged, and looked like a sailor, though he had
never seen salt water. "No, I did n't, an' what's
mo', I never counted on no preacher prancin'
aroun' in women's clo's. An' what's mo' yit, I
never counted on no young gals jawin' back at the
pul*pit* from the congregation. It's plum ridiculous. Saint Paul particular *said* that women-folks
wa'n't to speak out in the churches."

"Lord, pap," grinned young Joe, "I don't call that jawin'! I call it the cooin' o' honey-doves."

The old man followed the direction of his grandson's glance. His eyes rested for a moment on Margaret Ransome, lately returned from a girl's college in Kentucky, and her guest, Miss Wingate, who had accompanied her home. These were the culprits who had assisted at the novel service. Uncle Joe, if the truth must be told, had been startled out of his customary nap by their responses; hence his indignation.

The two young women stood arm in arm in the doorway of Peleg. Their pretty heads were bent in anxious consultation over those pages in the Book of Common Prayer devoted to the Ceremony of the Baptism of Adults.

"Waal! Waal!" chuckled Mr. Wyatt, his face clearing. "I reckon the 'Piscopals is ho'ped up by sech foolishness. Lord knows I don't blame 'em! We've got to make room for the 'Piscopals somehow, or somehow else," he added cheerfully. "They don't calc'late to come more 'n onct or twict a year nohow, includin' of the bishop. I'm a Soul-Sleeper myself, an' I'm mighty willin' to let 'em have a Soul-Sleepin' Sunday." Here Uncle Joe winked solemnly at the crowd. "I wish they'd hurry up the babtizin'," he wound up fervently.

"I'm plum on eedge about this here baptizin', an' that's the truth," broke out a tall middle-aged man standing near. This was Green Parsons, whose twin brother, Red, was the single candidate for baptism that day. "I don't keer nothin' 'bout Red jinin' the *E*-piscopals. I was with him over in San Antone when he heard the sermon that fetched his soul to grace. Bishop Elliott preached it. Bishop Elliott's a whale if there ever was one! But what in thunderation has Red set his-se'f up to be *dipped* for? I'm a Methodist my-se'f, an' sprinklin' is good enough for me. Ef he is so dead set to be baptized diff'ent, why n't he have pourin'? But no, the blame fool must be dipped, like a durn Baptis — 'scusin' of any Baptisses here present. An' I don't believe Bro-ther French *kin* dip Red. Look at Red Parsons yonder, an' then look at Brother French! I ain't afeared that *Red* 'll git drownded, but" — He pursed up his lips and shook his head ominously.

Red Parsons was seated on the ground not far away, with his back against a tree, his long legs stretched out before him. The twins were almost ludicrously alike, but just now Red's dark eyes had a far-away look, as different as possible from the fretful scowl in his brother's; his sallow lan-tern-jawed face was alight from some inner ecstasy. His lips moved in silent prayer, and he glanced from time to time toward the creek, as if impa-tient for the approaching ceremony.

"He 'lows Phil-up an' the eunuch is his eggs-ample," resumed Green, in an aggrieved tone, "but how does he know that Phil-up *dipped* the eunuch, when they went down *toe* the water? That's what I want to know! He might jest as well ha' poured, or sprinkled. *I* say sprinkled!"

The Reverend David French, on the farther side of the grounds, was walking up and down, with his hands clasped behind his back. His outer appearance betokened a calm which he was far from feeling. He was indeed a prey to an interior agitation which he prayerfully sought to control.

He was a small, delicate looking man about thirty years old, with reddish curling hair, a smooth, boyish face, and short-sighted gray eyes. He wore spectacles. His neat clerical dress excited hardly less comment among the Peleg people — whom he had addressed that morning for the first time — than the flowing gown and bands which he had worn in the pulpit. The eyes of most of those present were upon him as he paced back and forth — taking his measure, but with 'rustic dispassionateness withholding judgment until the facts of the case were all presented.

His lips, like those of the candidate for baptism, moved in mute prayer, and he too glanced from time to time toward the creek, but with an apprehension of which he was much ashamed.

"I am astounded at my weakness," he breathed, within himself. "But I have never even witnessed a baptizing by immersion. Will I be able to perform the sacrament properly? . . . I dare not risk making the Church ridiculous. . . . I do not know whether or not a priest under such circum-

stances should wear his robes. . . . Lord, forgive
me for dwelling, at such a moment, upon things
so trivial. And, Lord, help me to do my duty."

The women had gathered in a body on the shady
side of the church. The children raced unrestricted
about the slope. A few of the younger men had
ventured near the tacit line of demarcation between
the male and female folds, in the hope of attract-
ing the attention of the younger women. These
giggled together, flauntingly oblivious of this stra-
tegic advance.

"Ef Brother Whipple was here," observed Mrs.
Crouch, the postmaster's wife, "he'd make them
onrighteous boys keep their distance."

"I don't think it matters much about the boys,
Sister Crouch," said Aunt Lindy Wyatt sooth-
ingly; "they ain't supposed to have much sense!
But look at Red Parsons! He ought to be ashamed
of hisse'f makin' that pore little creeter resk his
life to *dip* him, — the gret, gangly darnin'-needle!"

"I've worked on Red all I could," said Mrs.
Red, feeling to blame.

"The Parsonses was born hard-headed," said
Mrs. Green apologetically.

Mrs. Red and Mrs. Green might have been
twins like their husbands, so alike were they in
appearance, — short, rotund, and perpetually rosy
from the exertion of keeping their lords reconciled
to each other, and their large families in order.

"Sech foolishness," reiterated Mrs. Wyatt;
"why n't he jine the Babtisses an' be done with it!"

"Where's Roy Hilliard?" demanded one of the group irrelevantly. "An' Jack Ransome?" All eyes were turned on Jack's mother.

"They promised to come," returned Mrs. Ransome, knitting her brows anxiously.

"I hope they ain't up to any mischief," said Mrs. Crouch. "Sence this bob-wire fence business" —

"Oh, Aunt Mary," interrupted Helen Wingate, hastening to Mrs. Ransome. "It is time. Mr. French has gone into the church with Mr. Parsons." The women were instantly on their feet, and the congregation hurried *en masse* to the creek.

The creek, in the rainy season, generally in February or March, deserved more than its name. Then it might well have been called a river; then, after the manner of West Texas streams, Mesquit Creek roared, foaming and frothing, along its deep bed, full to the brink; sweeping away bridges, eating cave-like hollows in the high banks, and tumbling the stones about on its uneven bottom. At such times, it was dangerous enough. But this tumultuous season overpast, it dwindled to a mere rill, which the drift of leaves choked up entirely in many places; the giant tree-roots, laid bare in flood-time, stuck out forlornly from the rifted banks; the fish and eels died on the sun-baked rocks. Only where the bottom-lands were low the water remained in reedy lakelets in the shade of the dense undergrowth, and in the more open country, a pool here and there defied the summer, and lay, deep, dark, and cool, beneath overhanging trees.

No-Bottom Hole, by Peleg Church, was such a pool. Parts of it were popularly held to be of almost measureless depth; even its upper loop, used as a baptizing-pool, was, according to some, a little "resky." It held no terrors for the Baptist brethren, however; their converts had walked down the slope these many years hand in hand with Elder Whipple, — a giant in body, as well as in soul.

But a tremor of anxious, not to say almost contemptuous, pity ran through the crowd which opened to let the Reverend David French and his companion pass to the grassy space on the edge of the pool. The Reverend David looked so little! He wore his black robe, and carried an open prayer-book in his hand. The sun glinted on his spectacles.

Red Parsons, towering above him, listened in rapt eagerness to the opening exhortation; and he answered "like a book" the questions put to him. Margaret Ransome and Helen Wingate stumbled and stammered through those parts assigned by the prayer-book to the people. All this seemed mysterious and almost unnatural to the multitude unused to such proceedings. But all stood bareheaded and respectfully silent.

Finally the supreme moment came. The little preacher's face was very pale; the muscles in his

temples twitched as he laid his hand on the arm
of his tall disciple and began with him the descent
of the steep bank; his knees trembled beneath his
fluttering gown.

Suddenly he began to sing: —

> " Soldiers of Christ, arise,
>   And gird your armor on."

His voice was not loud. It was in fact curiously
thin and bodiless, so to speak. But it came up
from the hollow of the creek like the fine far-away
call of a silver trumpet. It thrilled those who
heard. They pressed forward and gazed open-
mouthed and breathless on the singer.

> " Strong in the strength which God supplies,
>   Through His eternal Son."

The Reverend David had set his foot in the water.
His voice gained fullness as he waded on. The
big man beside him looked down at him with an
anxious, brooding gaze, as if he longed to take
him in his arms and bear him to safety. He
touched his shoulder occasionally, as who should
say like Hopeful to Christian in the river: "Be
of good cheer, my brother. I feel the bottom,
and it is good."

But now they had come to a halt and faced
about.

"He'll never do it, never!" muttered Amen
Bagley, noting that the water was breast-high to
the diminutive shepherd, while it barely touched
the waist of the sheep. Amen shut his eyes
tightly. The next moment he opened them. Red

Parsons's head with David's hand underneath was just rising from the surface of the pool. A second later he was firmly planted on his feet, and the preacher, reaching up, was gently wiping the water from his face.

"Amen! Glory to God!" shouted Amen Bagley. "Glory! Glory!" responded the people in an ecstasy; the triumphant cry echoed up and down the hollow of the creek. The Reverend Mr. French never heard it; his soul had withdrawn into itself in silent thanksgiving. But as they came up out of the water, he took up the strain again: —

> "Soldiers of Christ, arise,
> And gird your armor on."

The people, catching with ready ear both tune and words, joined in: —

> "Strong in the strength which God supplies,
> Through His eternal Son."

And they pressed forward, one by one, after their homely accustomed fashion, to give the right hand of fellowship to the man of God and the brand which he had rescued from the burning.

It was a great victory for the Reverend David, though in his simplicity he did not suspect it.

"Spunky little chap, ain't he!" beamed Mr. Wyatt to those around him. "Could dip Phil-up an' a whole rig'mint o' eunuchs, if he had to. Oh yes, we've got to make room in Peleg somehow, or somehow else, for the 'Piscopals."

The twin brothers had walked off together arm

in arm. There was unbroken silence between
them until they reached the black-haw thicket
where Red was to exchange his wet clothes for dry
ones. There, as he held aside the outstretched
branches for Red to pass into the heart of the
thicket, Green remarked: —

"The New Testament says that Phil-up an' the
eunuch went down *toe* the water. Now Phil-up
cert'ny baptized that eunuch. The question is,
how did he do it? *I* say by sprinklin'. But then
ag'in it *might* ha' been by pourin'."

This unexpected concession brought tears to
Red's eyes.

"I ain't got but one regret," continued Green
thoughtfully, assisting his twin to haul off his
dripping flannel blouse, "an' that is, that Elder
Whipple wa'n't here to-day to see what a powerful
dipper a *E*-piscopal can be — when he's *got* to
dip!"

The scene around Peleg Church was now one of
loud and familiar activity. Teams were being
harnessed, or, in the vernacular of the region,
"hooked up;" chairs for the married women set
into open wagons, and quilts thrown in for the
children to sit upon; dishes re-packed, feed-troughs
emptied of shucks and corn-cobs, dogs whistled in,
saddles girthed, riding-skirts adjusted. The unmarried girls waiting around the horse-block for
their horses followed the unwritten law of Peleg
and beamed with friendly eyes and coquettish
smiles on the young men, kept at so severe a dis-

tance all day; these, booted and spurred, stood
ready to leap into their saddles and make a mad
dash after the neighborhood belles. No open or
tacit engagements for the ride home were allowed
in the Peleg code; each man must take his chance
according to the speed of his horse, his own horse-
manship, or the diplomacy of the young woman in
question. And the fine art of "cutting-out" was
practiced almost as a profession at Peleg and all
through Crouch's Settlement.

Into this cheerful stir there came from far up
the winding road the clatter of horse's hoofs; and
a young man, riding at a hand gallop, turned a
bend and came into view. He was followed by
three or four other men.

"Hello, Roy!" shouted young Joe Wyatt, as
the foremost rider came up and threw himself from
his horse, which was reeking with foam. "What's
up? Where have you all been? Why n't you
come to church? You'll ketch it, you all!"

"There is nothing the matter," returned the
newcomer smiling. He lifted his hat as he spoke
to the group of young women, which included
Helen Wingate and Margaret Ransome.

Then turning swiftly, he added in a low undertone to the men who had hastened forward and
were gathered about him, "The news was cor-
rect. The wire fences have been stretched around
Vaquero Spring ever since Monday. Crawls's
Pond is shut in; Granny Tatums's whole place is
shut in. Three out of her little bunch of cattle are

dead. We counted fourteen of Uncle Joe Wyatt's, dead or dying, on Crawls's prairie. We have been over to the superintendent's camp and remonstrated with him and his factotum. But we got no satisfaction. They were not even civil " —

"Civil!" interrupted Jack Ransome, his black eyes flashing, "they threatened to shoot us if we ever came within five hundred yards of their camp!"

"That's not all," put in another of the riders; "there's another camp about fourteen miles east, about Haley's tank. They've run a fence there. I saw some freighters this morning; they said the dead cattle were lying around there, thick as honey-bees."

A chorus of angry exclamations had broken out among the listeners.

"Shet up, boys," growled Uncle Joe Wyatt, who had hurried over from his wagon. "Ain't ye got more sense than to skeer the women-folks to death? Come over to Crouch's to-morrow, all of ye. To-morrow at ten."

"What's the matter, pap?" called his wife in her shrill, high-keyed old voice.

"Nawthin', maw, nawthin'. The boys is jest makin' up a rabbit-hunt." The old man was walking off, but he turned his head to wink solemnly at his companions.

"Now, ain't that scan'lous," cried Mrs. Crouch from her seat in a spring-wagon. "'T ain't haffen hour sence the sperrit o' grace was fair hoverin' over Peleg. An' here's them on-Christian back-slidin' boys talkin' about huntin' jack-rabbits!'"

Her voice was drowned in the rush of horses' feet. The young women, already mounted, were off like the wind, looking demurely ahead of them, but quite conscious of the cavaliers riding after, with the jingle of silver spurs and silver-bitted bridles.

Leroy Hilliard and his squad had leaped again into their saddles. They had ridden hard all day; their horses were jaded and foam-flecked. But they pushed the fresher riders hard. Hilliard himself, neck and neck for a quarter of a mile with young Joe Wyatt, shot past him at length with a gay nod and drew alongside of Miss Wingate on her fleet bay filly.

The sun was near its setting; a yellow haze filtered through the scant foliage of the stubby post-oaks that covered the wide monotonous stretch of rolling country; it illuminated the flying caval-cade, bringing out vivid bits of color here and there, and turning into gold the powdery dust that arose from under the horses' feet; light laughter and the echo of youthful voices filled the warm air. It was such a scene as old-time poets loved to imagine, and old-time painters to put upon canvas!

The heavily-laden and more sober wagons rumbled away from Peleg Church in every direction. The last one to roll out was a big-bodied, many-seated freight-wagon, which carried the united

families of the Parsons twins. The Reverend
David French occupied the front seat in this with
Red and a couple of babies. The last gleam of
sunlight slanted across the slope as they drove off,
leaving the isolated church to its coming week of
silence and solitude.

VII

CROUCH'S WELL

BILLY CROUCH was a briar-breaker, that is to say, one of the pioneers in the settlement which bore his name. His small farm lay on the public road, about midway between the little town of Skipton and Rassler, the county-seat, some thirty miles apart. His unpainted frame house had two stories, — a circumstance which gave the family a certain distinction among their friends and neighbors, though some affected to decry the arrangement as unnatural, not to say iniquitous. "I don't see what call Sister Calline Crouch has to be so biggaty," Mrs. Green Parsons often remarked. "One room on top of another ain't no better than one room behint another, as I can see. And them child-breakin'-neck stair-steps is plum wicked."

Mr. Crouch's field stretched away in the rear of the house; its cultivation fell chiefly upon Mrs. Crouch and the children, Billy having other and more important business to occupy him. To the left of the front porch, and about fifty steps away, a grove of fine pecan-trees embraced in their shade Crouch's Well, with its high stone curbing, its great limestone slab cover with a circular opening in the centre for the pulley-rope, and its twin buckets. The road broadened as it approached the inward sweeping curve made by the rail fence at this spot; several hitching-posts had been set up, and a big wooden trough on sturdy legs was placed in a fence corner.

All teams which passed along the road going or coming stopped to water at Crouch's Well. The water, slightly milky from a superabundance of lime, was deliciously cool when it came up from the dark rock-lined bottom. The thirsty traveler, man or beast, could never get enough of it. There was an endless creaking of the rope over the pulley, a continuous gurgle and splash into the trough, and what with the comfortable lingering of those already there, and the arrival of fresh throats to be cooled, and fresh bottle-gourds to be filled, there was hardly an hour from year's end to year's end when there was not a rattle of trace-chains, a crunch of starting or stopping wheels, a cracking of long-lashed whips, an uproar of voices, and an echo of mellow laughter around Crouch's Well. Even at night the flare of camp-fires shone in the dip of woods beyond, and the pulley creaked at intervals between sundown and dawn.

Billy gave this water of life freely, without money and without price, and exceeding great was his reward!

Mr. Crouch's responsibilities as a family man sat lightly upon his shoulders; indeed, his smooth pink cheeks, blue eyes, and rotund little figure hardly seemed accordant with such burdens. He had eight children to be fed, clothed, and schooled, but the oldest of these, Lorena, a long-legged, soft-voiced girl of sixteen, took after her mother, who, according to common report, was a "buster," and between mother and daughter the place was "run" more or less successfully, while Billy sat on the fence and talked politics to the tune of his creaking well-pulley. Twice a week, on Monday and Saturday, his opportunities in this direction rose to a high level. These were mail-days. And Mr. Crouch was the postmaster.

On these days, soon after sun-up, the men of the settlement began to ride in after their mail. Some of them received a letter about once a year; several took the "Weekly Baptist Herald," "The Christian Advocate," or "The Observer;" others expected a pair of boots, a slicker, a pistol, or a bundle of axe-handles — for nothing seemed amiss in Crouch's mail; many had no correspondents, and no expectations. But all came with unfailing regularity. Pushing in by bridle-paths and wagon-roads, they rode up, dismounted, hitched their horses, drew a bucket of water, tipped it to their lips from the curb, took a deep draught, and re-marked, with an air of saying something never said before, that Crouch's well-water could n't be beat. Then they emptied the remaining water into the trough, and climbed upon the fence. There, like a row of vari-colored crows, in their blue, or

brown, or gray jeans trousers and white shirtsleeves, they perched, talking politics — national
preferred — with the delighted Billy, until the
mail came; and herein consisted Billy's profit on
his well-water!

Somewhere between eleven o'clock A. M. and
two P. M. the mail-hack rattled up from Skipton;
the dusty team stopped of its own accord at the
water-trough; Sam Whitehead, the mail-carrier,
spat ostentatiously from one side of the hack, and
threw the mail-bags from the other. Occasionally,
when he drove a hackful of drummers to Rassler,
he forgot to fetch the mail. Nobody, except Billy,
minded very much; and Billy was only exercised
for the dignity of his position.

When the letters and other contents of the mail-
bags had been distributed from the porch, and the
candle-box, sacred to post-office affairs, shoved
back under his own bed, Mr. Crouch returned
with renewed zest to his roost on his fence. Meanwhile, Mrs. Crouch, a tall, bony woman, some
years older than her husband, coming in from the
field, would have said to Lorena: "Go out yander,
honey, an' find out how many o' them mens folks
yo' pa has asked to stay to dinner."

The long-legged Lorena invariably brought back
word that pa had asked them all. A few, out of
consideration for Mrs. Crouch, a few others fore-
threatened by their own wives, might go; the
majority generally stayed; and for an hour or
more the clatter of coffee-cups and the rattle of

knives and forks mingled with the creak of the well-pulley.

"Billy is powerful sociable," Mrs. Crouch returned proudly to the sympathetic comments of Mrs. Parsons and others, "an' I cert'ny ain't complainin'. He kin ask the whole settlement, drummers into the bargain, twict a week, if he wants to."

But when some one suggested that Mr. Crouch ought to set up a store on his premises, where the settlement could trade, Mrs. Crouch interfered. "No, Lorena," she said, talking it over afterward with her help and mainstay. "I jest *had* to put my foot down. Ef yo' pa was to open a sto' as full of goods as the Ark was of animals, he'd *give* 'em all away befo' that sto' was open a week. No, Billy Crouch is too free-handed to keep a sto'!"

The morning after the Reverend David French's first appearance at Peleg Church, the men of Crouch's Settlement gathered as usual at Crouch's Well. Some came at daybreak, having letters to mail; no one lagged; nearly all wore a look of deep expectation on their sun-browned faces. Mr. Crouch, with unwonted forethought, had warned his wife that "sompn was up, and there might be a leetle company to dinner."

Each fresh arrival visited the well, drew a bucket of water, tipped it to his lips from the curb, and made the profoundly original remark that Crouch's Well water could n't be beat. Then, having poured a libation into the already overflowing trough, he sought his accustomed place on the fence.

No reference was made to the subject uppermost in everybody's thoughts. There was a tacit agreement to leave that untouched until all interested should be present. But there was always Congress and its nefarious doings.

"What!" demanded Red Parsons, frowning, "what do you make of this here new bill ag'in three-cent postage-stamps, Billy? Seems to me mighty" — here, his question being purely tentative, Red stopped and scratched his head.

"Ef cuttin' stamps down to two cents apiece means redoocin' o' Billy's salary, I think we ought to send in a petition," remarked Jesse Waldrup, giving Billy time to ask himself what he did think.

"N-o-o," admitted the postmaster, pursing his lips, "it don't redooce my salary none." Billy himself was responsible for the prevailing belief that the United States government paid him a handsome salary for running the candle-box. "I kin stand cuttin' down o' stamps to two cents ef the President kin. But what *I* think is scan'lous is the tariff. The tariff, gentle*men*" — And Billy, like many another politician before and after him, soared away into the azure region of import-charges, repaying himself a thousand-fold for all the delicious, milky, cool water that had ever quenched the thirst of the settlement.

The others listened gravely, putting in a word

now and then, with an air of vital interest. But
into the midst of Mr. Crouch's lucid peroration
there fell a sound which caused Uncle Joe Wyatt
to raise an interrupting hand. A moment later
Amos Bagley appeared, with Leroy Hilliard and
Jack Ransome riding at a smart pace beside him.
"'Light, boys, 'light," cried Mr. Crouch hospitably. "I'm jist th'oo explainin' of the tariff."

"Amen," responded Bagley soberly; he dismounted and led his horse to the moss-lined
trough. His constant and unconscious use of this
ejaculation had procured his sobriquet; he had
long been known in the neighborhood as "Amen"
Bagley. He was a spare, well-built man, upwards
of fifty; a bachelor, and distinguished from the
general run of briar-breakers by his inveterate
habit of wearing a coat. He owned a small flock
of sheep, and the only threshing-machine in the
settlement. Even at sheep-dipping, or when driving the thresher over the fields under a broiling
sun, he was never seen in his shirtsleeves. But
he was much respected in the community. It was
said of him that he never took a dare or told a lie.

Hilliard had dropped his bridle on the pommel
of his saddle, and sat quietly waiting for his companions to water and hitch their horses. Uncle
Joe had called Mr. Crouch to where he sat, and
was holding a whispered consultation with him.
Billy, at its close, nodded approvingly.

"Mr. Hilliard," began Mr. Wyatt, in a solemn
tone.

Hilliard started at this unusual address, and looked around inquiringly.

"It's the sense of this here meetin', as repersented by Billy an' me, Roy," continued Mr. Wyatt, dropping into his every-day style and manner, "for you to give yo' understandin' an' opinion o' this here bob-wire-fence business, that has jest crep' into Crouch's an' the a-jinin' settlements. Me an' Billy thinks you kin break the briars offn the subjec' better 'n anybody else in this community."

Leroy Hilliard, at the age of twenty-six, had more than fulfilled his early promise of manly beauty. He retained his striking likeness to the gallant soldier whose name he bore; he was taller and more slenderly built than the elder Hilliard had been; his complexion, though bronzed by constant exposure, was fairer. But the square face, the sensitive mouth and firm chin, the white forehead with its lengthwise furrow, the brooding yellow-glinted eyes — all these made of him a living counterpart of the dead Hilliard.

Looking at him and listening to his full, flexible voice when he spoke, it was easy enough to realize that he was the most popular man on Mesquit Creek. He had been considered by some a trifle too "studdy" when he first arrived from the States. His new-fangled improvements in farming had caused him to be set down as "biggaty." But it was not long before the men admitted that the newcomer could straddle a horse and shoot a rifle, sleep on the ground in camp, and sit on the fence at Crouch's with the pick of them. The women from the first mistrusted that there never was a nimbler pair of legs in a reel, or a pair of more skillful hands at a candy-pulling than Leroy Hilliard's. "He might be a briar-breaker" was the general verdict, — the highest praise known to the settlement.

"And if anybody can explain the bob-wire contraption, Roy Hilliard can do it," Green Parsons said, settling himself well on the top-rail of the fence to listen.

Hilliard had studied the subject carefully. It was one which had engrossed public attention in the surrounding counties for months past, and it took little sagacity to foresee that the swiftly spreading evil would sooner or later invade the whole of the western part of the State. Hilliard had turned from newspaper reports, and from the talk of passing drummers, who brought into Crouch's accounts of the affair in its wider aspects, to his law-books, over which he had lately begun to pore with keen interest. He had examined county maps, and located neighborhood claims and holdings; he had looked up title-deeds, burrowing into the earliest records of the county. Finally, the day before, in company with Jack Ransome and several others, he had ridden over a part of the county, and attempted to interview the superintendent of one fence-building gang. The case, as he briefly stated it, was this: —

The public lands of Texas, free from the earliest times to the cattle roaming over them, were offered in the early '80s for sale. These rich and fertile acres were eagerly bought, the purchasers being, generally, men of great wealth, and many of them strangers who had no interest in claims or communities already existing. The building of wire fences to inclose vast tracts of these newly acquired lands had now been going steadily forward for more than a year. Gangs of laborers were at work putting down cedar posts, and stretching interminable shining lines of barbed wire in every direction. There was a certain recklessness in the proceeding, a disregard both of possible ownership and of propriety, which excited profound indignation. In some quarters the public roads and familiar byways were closed up; many small freeholds, belonging to the poorer men, were fenced in; even larger places were practically barred from communication with the common highways. But worst of all, the water supply, scarce at all times in this region, was in many instances cut off; springs, ponds, and water - holes were ringed about with the formidable wire. Sometimes this was a legitimate proceeding on the part of the new owner, sometimes it was the ignorant or the willful misconception of an agent or a squad of workmen. Thousands of cattle had already perished, but the indignant remonstrances of the people were met with indifference or contempt.

The feeling everywhere inborn in man, that

water belongs to God, and therefore to all his creatures, was heightened among old frontiersmen by the fact that from the days when the redskin roamed the prairies and the hardy pioneer disputed the ground with him inch by inch, these springs and waterways had been free alike to man and beast. Excitement had already risen to fever heat in the neighboring counties, and the wire fences had been cut in hundreds of places. But this part of the country, divided into scattered settlements and therefore less desirable, had until lately escaped the surveyor, the loud - mouthed workmen, and the invading wagon-train with its great spools of gray barbed wire.

Now, however, the outlook was becoming daily more irritating. As the scouting party had reported at Peleg Church on Sunday, Vaquero Spring, a perennial pool which welled up in a shaded depression of the open prairie about sixteen miles away toward the northeast, where numbers of cattle watered, had been inclosed; a pond, known as Crawls's Water-hole, on the prairie of the same name, nine miles westward, had shared the same fate. Granny Tatum's little property — cabin, turnip-patch, and field — now lay a forlorn dot in the midst of an enormous fenced pasture. Her out-thrust cattle were dying of thirst.

"We appealed to the superintendent at Vaquero for justice," concluded Hilliard. "He laughed in our faces. We then warned him that the men, in this settlement at least, knew their rights in the matter, and would guard them. I am prepared to prove that in the special cases cited there has been a direct encroachment upon property belonging to our people. The law " —

"D—n the law!" shouted Uncle Joe. "I ain't goin' to wait for no law case to be drug an' drug th'oo the court, whilse my cattle dies an' rots on the prery for want of water."

"All right, Mr. Wyatt," said Hilliard respectfully, lifting his hat. "I'm in line with you. I told the superintendent that we would give him twenty-four hours to open the wire to Crawls's Pond and to Vaquero Spring. And that if he did not see his way to doing this — out of common justice and common humanity, we should come and take down his fences for him. That was at eleven o'clock precisely, yesterday morning. He swore that he would shoot us down like dogs if we came on any such errand."

A buzz of angry ejaculation passed along the fence. Hilliard sat on his horse, awaiting the result of the man to man conference which followed.

"Gentlemen," cried Tom Roper, a stalwart young farmer, presently, "I move that we ride over to-night toward midnight and see if that wire's down, and if it's not down, to cut it."

This proposition was greeted with a shout of approval. The men got down from the fence to stretch their legs; there was a general movement in the direction of the well.

"I beg your pardon, gentlemen." Hilliard's voice arrested speech and movement. "I suggest that whatever is done should be done in open daylight, and under fire, if necessary. We have justice on our side, and we don't need to work under cover of darkness. I am myself willing to be one of a party that will leave here within the hour."

An absolute silence, not of timidity, but of rumination, followed this speech. "All right," said Roper carelessly. "Daylight suits me. I'll go."

Nearly every man present volunteered; but a committee, composed of the elder Wyatt, Crouch, and Bagley, decided that the delegation should consist of six of the younger men under the conduct of Hilliard. These men were chosen by lot. It was found, upon inquiry, that all of them except Hilliard himself were already armed. He accepted the loan of a pistol from Bagley. "But I will carry the nippers, also," he said, laughing, slinging the short, thick shears to his saddle-bow. "This is the weapon just now most dreaded by Jellson and his sort."

It was half past eleven; Sam Whitehead drove up from Skipton with the mail as they swung into their saddles. He reported the wire on Crawls's prairie still in place, and the cattle a-bellowin' for water.

"Good luck go with ye, boys," sung out Uncle Joe, as Hilliard and his men galloped away.

"Amen," responded Bagley, according to his custom.

An inspection of the cordon of wire which crossed one of the county roads and cut off access to Crawls's Water-hole was the first bit of work laid out by Hilliard. This road branched off westward from the main highway, a short distance beyond Crouch's; it passed for several miles through a tract of post-oak rough, dipped across Mesquit Creek, near Hilliard's place, and wound around a corner of Mrs. Ransome's farm. Beyond, a gradual rise ended in the broad plateau-like prairie. A wagon-road leading from Skipton to Peleg Church here intersected it. Exactly at the point made by these cross-roads, a cedar post had been planted; five strands of heavy barbed wire stretched away from it in either direction.

Here, the first fence-cutting in Crouch's Settlement took place — without let or hindrance. Not a human creature was in sight. The mouse-colored road wound its way, visible to right and left, for a long distance. The cattle, known by their brands as Wyatt's, Ransome's, and Roper's, roamed forlornly over the level plain, or lay panting and exhausted on the hot ground. Many were already dead, and the west wind blowing over the prairie was heavy with the stench of putrefying flesh.

After the first howl of rage, the men dismounted and went to work, grimly silent. Hilliard himself set the nippers to the wire, while the others uprooted the post and flung it aside. From this point they proceeded westward; the fence was cut in a dozen or more places within the stretch of a couple of miles. The cattle were driven through the gaps thus made and headed toward the pond. Their hoarse bellow, as they charged pell-mell across the prairie, shook the silence with a sound like muttering thunder. With tails erect and heads down, their parched tongues lolling from their mouths, their eyes rolling furiously, they pitched headlong into the open pool, many of them perishing even as they slaked their thirst.

The wire-cutting was repeated where the fences had been so drawn as to shut in Granny Tatum's place and shut out her small bunch of cattle. This done, the horses' heads were turned nearly due northward, in the direction of Vaquero Spring, where Jellson, the superintendent of the new Cottonwood Ranch, had his headquarters.

An abrupt rise from the plateau led to another, whose farther boundary north and northeast was a chain of flat-topped pyramidal hills, with occa· sional clean-cut gaps between the mesas. Hilliard called a halt as they mounted the rise and came in sight of the grove of cottonwood-trees clustered above Vaquero Spring, and the tents gleaming white beneath them. The mesas beyond were wrapped in purple haze.

"Now, boys," said Hilliard gravely, "I claim the rest of this business for myself."

A protesting murmur ran through the group around him. "You will follow me," the young leader continued, paying no attention to the inter-

ruption, "as far as the bend in the road yonder.
I will ride on to the camp alone. I wish to say
a few words to Jellson. If he fails to listen to
reason, I will dismount and argue with him further — peaceably, you understand. You will remain on your horses, and you are not to shoot
unless I give the word. Is this understood?"

His authoritative yet winning manner compelled
a hearty "Yes" from his listeners. They all rode
rapidly to the point indicated, a curve in the road
about one hundred yards from the camp. Thence
Hilliard proceeded alone. He halted in front of
the wire fence which inclosed the camp and guarded
the disputed spring. In response to his loud halloo Jellson himself came out of one of the tents,
followed by three or four men. All appeared to
be armed. Jellson, a tall, powerfully-built man
of middle age, bull-necked and straight as an
arrow, carried a shotgun.

"What in h—ll do you want?" he growled,
approaching within easy speaking distance, but
signing his men to keep back. "I've had enough
of your impudence already, young man, and I
have already told you" —

Hilliard lifted his hat. "Mr. Jellson," he interrupted politely, "I have already told you that
you have trespassed — unintentionally, no doubt
— on private property, and we have come to
ask" —

"Leave this place, sir!" thundered Jellson,
purple with rage. "If you" —

"— to ask you," Hilliard went on imperturbably, "whether you will remove this fence, which you have unlawfully placed around land which belongs to another."

"No," roared Jellson, "I will not."

"The owners of this and other private property fenced in by you and your men intend to compel you by law to keep on your own land. In the mean time, we mean to save our stock. You have refused any consideration whatever to justice or humanity. I have the honor to inform you that your fences have been cut wherever they encroached upon property belonging to other people — except this one. And I now propose to cut this."

He leaped from his horse as he spoke, and began coolly to handle the shears.

Jellson had preserved a contemptuous silence throughout Hilliard's last speech. For a full second afterward he stood as if paralyzed by the audacity of the whole proceeding. Then, with another volley of oaths, he threw his gun to his shoulder and fired. His hand, trembling with rage, was unsteady; the shot flew wide of the mark, spattering the post and digging into the ground several feet to Hilliard's right.

"Don't shoot, boys!" Hilliard called over his shoulder, hearing the beat of horses' hoofs behind him.

Jellson jerked a pistol from his belt and fired again. The bullet whistled past Hilliard's ear.

"Don't shoot, boys!" he cried again. The last

strand of wire snapped in the sharp nippers, sprang apart, and curled up with a whizzing sound.

Hilliard's foot was already in the stirrup; his men had closed around him with a cheer. "Forward!" he cried gayly; and a moment later they were flying across the prairie, shot after shot ringing, impotent, behind them.

"No, not a shot!" insisted the leader, as once or twice his companions turned threateningly with their hands on their pistols. "That last exploit was pure bravado on my part," he added, laughing. "I can't say that I am particularly proud of it! But it may set Jellson to thinking, and things may straighten out. In the mean time, the poor beasts have had water. Of course the fences will be put up again."

"And of course we'll cut 'em again," said Roper.

VIII

THE next morning Hilliard was stirring early. There was barely dawn-light enough when he climbed into the stable-loft for him to find what he wanted, — a broken bolt and a piece of tubing which needed the blacksmith's craft; and the sky was just throbbing with the first faint premonitions of sunrise when he mounted his horse and rode across his own bit of woodland toward the Branch road. The tall flowering horse-mint, crushed beneath Hector's hoofs, filled the fresh air with a homely, wholesome fragrance. The love-vine, knotting its yellow links over the sumach bushes, was threaded with shining globules; the post-oak leaves, brushing his cheek with their rough, wet surfaces, filliped the woodsy dew into his eyes. There was a pleasant twitter of birds among the treetops. He bared his head and hummed a half-remembered tune; then he sang lustily a fragment of the old ditty which Miss Wingate had sung for him the night before: —

> " When from my window-pane
> I look on night again,
> I still am lonely, my love, mine only."

The melancholy refrain had nothing in common with Helen Wingate, in the full flush of her beautiful young womanhood — nor with him!

For life was at high tide with Leroy Hilliard that June morning. He glanced back as he repeated the last phrase of the song, "My love, mine only." He could see, down a lengthening vista of the woods, a corner of his larger field, the zigzag rail fence and the clean well-grown cotton, beyond. His house was not visible, but the joyous barking of dogs indicated its whereabouts, and he knew as well as if they were under his eyes how old Manuel at that moment was stalking, stiff and taciturn as a Spanish hidalgo, to his day's work, with Juan, hoe on shoulder, chattering like a brown young monkey at his heels.

He touched the breast-pocket of his light woolen blouse, where Mrs. Blackmore's last letter, full of affectionate encouragement and brimming with delightful home news, kept guard over some crisp bank-notes. The ride to Skipton for the purpose of sending home that first sum of money had been anticipated for weeks with an almost boyish eagerness. To-day, the very motion of his spirited horse under him filled him with joy. He recalled with keen satisfaction the rousing cheer which greeted Jack Ransome's account at Crouch's, the preceding afternoon, of his, Hilliard's, successful leadership of the fence-cutters, and of his dramatic "interview" under fire with the superintendent, Jellson. A pleasant sense of power, not unmixed with self-gratulation, pervaded his being.   To this was added a delicious quickening of his pulses before a mental vision of a pair of violet-blue eyes, long-lashed, tender, beautiful.   They seemed to smile upon him, to beckon him on.   "My love, mine only," he sang, flushing consciously in the solitude of the forest.   Yes, life was at high tide with him!

He emerged from the post-oak rough into his unfenced prairie pasture.   The morning light had grown stronger, the eastern horizon was reddening; the grass, which after the long drought hardly retained a vestige of green, was already alive with grasshoppers jumping incessantly and aimlessly about; Hector recoiled with a frightened snort from a centipede — a brilliant span of yellow, brown, and red — crawling across the bridle-path. "Steady, old boy," admonished his rider.   "Hello! what's in the wind!"   His eye had been caught by some cattle who were pawing the ground and lowing excitedly near one end of the small prairie. They scattered at his approach, and peering down from his saddle, he saw that the trampled ground, elsewhere parched and cracked with the heat, was here moist; the grass about this particular spot was fresh and green.   He could follow by this agreeable verdure the course of what was probably a hitherto unsuspected underground spring.   The shallow depression dipped a few paces away into a wide, deep hollow between some bluff-like knolls, whence the ground fell off toward Mesquit Creek, whose bed was now dry as a bone.

"There is certainly water here, and the cattle, as usual, have discovered it," Hilliard mused as he rode on.

Mrs. Ransome's house stood near the Branch road, about four miles from Hilliard's farm. It was a low, weather-beaten, peak-roofed structure, sitting comfortably in the midst of an ample yard. The wide gallery was shaded by a giant jack-bean purple with bloom and thick with honey-gathering bees. A row of hollyhocks intermixed with petunias and ragged-robin bordered the walk to the front gate. There was an orchard back of the house; the fruit-trees had the gnarled and knotty look of age. Both house and orchard were, in fact, older than any other work of white man on Mesquit Creek. Mr. Ransome, now dead, had taken precedence even over Uncle Joe Wyatt as a briar-breaker, being among those settlers in the county who had heard the savage yells of the Comanche, and gazed on the shaggy heads of the last of the buffaloes. They were thrifty folk, the Ransomes, with ideas of comfort and convenience not common at that time in the settlement, and Ransome's had been for many years regarded as the likeliest place on Mesquit.

Hilliard could not forbear turning into the Peleg road, which passed directly in front of the house. Jack Ransome, hearing the sound of a horse's feet, came out of the stable. "Hullo, Roy," he cried, his ruddy young face lighting with pleasure. " 'Light, and come in."

"No," returned Hilliard, secretly longing to accept the invitation. "No, I must get over to Skipton and back before noon. Besides, it is too early."

"Oh," said Jack, resting his arms lazily on the fence. "Everybody's up. We've had breakfast, long ago. I am hooking up a team to drive mother over to Mrs. Crouch's to spend the day. Better 'light."

"No." Hilliard glanced again at the house, where he heard the sound of voices. "No," he repeated resolutely, gathering up his bridle-reins. "I may stop as I come back," he added, his heart already leaping forward to the noontide halt in the leafy shadow of the flowering-bean, with —— !

He found himself, almost before he knew it, nearing the spot where the day before the cedar post had been uprooted and flung aside, and he himself had cut the first strands of fence-wire. An hour had passed since he had left Jack Ransome at his gate. The sun was already hot, the black dust whirled in clouds from under Hector's feet. The wide, treeless plain looked dreary and desolate under the vivid blue sky. Innumerable buzzards hovered in the air, rising slowly from their disgusting feast, opening and closing their great black wings, and settling again upon the heaps of half-picked bones. The sight grated upon Hilliard's high-strung nerves; he dug his spurs unconsciously in Hector's sides and jerked the bridle-bit. The horse sprang forward a length or two, then he swerved to the side of the road, and reared so suddenly that his rider was nearly unseated. Recovering himself in an instant, Hilliard soothed the trembling animal with voice and hand. At the same time, a glance ahead showed him a man lying directly across the road, motionless and apparently dead, his face upturned and ghastly white in the sunlight. A horse saddled and bridled was standing a few paces beyond. Hilliard leaped to the ground and ran forward. As he knelt beside the prostrate figure his knee sank into a pool of blood. A hasty examination convinced him that the man — a stranger to himself — was not dead, but had fainted, probably from loss of blood. His face, lacerated by the barbed wire dragged across it, had bled profusely; the fair hair was clotted with blood and dust; one arm was thrown out, the hand clutching the dry grass; the other, twisted under him, had bled at the shoulder; a rent in the coat sleeve showed the riven flesh. In the barbed wire which coiled around his neck and shoulders like a steel spring and trailed off to where the horse was standing, Hilliard read the story. The horse had doubtless stumbled in the loose wire carelessly left in the road by the fence-cutters, then reared, in an effort to disentangle himself; the rider, taken unaware, had pitched forward and fallen heavily into the mass of quivering wire.

Hilliard rubbed the slender wrists, white and delicate as a woman's, and chafed the fair fore-

head, noting as he did so the extreme beauty of
the pallid face. A tremor of returning life soon
ran along the graceful limbs. He forced a few
drops of brandy from his own traveling flask between the man's set teeth; in a few moments his
heavy eyelids slowly lifted and his blue eyes rolled
about with a dazed expression. But as Hilliard
attempted to move him, he uttered a sharp cry.
"I think my arm must be broken," he murmured
faintly.

It took Hilliard some time, working with infinite patience and gentleness, to extricate him from
the jagged and dangerous wire. The left arm,
upon examination, proved to be broken between
the wrist and elbow; the shoulder, torn by the
wire, was also dislocated. Tearing the sufferer's
linen coat into strips, he improvised sling and
bandages, and knotted his own handkerchief about
the forehead, which continued to bleed freely.

This done, he drew the fatal wire clear of the
road, and stood for a while looking anxiously in
every direction for possible help. There was no
one in sight. He returned to the disabled man
with an air of decision. "Do you think," he
asked, kneeling again beside him, "if I lift you
into the saddle, do you think you can ride? I
must get you out of the sun and to some place
where your arm can be set, and these cuts attended
to."

"Oh, yes." The stranger sat up bravely, making a visible effort to control himself. "Of course

I can ride. I was going " — The words ended
in an involuntary groan. He sank back.

"Don't talk," said Hilliard kindly, "and don't
try to move. We shall manage somehow." He
whistled; Hector, grazing a few rods away, trotted
up, his beautiful young head lifted, his eyes shining.

"I am going to put you on my own horse," Hilliard continued, slipping his arm carefully under
his companion's shoulders and rising to his feet
with him, an almost helpless burden in his arms.
"I know that his gait is easy. Yours " —

"Oh, he 's not mine. He 's a Skipton treasure."
The stranger steadied himself with an effort in the
saddle. A gleam of humor played over his pale
face. "And he trots like a pile-driver."

The ride seemed almost interminable to Hilliard. He guided the two horses with one hand,
while with his free arm he supported his charge,
who had become feverish and slightly delirious.
He was obliged to stop again and again to adjust
the sling, or moisten the trembling lips with
brandy. The morning was far advanced when he
finally reached Mrs. Ransome's gate. "Miss
Margaret," he called in a quiet tone. There was
a surprised movement behind the vines on the gallery; he caught a fleeting glimpse of two girlish
figures. One of them instantly appeared on the
step. "Oh, Mr. Hilliard, what is it? Who is
hurt?" cried Margaret Ransome, running bareheaded down the walk.

"Do not be frightened. It is nothing serious," returned Hilliard. He had already dismounted and taken the unconscious man in his arms, and was pushing open the gate with his knee. He explained the situation hurriedly as he passed up the walk. The girl, flying ahead of him, led the way into her mother's room, where he laid his patient on the bed, and began at once to loosen the improvised bandages, and tear away the bloody shirtsleeve. Margaret brought a basin of water, linen cloths, and home-made ointments; and assisted with deft and quiet hands in the operation of setting the broken arm, and in dressing the wounds made by the barbed wire. She paled now and then, but followed Hilliard's directions bravely.

They were both unskilled in surgery, but the shoulder was finally pulled in place, the broken arm set and splinted, the blood and mire washed from the matted hair and the pale face, and the bandaged head laid back on big, white pillows. Hilliard, blood-stained and dusty, with uprolled sleeves, and an unwonted expression of fatigue about him, stood looking down at the face on the pillow. It was a very beautiful face, — blond and delicate and spirituelle. The white brow was shaded by curling hair, absolutely golden in color; the eyebrows, the long, upturned lashes, and the light mustache drooping over the handsome mouth — which seemed made for smiles — were a shade darker; the hands crossed on the breast were exquisitely moulded, long and slender, with tapering fingers, — the hand of a girl, yet conveying somehow an idea of strength.

"He seems very young. I wonder who he is," mused the watcher. He turned at the sound of light footfalls on the bare floor. Margaret, who had gone out a moment before carrying basin, towels, and stained bandages, had reëntered. Helen Wingate was with her; an involuntary thrill stirred Hilliard's pulses at sight of her.

This was suddenly arrested by the look which overspread her face. She had paused at the foot of the bed; a vivid blush flooded her brow and cheek. She drew back with a surprised exclamation.

"You know him?" demanded Hilliard quickly.

"Yes — he — they are neighbors of ours in Kentucky. His mother lives quite near us. His name is Allan Deerford."

Hilliard's brows contracted in a sudden effort of memory; the furrow on his forehead deepened; the scarlet line, as always when he was under the influence of painful emotion, leaped along his left cheek. "Where have I heard that name? What have I to do with Deerford? *Deerford! Deerford!*" These inward questionings, which proved fruitless, passed like a flash of lightning through his brain.

At the same moment Allan Deerford opened his eyes — blue as forget-me-nots.

It would be difficult for a man coming out of a swoon to find awaiting his first bewildered glance a fairer picture than that presented by the two young women standing at the foot of the bed whereon Deerford was lying. Their pretty heads were close together, their arms were intertwined. The contrast between the two types of beauty heightened the charm of both. Both girls were tall and slender, and exquisitely proportioned. Helen Wingate was wonderfully fair; a wild-rose color in her cheeks and the deep scarlet of her lips gave her oval face a vividness almost belied by the gravity and luminous softness of her dark violet eyes. A mass of reddish brown hair waved away from her low brow, and from the loose, heavy coil on the nape of her neck little strands escaped, to lie like rings of burnished copper against her white skin. There was an air of repose about her slow, almost majestic, movements, which seemed hardly in keeping with the airy and winning grace of her manner, and the joyousness of her speech and laughter. A little pale from a recent illness when she first arrived from her home in Kentucky, on a visit to her friend and classmate, she now bloomed with radiant and buoyant health.

Margaret Ransome's skin had the delicate transparent whiteness of a yucca bloom; her long-lashed eyes were gray. Her abundant hair was intensely black, perfectly straight, and so long that it fell when unbound far below her knees. Her features were irregular, but of a cameo-like fineness; her voice was soft, but singularly clear and penetrat-

ing. Lithe but vigorous, she seemed surrounded
by an atmosphere of vitality.

But it was not upon this rare and gracious picture that Allan Deerford's eyes first fell. They
opened full upon Hilliard's face. Pain and de-
lirium had hitherto prevented him from taking
note of his deliverer. He now seemed to see him
for the first time. He frowned. His fair face
clouded. He also struggled with some dim, intangible, antagonistic memory.

The two brothers, each utterly unknown to the
other, gazed at one another silently for a long
second.

Then Deerford's eyes wandered, and opened
wide with surprise. "Miss Helen!" he cried joyfully, attempting to rise. The sudden movement
wrenched from him a suppressed groan. "Ah, I
had forgotten," he said. "What a hole you
pulled me out of, to be sure!" He turned his
glance gratefully on Hilliard, the momentary dis-
trust vanishing. "I don't know where I would
have been by this time, but for you!"

Hilliard's face had also cleared. "I was in
honor bound to look after you," he said smiling,
"since I was indirectly the cause of your mishap."
He explained, without going into detail, the wire-
cutting of the previous day.

Deerford's fall, it appeared, had occurred precisely as Hilliard had conjectured. He had left
Skipton before sunrise, and must therefore have
been lying unconscious in the road some time be-

fore Hilliard's timely arrival. He remembered
nothing after his fall and the sharp prick of the
wire on his forehead, until he opened his eyes to
the face bending over him, and felt the painful
rush of renewed life through his veins. "I should
certainly have bled to death if you had not found
me," he concluded.

"Oh, somebody else would have happened along.
It is a traveled road," said Hilliard hastily.
"You will have to keep quiet for a few days," he
added. "But you will soon be on your feet
again."

Miss Wingate, who had recovered from her
momentary embarrassment, here interposed with
formal introductions. This ceremony ended, she
asked, "When did you leave The Bluffs, Mr.
Deerford?"

"Oh, about three weeks ago. I stopped at
several places *en route*. I came out to see about
some property — some disputed property — I have
somewhere around here." There was an undertone in the speaker's voice — mocking or malicious
— which did not escape Hilliard's sensitive ear.
Deerford had looked with smiling boldness at
Helen as he spoke. She dropped her eyes, and the
color in her cheeks deepened.

"I hope you have not come as a fresh ' bob-'
wire emissary," said Margaret gayly. "But your
home-news must wait, Helen. I think our patient
had best stop talking now, and sleep if he can, or
he will be having fever in downright earnest. He

may have a plate of chicken broth presently.
Oh," as a hungry protest came laughingly from
the patient himself — "if you think my reign a
tyranny, wait until you fall under my mother's
iron despotism! She will take possession of you
this afternoon the moment she returns. Come,
Helen."

The girls withdrew. Deerford fell almost instantly into a profound slumber. Hilliard remained by the bedside, watching him. His own
vague uneasiness had returned. He wrestled with
it manfully, looking down on the youthful face
which in sleep had lost the disingenuous expression
which alone marred its expression. But the feeling remained in spite of his resolution.

"The fellow has come to Texas for the sole purpose of seeing her, confound him," he said to himself, as he rode homeward late that afternoon.
"And I may as well admit to myself at once that
that is the ground of my prejudice! I wonder if
she " — he paused, not wishing even to frame the
thought. But he sighed; he found himself curiously tired and out of sorts. A jarring note had
somehow disturbed the harmony to which, a few
hours earlier, all his being was set; a discomfort
hitherto unknown to him in all his vigorous,
healthy life pervaded his mind and his body.
"What is the matter with me!" he exclaimed
aloud. "Have I so little backbone that I go into
a jelly at the mere sight of a little yellow whipper-
snapper from the States? Ho! ho!" He pulled

himself together, and his cheery laugh rang through
the silent woods and came echoing back. Hector
pricked up his ears and moved forward with a
lighter step, as if he, too, had shaken off some
invisible burden. Suddenly he threw up his head
and neighed softly. "Not another Kentucky rival,
I beseech you, Hector," said Hilliard whimsically.
Hector neighed again, trotted on a few paces, and
stopped still.

"Hey, boy! Hi, boy!" The voice came from
a clump of sumach by the roadside. Hilliard
recognized it before its owner lifted his long length
from the ground, and laid a hand on the horse's
glistening neck. "How do you do, Mr. Croft,"
he said in a cordial tone.

Abner Croft was a tall, thin, shambling fellow,
with bent shoulders, who, at a glance, looked
twice his thirty years. Close observation revealed,
however, the powerful muscles of youth, and the
bone and sinew of an athlete. There was something uncanny about his appearance. Supersti-
tious people were afraid of his pale blue eyes,
which pierced, they said, like a brad-awl from
under their stiff, shaggy eyebrows. But, as is
often the case with a certain sort of terrifying and
mysterious folks, children and animals were fascinated by him. These, by the way, have apparently no sense of what we call beauty, — that fair-
ness and proportion of form and feature which
makes the exterior attractive, and by which we,
confessedly, are sometimes deceived. The dog

following his hunchbacked master with inexhaustible devotion; the child pressing its blooming cheek to a scarred and withered bosom, or cooing caressingly into a monstrous black face — such things prove that there is a subtle divination in unsophisticated creatures which reaches beneath the envelope of flesh and finds something which more perverted eyes cannot see.

Hector, whom he had bred from a colt and sold to his present master, ran to Croft always upon sight, and found him when his presence was unknown to others.

Croft was the chimney-builder, the well-digger, and the grave-digger of Crouch's Settlement. He held a pick in his hand now, as he stood on the roadside; a long dogwood switch denuded of its leaves was stuck in the band of his ragged wool hat.

"Have you been looking for water, Mr. Croft?" asked Hilliard, glancing at the switch.

"No," Croft returned, with a quick upward scowl, as if ready to resent any approach at jocularity on the subject. Seeing the soberness of the young man's face, he added, "I've been diggin' a well over at Red Parsons's. His old one has gone plum dry. It's cur'us, Mr. Hilliard, how water acks in this county, dryin' up in one place, an' breakin' out all to onct in another. Now that there well of Tip Elliott's — seventy feet deep. I dug it myse'f. Water ez good ez Crouch's, ef not better. An' plenty of it. Well, sir, whenever the north wind blows, that well of Tip Elliott's goes dry. What do you make of that, out'n yo' schoolin', Mr. Hilliard?"

Hilliard answered absently. It was not the first time Croft had commented on the phenomenon and asked his opinion. "Abner," he broke out abruptly, "would you mind stepping over to my prairie pasture with me? It isn't far, you know. Have you time?"

"Why, cert'ny," returned the well-digger, looking pleased. "I've got all time. I was jest loafin' along, so's not to get home afore nighttime. Old Ma'am Croft might put me to churnin', or sompn." He winked slyly to himself. Old Ma'am Croft was his mother, to whom he was known to be very devoted.

Hilliard dismounted, and the two men walked on together, Hector following at a little distance like a pleased dog. There was no further conversation. Croft, used to being shunned by his neighbors, and to holding himself aloof from them, had an uneasy look at finding himself actually alongside of one of them. His brief talks with Hilliard had heretofore been held in passing, as it were, and with that gentleman astride of Hector. A half hour or so of brisk tramping brought them to the small prairie set like a treeless island in the heart of the surrounding rough.

The little bunch of cattle were gathered as before near the edge of the slope falling away to the creek. They retired slowly as the two men came up. "What do you make of this, Mr. Croft?" demanded Hilliard, indicating the moist hollow. "An underground spring?"

Abner had taken the dogwood switch from his hat-band and held it thoughtfully in his hand. "I don't know," he said, with a doubtful sidewise look at the questioner. "Looks like it. This here is a funny country. Water is all the time wellin' down in one place, an' wellin' up in another."

"Try the switch," suggested Hilliard, in good faith.

Croft nodded, and stepped back without a word to the knoll above the depression. He placed the butt end of the switch against his breast, holding it in place with the thumb and forefinger of his left hand. He walked steadily forward, stepped across the band of green grass, and turned a pace or two to the right. The flexible end of the switch dipped suddenly downward, sprung up, and dipped again almost imperceptibly. "There's water," said the diviner carelessly over his shoulder, "but not over an' above much of it."

"Well," said Hilliard, secretly convinced that he was mistaken in his last statement, "I have been thinking that if there is water here, what a fine tank we could have. You see this hollow;" he paused to tilt back his straw hat and thrust his hand into his pocket for his handkerchief. At sight of the blood stains on the square of linen — for the handkerchief had served as a bandage for Deerford's forehead — Croft uttered a hoarse cry, and leaped backward. His eyes were terror-stricken; he trembled from head to foot. "Why, Abner," exclaimed Hilliard, amazed, running to him, "What is the matter? Are you sick? Are you hurt?"

"No, no," stammered the man, turning his face aside. "Don't mind it, Mr. Hilliard," he continued, setting his teeth together impatiently. "It's the blood. I can't help it. They say that my father was killed under my mother's eyes jest afore I was born. She ain't never spoke of it to me, pore little creeter. But I reckin it's that. I dunno. It plum skeers me into fits to see blood, or a corpse. An' me a grave-digger by perfession. That's why I do it. I'm wrastlin' with that white liver o' mine. An' I'll down it, or die!"

"Give me your hand on it, Mr. Croft," said Hilliard, touched by a confidence which the reticent man had never offered to any one before. He grasped the horny hand held out to him, warmly, and affected not to notice Croft's emotion. "You see this hollow," he proceeded, as if there had been no interruption. "Don't you think by throwing a dam yonder, and another here," indicating two gaps in the deep natural basin below the slope, "that we can get a fine head of water?"

"Cert'ny," responded Croft promptly. "I don't think you'll get it from the onderground spring," he added honestly. "But you make the dam, an' one of our hell-roarin' rains — ef we ever git one ag'in — 'd fill her chuck full. It's a good idee,

Mr. Hilliard. Then I s'pose you'd fence in yo' paster."

"Eh? Why, no, of course not," said Hilliard. "I propose to have water enough to water all the cattle around here — at least all the home-cattle — until this wire fence outrage is abolished."

"Lord, Mr. Hilliard," muttered Abner, gazing at him quizzically, "the fool-killer is cert'ny layin' fer sech as you!"

"Can you" — began Hilliard.

"Cert'ny," interrupted Croft, "I'll take the job. I ain't got nothin' to do. I'll git Red 'n' Green Parsons's children to he'p gether rocks, 'n' — you jest leave it to me, Roy, I'll commence termorrer. But you ain't goin' to git over an' above much water out'n this onderground spring," he concluded obstinately. "You'll have to wait for a hell-roarin' rain."

"All right," laughed Hilliard. "The rain will do — if it ever comes. Come over to my house in the morning, and get what you need. I'll send Juan with a mule and cart back with you."

He shook hands again with the digger, who shouldered his pick and trudged away. Then he mounted and rode home through the waning light.

"Deerford. *Deerford*," he mused, tossing sleeplessly on his bed that night. "Where have I heard that name! And this stranger — pshaw, why do I think of him? What have I to do with him, or he with me?"

What indeed!

IX

A WEEK passed before Hilliard saw his friends, the Ransomes, or the newcomer, Allan Deerford, again. His crop was nominally laid by, but the weeds and the tie-vines, which flourished in spite of the long-continued drought, demanded unremitting attention. He took his place, as usual, by Manuel's side, hoe in hand, under the blistering sun, while Juan hauled stone and earth for Abner Croft at the new water-tank. He did not go to Crouch's for his mail, and the remittance for Mrs. Blackmore still waited to be forwarded from Skipton; the unmended bolt had been cast aside. Rumors reached him, through Croft and others, of fresh complications arising from the barbed wire which was still creeping like a steel centipede across the prairies; but he learned that Jellson had at least left Crawls's Water-hole open to the cattle, and this important concession was, he thought, all that could be expected at the moment.

He avoided as much as possible the thought of Deerford, whose very name aroused undefinably unpleasant sensations; he heard no mention of the

man, and he conjectured that he had left the neighborhood. He had no mind, however, to banish
from his thoughts the vision of Helen Wingate
which hovered star-like and lovely over his sleeping and waking dreams. She was the first woman
who had come to stir the inner depths of his nature. He had been singularly free from even the
callow and fleeting affairs considered inseparable
from the schoolboy and young collegian period of
life.

An electric shock had thrilled him when, riding
slowly along the Peleg road one day in the early
spring, his head bent in deep meditation, he looked
up and found himself face to face with a stranger
— a young girl — also on horseback. She was
alone, and had approached so quietly, her horse's
hoofs falling lightly on the deep sand, that she
had upon his startled senses almost the effect of
an apparition from another world. She wore a
close-fitting habit of gray cloth, ornamented with
brass buttons; a wide black-plumed gray hat
shaded her brow, and a pair of long gauntlets of
undressed leather covered her hands. Hilliard's
heart leaped. A swift but vivid memory of a
commanding figure in Confederate gray uniform,
with proud face and deep, tender eyes, swam between him and the beautiful young stranger
mounted on Jack Ransome's bay filly. Recovering his self-possession, he had barely time to lift
his hat courteously and give the road, for the girl,
touching her horse lightly with her whip, had

darted past him, and was already disappearing. He could not at once define his feeling for Helen Wingate, whose acquaintance he immediately sought. He had a passionate desire to serve her, as if in return for some inestimable act of grace to himself. "For just condescending to live and be, I suppose," he laughed to himself with a fullness as of tears in his throat. This exalted worship continued, remaining a thing apart, in the midst of the overwhelming but explicable love of a man for the woman whom he wishes to make his wife. The latter feeling came more slowly — yet it was not long in coming.

He had seen her almost daily, for Jack Ransome, younger than himself by several years, was one of the earliest friends he had made in the settlement, and Mrs. Ransome and Margaret stood almost in the relation of mother and sister to him. He had not put his fate to the final test; he had been restrained from this step by several reasons, chief among them being the knowledge, accidentally acquired, that Miss Wingate, the only child of a widowed mother, was heir to great wealth. A sense of delicacy, moreover, forbade him to press his suit while she was absent from her own home. He had determined to follow her there and demand permission to woo her frankly and openly. He had so far thought himself, if not secure, at least not in danger of formidable rivalry. Now, a competitor had appeared. He might banish the fair face of that competitor from his mind, but the rival was no less in the field. "I shall not wait," he now decided. "I cannot afford to wait." His self-conflict and very desire to settle the matter once for all had as much to do as the needs of his cotton crop with his absence from Mrs. Ransome's during the week following Deerford's arrival. It went far, also, toward explaining his feverish activity in the construction of the water-tank.

This work had progressed rapidly. Croft, who developed unexpected engineering talent, had gone beyond Hilliard's original simple scheme. The dam was really a fine piece of rough masonry, — a rock wall carefully cemented, and protected by a wide embankment of earth, inclosed the outer and open side of the enlarged hollow, making a pond-like basin. Easy approaches for the cattle to the hoped-for supply of water were made. A shaft was sunk and water found, though as the experienced well-digger had predicted, in no great quantity, at the head of the moist grass-lined depression on the prairie; from this shaft, a rude pipe had been laid to the basin, and both shaft and pipe were well covered with earth to prevent injury by the trampling cattle.

When Hilliard at the end of the week made his usual daily visit, he found Abner leaning on his spade and surrounded by a ragged battalion composed of Red Parsons's boys and their cousins, the Green Parsons girls — all as hardy and handy at rock-gathering as at cotton-picking or coon-hunting. A thin stream of water from the pipe trickled down the upper side of the tank; and a small pool continually soaking into the dry earth, and as often renewed, showed on the bottom. Abner received Hilliard's thanks and congratulations with becoming modesty. "I think she's a fair job, myse'f," he admitted. "But you'll have to stretch a wire fence around the tank, Mr. Hilliard, to give the water a chanct. Ef you don't, the cattle'll be tumblin' over the eedge after that cupful o' water down there. There won't be no water wo'th talking about no-how ontil we get a hell-roarin' rain. Then you kin take down the fence an' turn her loose. You'll have a tank that'll set the settlement to shoutin' hallelujah."

He readily undertook the further business of putting a temporary fence around the tank. "Step lively, gals," he cried gayly, as Hilliard rode off, for the Red Parsonses, at the suggestion of more work, had sneaked to the creek bottom. "Step lively, an' he'p dig these post-holes."

A new element had come into Abner Croft's lonely and colorless life with that first hearty and sympathetic handshake from Leroy Hilliard. His peculiarities, real and imagined, had set him apart from the open and expansive people around him. He had lived among them more than a dozen years, building their chimneys, digging their wells and their graves, lending a hand at their house-raisings, and "yearning" (*i. e.* charming) their children, but utterly aloof from themselves. His mother — whom few in the settlement had ever

seen, and who was vaguely understood to be a little
"cracked" — had hitherto been the sole grown-up
human being with whom he ever held voluntary
speech, except in the way of business. Even the
few words he had exchanged with Hilliard from
time to time in passing had been a matter of
wonder to himself. Now, in one moment a sealed
fountain had been opened, and Hilliard had become unwittingly an object of almost passionate
veneration to the "yearner." "Sompn inside me
busted loose when I seen the shine of his eyes that
day," he said long afterward to Margaret Ransome, "sompn cert'ny busted loose."

Strange to say, Margaret understood this obscure explanation.

Some days after the water-tank was pronounced
finished, Hilliard rode to Skipton and transacted
his interrupted business there. He passed a corner of Mrs. Ransome's place after daybreak; he
could see a flutter of white dresses in the garden;
he fancied he heard the echo of girlish laughter,
but he galloped stolidly on, not even turning his
head. He made a circuit on the open prairie to
avoid the spot where he had found Deerford —
this, however, under pretense of examining Jellson's new line of wire. His satisfaction in finding the water-hole still open to the cattle helped
to dissipate a slight bitterness which for several
days had been stealing into his soul. "As if anything could be wrong!" he exclaimed in a tone of
self-reproach. "I will stop on my way back."

About mid-afternoon he drew rein at Mrs. Ransome's gate. The thought came back to him in spite of himself as he dismounted, that Jack Ransome had not crossed his threshold for nearly a fortnight. Such a thing had not happened before since he had settled on Mesquit Creek. Jack Ransome, sitting on his porch, sprawling on his home-made lounge, Jack smoking his pipes and roaring over his comic newspaper-weeklies, Jack borrowing his guns, or sitting at the foot of his dinner-table — he had not until now realized how large a part of his daily life the lad had become, for Jack, though twenty years old, was but a great boisterous affectionate boy. He felt an unwonted embarrassment as he strode up the flower-bordered walk to the house. His approach had evidently been unnoted. He paused at the foot of the steps, and stood there — it seemed to him a long time, before any one observed him. Deerford was sitting in a large rocking-chair; his arm was still in a sling, but his face had regained its healthy color, and the wounds on his temple had healed. He looked bright and joyous. Helen Wingate's guitar lay across his knees, and he swept his right hand occasionally across the strings to emphasize the story he was telling. The two girls, side by side on a bench, were leaning forward eagerly. Jack sat on a low stool, literally at the stranger's feet. Mrs. Ransome, in the shadow of the vines, had dropped her sewing in her lap, and was listening. "And so," concluded

Deerford gayly, "L'Eclair won by a couple of
lengths, proving that — like the family doctor — a
good jockey drunk is better than a poor one sober."

Margaret Ransome drew back, a distinct shade
of disapprobation crossing her expressive face.
She seemed about to speak. But Jack had caught
sight of Hilliard. "Hello, Roy," he cried, springing to his feet, "where did you drop from, old
man!"

"Good morning, Mr. Hilliard," called Deerford
in the same breath. "Come in. Come in!" He
had, Hilliard thought afterward, quite the air of
a man doing the honors of his own house. At the
moment, however, in the passing of his own slight
embarrassment, this escaped his notice; he found
himself shaking hands all around as usual, and
responding lightly to Margaret Ransome's banter.

"Why haven't you been here!" she demanded.
"Where have you been keeping yourself? When
last heard of, you were in conference with the
silent and lugubrious Croft. We had about concluded that you had ordered your own grave, and
descended into it for a fixed period, like a self-
resurrecting Mahatma."

"We have missed you, Roy," said Mrs. Ransome, with motherly gentleness.

Hilliard looked quickly at Helen; she was
absorbed in a half-whispered conversation with
Deerford. "Oh," he said, turning to Margaret,
"you bright-winged butterflies that flit from ear
to ear — of corn, for a brief season only, cannot

understand how a cotton-grub has to toil. I can show you the regulation July hoe-handle blisters on my horny palms."

"We have heard about your new water-tank," said Margaret, suddenly serious. "It is a beautiful idea" —

"You are setting up as a public philanthropist, for man and beast, eh, Mr. Hilliard?" Deerford broke in. The sneer in his voice was unmistakable, though he looked airily unconscious, swinging himself back and forth in the rocker.

Hilliard flushed and bit his lip. "For beasts only, Mr. Deerford," he returned, looking full into the speaker's face. But, ashamed in an instant of this brutal allusion to the service he had rendered a helpless stranger, he continued without showing the effort the words cost him, "you must ride over as soon as you are able to do so, Mr. Deerford, and inspect the Croft masterpiece — the water-tank, which, by the way, has no water in it! and spend a couple of weeks with me, or as long as it may be agreeable to you to share my bachelor quarters."

"Thanks." The sneer in Deerford's voice had given place to a hardly veiled antagonism.

The others apparently had not caught the meaning of this slight passage-at-arms. It went no further, for Jack Ransome broke in, "Able! Shucks! He has already been on horseback several times. He rode over to Crouch's with the girls yesterday morning and came home by way of

Peleg Church.   Allan stood the racket better than
any of us."

Allan ! Hilliard felt as if the earth were breaking under him, knocked to pieces by the slender
hand which he had warmed to life a bare fortnight
ago!

"And that reminds me, Roy," continued young
Ransome, "there is a meeting of the fence-cutters
called for to-morrow.   At Crouch's.   Ten o'clock.
I promised Billy and Uncle Joe Wyatt that I
would ride by your place yesterday and notify you.
But I forgot it.   Allan and I are going early."

"Yes," said Deerford lazily.   "I want to study
the barbed-wire controversy — and the natives."

"Take care!   The natives may do some study-
ing in return."   Hilliard thought he detected some
sarcasm in Margaret's shot, and he glanced gratefully at her.   He had arisen to go, feeling oddly
out of place in the familiar group.

"Why, Roy," remonstrated Mrs. Ransome,
"are n't you going to stay to dinner?"

"Of course you will, old fellow," cried Jack.

"You have not told us the Skipton news," urged
Margaret.

Again Hilliard cast a covert glance toward
Helen.   She had hardly spoken at all during his
brief visit.   She did not now lift her down-dropped
eyelids.   Deerford kept his smiling face turned
toward hers, completely ignoring the debate.

"I must go," Hilliard said quietly, turning
away.

"Be sure and meet us at Crouch's to-morrow,"
Jack called after him, not moving from his place.
Margaret walked beside him to the gate. He was
so blinded by anger, disappointment, wounded
pride, — a thousand conflicting emotions, — that
he did not even see her. She, on her part, could
think of nothing to say, though her heart was
throbbing with sympathy and indignation. Only,
at parting, she put out her firm white hand; he
clasped it in his own. And when the angry tumult
in his breast had a little subsided, he tried to remember what it was that had sent something like
a healing thrill along his bruised nerves.

Crouch's Well presented a lively appearance
the next morning towards eleven o'clock. The
usual mail-day crowd was augmented by numbers of
men from outlying settlements, who were suffering
from the barbed-wire outrage; many of these had
brought their shotguns with them, and their belts
bristled with small arms. A dozen or more passing teamsters and drummers had stopped for the
meeting; and there were as many idlers from
Skipton and Rassler, who had come over, avowedly
to see the fun. Mrs. Crouch, making no pretense
of farm-work for the day, was already in the
kitchen with Lorena and the younger children;
the appetizing smell of frying bacon and boiling
coffee pervaded the air. Billy was in his glory.
He kept slipping from his place on the fence to
greet fresh arrivals; and he drew water from the

well at a rate which left his round face purple and his short arms limp. It may be remarked in passing that Billy never dreamed of drawing water for Mrs. Crouch.

Uncle Joe Wyatt was haranguing the crowd when Hilliard rode up. Among the most attentive and respectful listeners was Allan Deerford. He looked very handsome and picturesque. He was in his shirtsleeves. A light blue silk handkerchief, coquettishly knotted, served as a sling for his left arm; it also served to intensify the clear blue of his sparkling eyes. His white flannel trousers were tucked into high boots and girdled by a leather belt. In the latter he wore conspicuously a small dagger with an oddly-shaped silver hilt. On the heels of his boots jingled a pair of silver spurs. Many of the older men had grunted disapproval when this dashing figure had galloped up alongside of Jack Ransome; the younger ones, sneering openly, secretly admired his theatrical appearance.

"I hain't no call to palaver," concluded Mr. Wyatt, "no more 'n to say, that bob-wire has been wound worse 'n a spider-web th'oo an' th'oo this county. Water has been shet in, an' cattle has been shet out, as Roy Hilliard has explained nigh a month ago. It gits mo' an' mo' aggravated every day. That job o' wire-cuttin' was good as far as it went. But 't w'an't enough. Ef this thing keeps on, there won't be a steer left in the county."

An angry murmur ran like a low growl of thunder along the fence.

"What's to be done, gentlemen? That's the question. That's what we've met here ag'in to consider."

"Cut the wire! Cut the wire!"

"Drag the posts an' the d—d post-setters out of the county."

"Blow the cussed agents into kingdom come."

"I'm ready to start, right now."

"So am I."

"And I."

"And I."

"Let's start with the wire across Burke's prairie."

"Wait a minute, boys. The captain has got a word or two to say." This last sentence came from Roper, who had been lounging against the fence near where Hilliard sat. There was instant cessation of noise.

"I wish to say, friends," said Hilliard, in a quiet but emphatic tone, "that I think this is a matter to be carefully considered. As I said at our last meeting, wherever the wires are stretched upon private property, or block public roads, we have, according to my opinion, the right to protect ourselves. I have already joined in one expedition of this kind. I stand ready to do so again. But we have no more right to destroy other people's property than they have to destroy ours. To all of the places just mentioned — begging your pardon, Mr. Wyatt — I happen to know that the men who have fenced in have acquired legal ownership. Burke's prairie is a part of the Cottonwood Ranch. I would suggest that " —

"I move we pull up every strange post and cut every strand of new wire in the Settlement."

Everybody turned, amazed, at this interruption. It came from Deerford. He had sprung upon the half-empty water-trough and was standing in an easy attitude, with his straw hat in his free hand, and his blue eyes roving over the crowd.

"What the devil has that jack-in-the-box got to do with it," growled Bagley.

This feeling was shared for one second by nearly every man present. But Deerford had unquestionably struck the popular chord. A brief silence was followed by a loud approving cheer.

"I know," continued Deerford gracefully, "that I am a stranger — and thanks to this same barbed wire — a lame one, at that. But this does not keep me from seeing what is just and right. The barbed-wire business from first to last is a damnable outrage. If it is allowed to go on, as the last speaker has so justly and forcibly observed, there will not be a steer left in the county, — neither beef-meat, milk-cow, or beast of burden! By what right — I ask this of intelligent and high-minded citizens — by what right does the bloated capitalist of the far north and the far east, with his millions and his minions, dare to invade the sacred homes and the inviolable birthright of the poor, perhaps, but free and manly Texan?"

The speaker was interrupted by wild and almost savage yells of indorsement. With rare skill he had found and played upon the dominant key of the pioneer character, — an almost unreasoning mistrust of the rich and a dread of his encroachment upon their rights.

"I am a stranger," he resumed when the applause had a little subsided, "but time will remedy that, for I propose to cast in my lot with the people of Crouch's Settlement. Moreover, I claim the right to lead a party this very night to riddle the fence on Burke's prairie to atoms."

Bagley fairly gasped at the audacity of the man. Hilliard had turned pale; the red line shone like a sword-cut on his cheek. But his voice was steady and his acknowledged influence compelled attention as he said: —

"I beg to utter my protest against what Mr. Deerford has just said. I think he is mistaken, even if the matter be considered from the standpoint alone of public policy. And I claim no right over any man's conscience, — but I for one will not take part in setting an example of wanton destruction of property which is not mine."

"Amen," said Bagley emphatically.

"I have already given my views on the subject of night raids," continued Hilliard, "and I warn those proposing to lead such that they will be directly responsible for consequences probably dangerous."

There was a dead, uneasy silence. Red Parsons unwound his long legs from the rails where he sat, got down and walked over to Hilliard and stood by him in solemn allegiance. Bagley grinned understandingly and moved up near them; Abner Croft followed, dragging a long-handled pick after him.

The others looked at each other, anxious and uncertain.

"Meet me at nine o'clock to-night, on the Peleg road, near Blackbird Gully." Deerford spoke with assured authority. "And — down with the wire-pullers!"

The phrase caught the fancy of his hearers; the sentiment chimed but too well with their own exasperated feelings. "Down with the wire-pullers!" The idlers joined lustily in the shout; even the freighters, hitherto but mildly interested in the proceedings, caught the contagion and cried, "Down with the wire-pullers!"

"The signal for the start will be" — Deerford interrupted himself, and looked around with affected apprehension. "I take it for granted, gentlemen, that there are no *informers* present." His glance rested as if by accident on Hilliard — "the signal, I repeat, will be two pistol-shots at half past nine at Blackbird Gully on the Peleg road. Do you agree, gentlemen?"

"Yes, yes. Hurrah for Deerford! Down with the wires. Down with the wire - pullers!" A frenzy of enthusiasm possessed the crowd. They swarmed about the young stranger, shaking his hand, overwhelming him with compliments, and showering invitations upon him.

Hilliard stood apart, wondering at the easy grace with which he received this rough ovation, wondering still more at the surprising quickness with which he had become acquainted with the lay of the neighborhood and its roads.

This knowledge in truth was superficial. Deerford possessed a certain alertness of mind, and a trick of catching and weaving together floating threads which, to an ordinary observer, had no connection with each other. He had also a retentive memory, a natural fondness for adventure, and great personal courage.

Rich, idle, and unscrupulous, he had in all his life known but one really honest feeling. This was his love for Helen Wingate. It had been his avowed determination since his early boyhood to make her his wife. Meantime, there were other things to make life worth while! He had followed her to Texas as much for the excitement to be had in a semi-frontier neighborhood, as for the desire to be near her. He had for years counted her as already won, though he had not as yet committed himself by open speech. Young, beautiful, and rich, she had had many suitors. But in Hilliard he had encountered the first rival who appeared to him worth the unsheathing of his sword. Moved less by jealousy than by an instinctive hatred, he had drawn his weapon the very first day. Meantime, again, there were other things to make life

worth while on Mesquit Creek! It was not opposition to Hilliard alone which had caused him to
propose himself as a leader of the fence-cutters.
Every fibre of his reckless nature tingled with
rapture at the prospect of the wild midnight raids,
the dash into probable danger, the quick doublings
and turnings on the homeward route, with the
baffled pursuer at his heels!

"To-night, boys," he cried at length, springing
on his horse without regard to his lame arm.
Hilliard noted with an angry pang that he was
riding Diana, the bay filly which had been sacred
to Helen ever since her arrival.

The first batch of diners were trooping into the
house, escorted by Billy. The belated teamsters
were watering their horses and getting ready to
move off. There was some trading of horses
among the idlers, and not a few small but lively
quarrels. Hilliard made his way through the
confusion to where Jack Ransome sat his horse,
gaping with admiration at Deerford.

"Jack," he began in a low voice. Young Ransome turned a reluctant face toward him. "Jack,
I want you to promise me that you will not go on
that raid to-night."

"The h—l you do," returned Jack, in genuine
astonishment. "I hope you don't think I'd miss
it. No, sir, not for a million!"

Hilliard lost control of himself a little. "Listen, Jack," he said impatiently. "The trouble is
this. Your friend Mr. Deerford" —

"The trouble with you, Mr. Leroy Hilliard," interrupted Jack with boyish impertinence, "is that you are jealous of my friend Mr. Deerford."

Hilliard drew back as if he had received a blow. He turned Hector's head and rode away without another word.

"Roy," said Red Parsons, riding up beside him, in company with Bagley, "I 'm a thousand times er-bleedged to you for expressin' of them straight-out principles to-day. I seen 'em clear enough in my mind whilst Uncle Joe Wyatt was jabberin', but I could n't of laid 'em off plain an' Christian, like you did. Them principles is my principles."

"Principles!" chuckled Amen. "Oh, yes. I am proud to say, Roy, that your principles are sound to the core. But I am also bound to say that if that cavortin' blue-silk-handkerchief, white-breeches young monkey owned a stack of principles as high as the Tower of Babel, I would n't ride after *him* to cut a wire across my own sheep-pen."

"I don't like the way Green is actin'," mused Red, shaking his head gravely. "I 'm afeared he 's goin' to be led away by the weak an' beggarly elements o' that yander yaller-headed sojourner from the States."

"Don't worry, Mr. Parsons," admonished Hilliard. "Things will come out all right, I hope."

"Amen," said Bagley.

That night Hilliard sat alone in his small smok-

ing den, vainly trying to fix his attention on the
law book open on the table before him. The night
was unusually still; his ear was painfully alive to
every sound. He started at the hoot of an owl in
the creek bottom, at the dreaming whine of his
dog Bruce on the porch, at the swish of a dew-wet
cabbage-leaf under the leaping passage of a jack-
rabbit across the garden. When the echo of the
distant double pistol-shots came sharp and clear
on the warm silence, he sprang up and ran to the
porch. It was inconceivable that he should be
there alone, like a man unfriended and forgotten,
while his neighbors, his comrades, the men in
whose company he had labored and frolicked,
camped, hunted, sung, and voted, were following
at the heels of a stranger! The dull trampling of
many horses on the road sounded faint, faint, in
the direction of Blackbird Gully, then loud, louder,
coming on, then faint, fainter again, dying off
into the distance. For one second he had a wild
desire to throw himself upon his horse and follow
— no, by the gods! lead; for he could yet lead, if
he so willed — right or wrong.

The temptation was brief. "Come what will,"
he muttered between his clenched teeth, "I know
I am in the right." And turning resolutely into
the house, he took up his book.

The neighborhood for the next few days rang
with the successful exploit of the fence-cutters.
They had chopped the wire on Burke's prairie to
bits. They had been fired upon by the men guard-

ing it; they had returned the volley with interest. They had been pursued; they had plunged aside into the cover of a thicket, until the armed squad galloped by, then, becoming pursuers in their turn, they had chased the terrified wire-pullers back to their holes. Deerford was a born leader and a tip-top good fellow! Down with the wire-pullers!

The next Sunday being the Sabbath sacred to the Baptists of the congregation, Elder Whipple preached at Peleg Church. There was much talk concerning the wire-cutting raid, between the sermons. Hilliard forced himself to listen quietly to the boastful descriptions of sundry of the participants. Not so Red Parsons.

He quarreled violently with his brother, who had, according to his gloomy forebodings, been led away by the weak and beggarly elements of Deerford. He scolded him soundly for his inattention to principles.

"Principles!" shouted Green at length in high dudgeon. "I thank my Maker I ain't got no principles, Red Parsons. You 'tend to yourn, ef you 're so proud of 'em." And he turned his back on his twin. Upon this but too-well-understood signal of hostility, Mrs. Green and Mrs. Red tearfully divided the dinner-baskets, the quilts, and the children, and withdrew each to her own wagon. For when the twins quarreled, the making-up was a question of time.

Deerford was present, but took no part in all the excited talk. He walked about from group to group, putting in a quiet word here and there, telling a joke, or relating some personal experience. His lightest expression was everywhere received with profound respect.

Strange to say, the women did not share the infatuation of their men-folk for the handsome young stranger.

"Yes, he's personable," admitted Mrs. Crouch, "an' so I tell Billy. But he's too soft-soddery, an' there's sompn in his eye fair turns my stomach. Roy Hilliard is wo'th a ridgment of him. That's my jedgment, an' Loreny's, too."

Mrs. Crouch, indeed, voiced the general sentiment of the Sisters in Zion, young and old, seated on the grass around her on the women's side of the Peleg Church grounds.

When the time came for the afternoon homeward ride, Hilliard took the lead, as usual, in the gay dash after the flying nymphs. But a short distance from the church, his saddle-girth broke. Hector, feeling the loose leather whipping his legs, gathered his feet together and pitched violently. When his rider had succeeded in controlling him and dismounted, Deerford, far ahead, had joined Miss Wingate and laid his hand, with the air of a master, upon her bridle.

Abner Croft, lounging along the roadside, stepped forward to help with the broken girth, and Margaret Ransome fell back, reining up her horse. Hilliard looked up at her with a smile.

"Mr. Hilliard — Roy," she said abruptly, bending her dark gray eyes seriously upon him, "I hear that you did not go out with the fence-cutters, Thursday night."

"No," he returned, "I did not."

"Why?" she insisted.

A torrent of words rushed to his lips. He longed to utter them, to justify himself for seeming obstinacy, if not for seeming cowardice. He longed for the intelligent sympathy which he felt sure he would receive from this trusted friend; above all, he longed, through her, to be set right with Helen. But he restrained himself and answered carelessly, as he buckled the saddle-girth, "Oh, I had important business to attend to at home that night."

He accompanied her to her gate, but did not enter, not wishing as yet to trust himself in the presence of Deerford.

Monday, a little past twelve o'clock, Croft opened the front gate at Mrs. Ransome's and walked in. "Good-day," he said rather gruffly, taking in at a glance the group assembled on the gallery, and piercing at least one present with his brad-awl eyes.

"Good morning, Mr. Croft," said Margaret pleasantly, but even she could not quite conceal her amazement at his visit. Abner Croft deliberately entering any house except his own — especially any house where there were women-folk! Such a thing was unheard-of!

"Take a chair, Mr. Croft," urged Mrs. Ransome hospitably; "Jack, get Mr. Croft a glass of cool water."

"No, ma'am," said Abner, "I don't want no drink. An' I'll set on the steps." He seated himself on the top step, took off his shapeless wool hat, and remained abnormally silent, his eyes fixed absently on the vines which wreathed the pillar opposite. Deerford, who was polishing the hilt of his little dagger, glanced at him with an amused smile, and presently began to poke open fun at him. "The Knight of the Spade," he said airily, "better known by his additional title, the Baron of the Crypt, seems to have some unusual weight on his mind, or can it be his heart? Shall I encourage him to unburden?"

Croft turned a stolid face toward him.

"Perhaps," Deerford continued, "he has some message from his virtuous Highness of the Philanthropic Water-works."

Jack laughed, but Margaret flushed indignantly, and turned to the strange visitor with a gentle inquiry about his mother.

Seeing that he had gone too far, Deerford veered about and talked lightly on, ignoring Abner altogether.

Croft stayed on. The afternoon wore away; Helen slipped off into her own room; Mrs. Ransome had long since bustled out to her preserve-kettles in the kitchen-yard. Deerford finally got up with a yawn. "Come, Jack," he said, "this becomes oppressive. Let us quit the atmosphere of the mausoleum and seek a less melancholy region. Signor of the Mould, I bid you adieu."

Croft paid no more attention to the exaggerated bow than to the mocking address.

He waited quietly until the gate closed behind the two young men, then he turned to Margaret. "Miss Margaret," he began, his face for the first time losing its impassiveness, "I heard you ast Mr. Hilliard, yistiddy, why he didn't jine them raiders Thursday night."

"Yes." Margaret leaned forward, startled.

"Well, 't wa'n't because he was afeard, an' 't wa'n't because he wa'n't wanted ez the leader o' that gang, an' 't wa'n't because he had any business that kep' him at home. He didn't go, Miss Margaret, because his principles was ag'in it. An' he warned the others not to go."

He paused a moment, then went on in homely but vivid language to describe the meeting at Crouch's, and what had happened there, including Hilliard's downfall in popularity, and the sudden rise of Deerford in public favor. "An' whether he's right or wrong, Miss Margaret," he concluded — "an' *I* think he's right, an' Mr. Bagley an' Red Parsons thinks he's right — but whether he's right or wrong, he's actin' from principle. An' *ez* for that wall-eyed peccary, barkin' aroun' Crouch's Settle*mint*, I hate him worse 'n blue pizen!"

"Thank you, Mr. Croft. Oh, thank you!"

cried Margaret. She reached down and grasped his hand fervently. How much of the handshake meant friendship for Hilliard, and how much dislike for Deerford, Croft could not afterward divine. But that she added the well-digger to the small circle of her adorers, he had no doubt whatever.

That night, after they had gone to their bed-chamber, she sat on a couch silent for some time, watching Helen comb out her long shining bronze hair. "Helen," she demanded at length, "do you know why Abner Croft came here to-day?"

"Why, no," returned Helen smiling. "I confess that it *looked* as if he had come to ' set out ' Mr. Deerford. This is a serious matter, Margaret, and your mother ought to " —

"He came," Margaret continued, ignoring her friend's playfulness, "to tell me why Mr. Hilliard did not lead the wire-cutters Thursday night."

"Did he? Oh, why?" Helen clasped her hands, instantly serious.

Margaret repeated the substance of Abner's talk. "You must forgive me for saying so, Helen dear, but I fear that your friend, Mr. Deerford, will lead Jack — and others — into trouble."

"I know he will," said Helen quickly. "I — I do not like Allan Deerford, Margaret," she added in a hushed voice, almost as if afraid. "I have known him all my life, nearly. And I know, of course, that he wishes to marry me. But I would not marry him for " — she shuddered — "for

worlds. My mother favors his suit; so does his
mother, who idolizes him. The Deerfords are
enormously rich. There is another son, and there
is one daughter. But by the terms of his father's
will, Allan, as the oldest son, will inherit the bulk
of the property. The father, who died many
years ago, it seems, had the English idea about
property. Oh, no, I never could love Allan.
But — Margaret, this, I know, will seem silly and
childish to you. But I cannot reason it out, or
reason it away. He has a curious influence over
me. I am afraid of him. I feel, when I am in
his presence, as if I were half-paralyzed. I was
terrified when I found he had followed me here.
I have not been myself a moment since he came!"
She burst into hysterical sobs and buried her face
in her hands.

"I understand," said Margaret, "I understand
perfectly, dear. He is like a serpent. He does
not charm me, nor " — Hilliard, she was about to
say, but checked the name on her lips — "nor
Mr. Bagley, nor Abner, nor Mrs. Crouch. But
look at his influence over Jack. Jack is changing
from day to day. Oh, Helen!" —

The two girls fell weeping into each other's
arms, the intangible coolness which had hovered
between them for a week past melting instantly.

Hilliard's name was not mentioned in the long
confidential talk which followed. But he was uppermost in the thought of both. When, about
midnight, a reverberating clap of thunder shook

the shutters and a dash of rain scurried across the roof, Helen said naïvely, "There will be water in his — in the water-tank, now."

"Yes," said Margaret.

It was one of those flooding rains which usually break the drought in that western region, a solid downpour that lasted, with incredible fury, for hours, raising Mesquit Creek to a roaring water-course, and washing down bridges, pens, and fences. The creek soon ran down, leaving only the well-known water-holes here and there. But Hilliard's water-tank was full to the brim, and the strengthened underground spring continued to pour into it a vigorous helping stream.

X

LITTLE MARGARET

THE long drought had been broken — but only in two. The middle of September saw the country as parched as if a drop of rain had never fallen; the winds blowing over the prairies were heated as if by a furnace. Only the fat, pale-green juicy leaves of the prickly-pear — which would seem to draw its nourishment from some secret and mysterious source; an occasional muddy water-hole, scorned or forgotten by the grasping barbed wire; and Hilliard's Pool, as the tank was now called, afforded any relief for the thirsty beasts around Crouch's Settlement.

Cattle-paths leading to the tank soon criss-crossed like the meshes of a net over the prairie-pasture, and through the adjoining woods. Numbers of gaunt, wide-horned creatures stood about the prairie all day, as if loath to get out of sight and hearing of the placid pool and the steady crystal stream which fell into it with a rushing musical sound from Croft's pipe. About sunset every day the milk-cows of the neighborhood came leisurely in from their several ranges — their bells tinkling, their heavy udders swinging — to slake their thirst, and to meet, as if by appointment, the barefooted urchins of either sex whose business it was to drive them home. The scene, a moment earlier drowsy and tranquil, became animated. The mere sight of the cows approaching the tank seemed to induce a fever of thirst among the stock already there, and who might be called the habitués of the place; they plunged instantly in the same direction. A jostling, hurrying, leaping, slipping mass of cattle struggled wildly about the edge of the tank. Croft, who made it a point of honor to inspect his handiwork at the close of each day, then had his hands full to preserve life and limb to the barefoot urchins, who dodged and danced about, flourishing their driving-sticks, and screaming with laughter. The performance afforded him keen delight. He was inordinately proud of the pool itself. The spring, he admitted, had turned out better than he had expected, keeping the water up to a certain level in spite of the constant drain upon it.

Hilliard visited the place but rarely. He was busy in his fields. The sun twisted the brown cotton-stalks and scorched the green leaves, but the new cream-white and the day-old pink blossoms sent a flush of color over the fields, and the bolls formed and opened rapidly. The crop, free as yet of cotton-worms, promised fairly well in spite of the drought.

A row of tow-heads — the Red Parsons boys and the Green Parsons girls — the family feud in

abeyance for the time being — went up and down
the even rows beside the owner, with their cotton-
sacks around their necks. Manuel and Juan in
the outer field where the stalks were more stunted
picked, after their own fashion, on their knees,
dragging the open baskets after them.

Hilliard had resumed, though with far less familiarity than of old, his visits to Mrs. Ransome's.
Deerford, urged by the infatuated son of the house,
was still a guest there. But the two were seldom
at home. They were riding about the country,
spending much time at Crouch's Well, — more
than ever a lounging-place for the men of the
neighborhood. Hilliard heard of them at Skipton
and Rassler, with companions and in places which
boded no good for a lad like Jack Ransome. He
had ventured several times when he could find
Jack alone, to remonstrate with him, kindly but
firmly, and he had suffered without resentment
his flippant and angry replies. More than once
he perceived that the boy had been drinking. He
saw the growing anxiety of the mother and sister,
but felt himself powerless to interfere or help.
Deerford's bearing toward himself in their infre-
quent meetings was intangibly insolent; his attitude toward Helen was one of arrogant ownership.
Her curious silence in his own presence when
Deerford was near continually outraged and puzzled him; her frank return to ease and confidence
when he found her alone, or with Margaret, as
continually renewed his faith. His pride, deeply

wounded by the inexplicable coldness of his other
neighbors, withdrew him more and more from all
but necessary contact with them. He applied himself with ardor in his leisure moments to a study of
the legal aspect of the question now agitating not
only Crouch's Settlement, but the whole of western Texas — the wire-fence war. He found time
to ride over to the county-seat to confer with law-
yers and legislators on the subject. And during
the fall sitting of the court there, he presented
himself for examination, and was admitted to the
Bar, with full license to practice the profession of
law.

Meantime, the fence-cutting went merrily on,
under the open leadership of Deerford. The raiders even made incursions into the neighboring
counties, leaving a trail of destruction and wrath
behind them.

"Oh, Jack," Margaret said imploringly to her
brother, after one of these nocturnal expeditions,
"mother and I are so anxious, so unhappy. Please
give up this life you are leading. At any rate,
give up the wire-cutting. It will end in trouble
for you, I am sure. Dear Jack " —

"So! " sneered Jack. "Leroy Hilliard has
been preaching to you, has he? Confound him!
I 'll blow his brains out, if he comes preaching
around me again."

"Mr. Hilliard has said nothing to me about you
or your affairs," replied his sister indignantly.
"But if you would only listen to him " —

Jack had already turned on his heel, whistling, and walked off.

He repeated this scrap of conversation at Crouch's Well, a little later, in the presence of his "crowd." "I'll let Roy Hilliard know that he can't bully me, d—n him," he cried, swelling with self-importance, and speaking with a thick tongue.

"Hilliard's too all-fired biggaty, anyhow," remarked one of the listeners. "He expects to sail his Ship of Zion plum into Heaven across that d—d free water-tank of his'n. I wisht to God he'd drop into it and drown hisse'f."

"His ship ought to be scuttled," laughed Deerford. "Why don't somebody knock down that dam and drain his Christian cattle-pool dry?" He looked around carelessly as he spoke, but there was a sparkle of deviltry in his eyes.

Bud, the oldest Red Parsons boy, dropped his cotton-sack in Hilliard's field one morning at the end of the first row. He was about thirteen years old, freckle-faced and sunburned, with a shrewd twinkle, got from his mother, in his small eyes, and a solemn twist of the mouth, like his father's. "Mr. Roy," he said, "I wisht you'd come over to the creek a minute. I've got sompn I want to show you."

"Why, Bud," said his employer, surprised, "what is it? Can't it wait?"

"It's a snake hung up fer rain," replied Bud.

"It's plum curious. I want to ast you about it. 'T won't take more 'n five minutes."

"All right," said Hilliard good-naturedly. He dropped his own sack and followed the boy across the field. The other children, previously warned and direfully threatened by Bud, kept their heads down and their hands busy.

Bud ran down the cotton-row, leaped the staked and ridered fence like a squirrel, crossed over to the edge of the dry creek, and stopped under a pecan-tree, awaiting his companion, who made no pretense of keeping up with him.

A huge chicken-snake, much swollen and glistening in the sun's rays, depended from a limb of the tree, its stiff tail touching the ground. "Well?" said Hilliard, eying the dead reptile with some disgust.

Bud set his back against the tree, spread his legs wide apart, thrust his hands in his breeches-pocket, spat on the ground, and looked mysterious. "Mr. Roy," he said at length, "th' ain't nothin' curious about that ole chicken-snake. But I got sompn to tell you, an' I don't want them blabbin' gals to hear it, nor them fool boys, neither. It takes a man to keep a secret."

Hilliard forebore to smile and listened gravely.

"It's a message from pa. He couldn't come hisse'f, because he had to go to Skipton this mornin'. But he told me to tell you, Mr. Roy, that they was goin' to raid our water-tank an' cut the dam about midnight to-night, so's to let out the water."

"What!" cried Hilliard, startled and incredulous. "Who? What for? Who told your father?"

"Hit's thes this-a-way," said Bud, delighted with his own diplomacy, and with the reception of his news. "You know pa an' Uncle Green ain't spoke for nigh six weeks."

Hilliard nodded.

"Seems like pa an' Uncle Green is always fallin' out an' not speakin'! Well, this mornin' we-all was eatin' breakfast an' we heard somebody comin' *buckety-buckety*, down the road. Pa, he swallered. Ma, she said she'd have to put off the washin' an' bake some cake, 'cause Uncle Green was comin' down the road, an' they'd be a fambly *re*-union to-morrow. Sure enough, it was Uncle Green, an' he shook hands with pa, an' he swallered, an' he didn't say nothin', an' pa, he swallered, an' didn't say nothin'. Then Uncle Green told pa that some o' them men about Crouch's was makin' up to cut our dam at our water-tank to-night about midnight. He said he was boun'-in-honor not to tell who they was, but he thought it was a durn shame. An' he told pa to tell you to-onct. Pa he had to go to Skipton, an' Uncle Green rid back home. An' pa told me to tell you. An' says he'll be over to set up at the tank to-night. Ma is bakin' fer a fambly *re*-union. An' so I fetched along that ole chicken-snake to blind them gals an' boys. An' I hung him up anyhow, seein' as we are a needin' of rain."

"Thank you, Bud," said Hilliard, shaking the dirty paw held out to him. He stood musing a moment, in deep thought, then turned toward the field. "Mr. Roy," — Bud had lost his important look; he was twisting his piece of a straw hat in his hands, and his eyes were lifted in timid appeal. "Mr. Roy I kin pop over a squirrel any time. I kin hanl'e a rifle as good as pa, an' a sight better. Won't you — won't you lemme come an' set up 'long o' you an' pa at our tank to-night?"

Hilliard started to pat the towhead, but remembered the diplomat's dignity in time, and slapped him heartily on the back instead. "Not to-night, Bud, not to-night. Tell your father from me that I am much obliged to him and to Mr. Green Parsons for the warning. I will be very glad if he will ride over about dark to my house and consult with me."

They went back to the field together, Bud walking soberly by his patron's side. He was elated, in spite of his disappointment in not being allowed to bear a hand in the proposed defense, and his work for the rest of the day, as Patty Green Parsons reported to his mother the next day at the *re*-union, "wa'n't worth shucks."

Hilliard felt strongly inclined to disregard the friendly warning. He could see no possible reason why the very men whose cows probably watered at his pool should wish to destroy it. But he finally decided, by way of precaution, to keep watch, with Red Parsons, — at least until after the hour named for the raid.

At dusk he sat alone on his porch; the sudden bark of Bruce at the gate announced an arrival. He walked out, expecting to meet Parsons. Instead, he was surprised to find the Reverend David French.

"Why, Mr. French," he exclaimed with genuine pleasure, "I am delighted to see you. Get down and come in. Give me your saddle-bags. I will have your horse attended to." He hallooed for Manuel, with his hand on the gate-latch.

"Thank you, Mr. Hilliard," replied the preacher, dismounting, and taking his saddle-bags over his arm. "I had intended to stop over Sunday with Mr. and Mrs. Red Parsons. But I came by there an hour ago, and found the house shut up. No one seemed to be about. I have therefore taken the liberty to coming on to throw myself, for the night at least, upon your hospitality."

"If you knew what a godsend it is to me to see a friendly face nowadays, Mr. French," said Hilliard, laughing, "you would not apologize for coming."

Mr. French noticed the slight bitterness which tinged the laugh and wondered at it, as he followed his host into the house.

The two men had met several times since the occasion of Red Parsons's baptism, but these meetings had been no more than a passing handshake and a polite greeting. They were now mutually surprised, sitting opposite each other at the well-appointed supper-table; the Reverend David at the culture and refinement of the young backwoodsman, and Roy at the wide range of the preacher's knowledge and his keen and liberal interest in every-day affairs.

It was with regret that Hilliard rose about nine o'clock to prepare for his solitary vigil at the pool. He accounted for the non-appearance of Red Parsons by the reconciliation of the twins, which had probably driven the appointment out of his head, or he might, he thought, have been detained at Skipton, or perhaps Bud had failed to deliver his own message.

"Will you make yourself comfortable for the night, Mr. French," he said, taking his gun from its rack over the door and fastening on his cartridge-belt. "I am compelled to leave you for some hours at least. You will find a small collection of books on the shelf yonder. Here are pipes and tobacco. And your bed " —

"Where are you going?" demanded French, with a ring of authority in his voice.

Hilliard did not resent the tone. Its frankness pleased him. "I will tell you," he said with equal frankness. And leaning on his gun, he related as much of the neighborhood history for the past three months as was necessary to explain his own present situation. "I have somehow managed to become personally very unpopular," he concluded, smiling a little sadly. "I give you my word I have not the least idea why. My only offense, so far as I know, has been my opposition to the promiscuous fence-cutting. This hardly seems to be sufficient ground for the persistent avoidance of me by my sometime friends and neighbors, which I confess has disturbed me no little. Certainly it is not sufficient ground for a malevolence which would seek to destroy my property. This, however, as I have already told you, I do not believe. I ought to have warned you before you came in," he added, "that you were running the risk of impairing your own influence by associating with me."

The minister laughed. "But," he exclaimed seriously, "I agree with you that these men cannot possibly intend to cut the dam. There could be no gain to any one in its loss. On the contrary " —

"No," returned Hilliard. "I believe it to be merely an idle threat, made, perhaps, in jest. But since a great deal depends on keeping that dam intact, I will not run any risk. Manuel will look after you " —

But Mr. French had already arisen, and was looking about for his hat. "Oh, I am going with you, if you will allow me, or rather, whether you will allow me or not," he said. "I suppose my cloth forbids me the use of a gun on such an occasion, but I should be justified, in a case like this, if it came to blows, in the use of my fists."

Hilliard, though pleased with his guest's interest, could not but be secretly amused at this speech. He cast a swift glance at the coat sleeve hanging loosely upon the thin arm, and at the small hand grasping a cambric pocket handkerchief. But he accepted the companionship gratefully.

They walked over to the pool, about three quarters of a mile from the house. The wood was very dark, the stubby post-oaks shutting out the clear sky, with its gleaming stars. The small prairie was light by comparison. There was no sound there except the measured breathing of the cattle lying about — formless heaps that hardly stirred as the two men passed — and the fall of the spring water into the tank. They seated themselves on the dry grass at the upper edge of the pool, lighted pipes, and took up the interrupted thread of conversation. Leaving Crouch's Settlement and its petty round of life far aside, they rode full tilt, as it were, into a broader arena, — books, music, statecraft, epoch-makers; Hilliard felt, breathing in this whiff of a delight long untasted, like comparing himself to the famished cattle that fought for a life-giving draught from his own pool!

The flow of talk was interrupted by a distant but unmistakable sound, — the beat of horse's feet. He sprang up, grasped his gun, and leaned forward, listening. It was plainly a single rider coming at a gallop down the Branch road, which ran some four or five hundred yards to the left of Hilliard's prairie. The sound drew near and passed on. The horseman, whoever he was, had turned aside some distance below and was apparently riding up to Hilliard's own gate. The barking of dogs, and above it the echo of a voice came clearly, borne on the night wind. There was a pause and then the rider returned more rapidly along the road and presently branched off across the prairie itself.

"Halt!" cried Hilliard, throwing his gun to his shoulder. "Who is there? Halt, or I fire."

The horse stopped abruptly, thrown on his haunches by the sudden tightening of the rein. "Don't shoot. It is I, Mr. Hilliard." The rider was a woman. Hilliard recognized the clear liquid voice of Margaret Ransome.

"Great God," he cried, dropping his gun and running forward. "What is it? What has happened? Helen?" —

"Helen is well. Nothing has happened — to any of us," Margaret called out. She waited for him to come up, then leaned down toward him, her face white and ghost-like in the starlight. "But, Red Parsons's baby, his only girl, little Margaret, is lost. Jack and Mr. Deerford are away. I fear there is another raid, for nearly all the men seem to be absent from their homes. Mother has gone over to stay with Mrs. Parsons, who is beside herself with grief and anxiety. Is that you, Jack?" she called sharply, catching sight of the indistinct figure standing by the pool. "Oh, I am so glad! Jack, dear, I need you so. Come! Come!"

Hilliard's heart throbbed with pity. He explained hurriedly, and invited French to join them. "They missed her about three o'clock," Margaret resumed, after greeting the minister and smothering a disappointed sigh. "And they have been searching for her ever since. Her father reached home about sundown from Skipton. He and Mr. Bagley are in Shinn-Oak Prairie now; Mr. Green Parsons and Mr. Croft are searching the creek bottom back of Waldrup's field. They will all meet at Blackbird Gully at ten o'clock, unless they find the child before then. She is my own namesake, Mr. French." She covered her face with her hands and wept silently. "She is only three years old," she said when she could speak again. "Such a little mite of a creature. Oh, Roy!"

He touched his lips to her hand, which he had taken in his own. "Do not despond, Margaret," he said confidently. "We will find her. It is nearly ten o'clock now," he added, striking a match and consulting his watch. "Have they lanterns, do you think?"

"Oh, yes," she replied, heartened by his cheery tone. "I came for you as soon as I had taken mother over to Mrs. Parsons. Mr. Bagley had left the message for you there. He knew that you would come. But there was no one to send after you, so I came."

"Thank you, Margaret. I will — you are not afraid to ride home alone? Well, then, I will get over to Blackbird Gully at once. Good-night, Margaret. God bless you, Margaret."

He had walked a few paces beside her stirrup as she rode off. He listened a second or so to the steady gallop of her horse in the homeward road. Then he returned to the tank. "I will conduct you as far as the field, Mr. French," he said, picking up his gun. "From there you can easily find your way to the house"—

"What!" interrupted French, with a frown, so to speak, in his voice. "Do you think I am going back to the house, while Red Parsons's baby—anybody's baby—is lost in the woods? I am astonished at you, sir!"

The words were gravely spoken and quite evidently intended as a rebuke. "I christened little Margaret the last time I was here," he pursued, more gently. "She was the first wee lamb of my small flock here."

Hilliard murmured an apology, and set off without further ceremony, with the little man at his elbow. They had but to follow the open road for about two miles in order to reach the rendezvous.

Hilliard at first walked slowly, fearful of wearying his companion. But in a few moments he saw by the steady swing of the Reverend David's gait that he could walk as well as preach, and he made no ado about quickening his own pace. They made the short journey in silence, each occupied by his own thoughts. As they approached the heavy line, densely black in the dim starlight, which indicated the dip of the road into Blackbird Gully, they saw the gleam of lanterns, like a small

procession of fireflies, winding in and out among
the trees on the right. Hilliard gave a quick
halloo which echoed lonesomely through the silence,
and they were soon in the midst of the searching-
party. This consisted of the Parsons twins, Amos
Bagley, Abner Croft, Bud Parsons, and Patty
Green Parsons. The last named, a sturdy, stumpy,
red-haired damsel of thirteen, had so stoutly maintained her right to join the party, — in the face of
stern opposition, Bud even threatening to "rock"
her back to the house, — that consent had perforce
been given.

Red Parsons grasped Hilliard's hand, and the
minister's in turn. He was unable to speak; the
tears were rolling down his cheeks; he looked
worn and haggard. Mr. French drew him apart.

The others had a hasty conference. So far, not
a trace or a token of the lost child had been found;
there was therefore no clue as to the direction
which her wanderings might have taken. When
last seen, she was quietly playing with her dolls
and dishes under a china-tree in a corner of the
yard. The fields and woods immediately around
the house had been carefully searched; the well,
and a water-hole near, had been dragged. Hilliard, taking the lead, now proposed to divide the
small party into three detachments and scour the
country, nook and cranny, until the child was
found. In case of failure, they were all to meet
at the Gully at daybreak for fresh consultation.
It was agreed that a single pistol-shot would an-

nounce the finding of the child. An additional
shot would mean that she was alive. In that case,
Croft and Patty were deputed to carry the news at
once to the stricken mother. But if —

"No! No! No!" cried the father, breaking
down utterly for the first time. "Don't ye say
it, Roy. Don't ye dassent to say it. My little
gal! My baby-gal!"

For a moment no one had the heart or the voice
to speak. "Come 'long o' me, Red," Croft said
gently, taking him by the arm, "an' don't ye
werry. Wher' ever that baby-gal is, the Lord's
arms is around her."

"Amen," said Bagley reverently, watching them
trudge off into the darkness, with Patty trotting
valiantly at their heels. Before he himself started
in company with Green Parsons, he took Hilliard
aside. "What in the name o' thunder did you
fetch the little parson along for?" he whispered.
"He's a powerful hand at dippin'. But dippin'
is one thing an' mesquit woods at midnight is
another. He'll git lost, sure as shootin', an'
you'll have a couple of infants to look for 'stead
of one."

This was Hilliard's own opinion, though he was
beginning to respect the parson's pluck. All he
said, however, was, "He would come. I will try
and keep him in sight."

Bagley, with Green Parsons and Bud, took up
the march toward the beat assigned them. Hilliard had chosen for his own scrutiny a long

stretch of Mesquit Creek bottom, — a desolate
crater-like glade which opened out, a couple of
miles below where he entered it with French, into
a piece of ground known as the Island. This was
a high ridge several acres in extent completely
surrounded by a deep moat-like, natural gulch,
with precipitous rain-furrowed sides.

The glade, studded with enormous trees and
hung with a matted tangle of grape and bamboo
vines, was almost impenetrable. After a freshet,
it was a swirling and dangerous pool; the ground,
now dry, was honeycombed with treacherous fis-
sures, which were hidden by a thick undergrowth
of bushes and weeds. The midnight darkness of
this unfrequented place was terrifying. Hilliard
felt the hair rise on his head at the slippery glid-
ing of a snake under his feet, or the furry weight
of a spider against his cheek. More than once he
saw the gleam of fiery eyes, or heard an ominous
rattle at his elbow. He swung the lantern low,
throwing its pale light upon every inch of ground.
A second unlighted lantern hung over his arm,
designed to be left as a beacon at a certain turn
of the bottom.

"I will take the other lantern, Mr. Hilliard,"
the minister said, after an hour of this minute
examination, "and bear off to the left. We can
in that way cover more ground."

Hilliard stood up, dismayed by this request.
"I — I fear you are not sufficiently acquainted
with these parts, Mr. French," he stammered;
"you might" —

"Get lost," he was about to add, but in truth he did not dare!

"Give me the lantern." The Reverend David's tone was severe. "If I find myself at a loss, I will halloo."

Hilliard meekly lighted the lantern and handed it to him. "I have come to the conclusion," he muttered, looking after the twinkling light as it bore off slowly to the left and disappeared in the underbrush, "that the little parson, whatever he may lack, has got a will of his own."

His own search was fruitless; as much as he dreaded to find any trace of the child in this wildcat haunted cove, he was beginning to grow sick with apprehension. He kept his ear strained for the hoped-for signal from the others. But none came, and the night was wearing away.

At the end of another dreary hour, he came suddenly in sight of French's lantern, and peering intently forward, he made out the figure of its bearer.

"You need not cross that gulch, Mr. French," he shouted at once. "A cat could hardly get over to that island, much less a baby — or a preacher," he added impatiently, under his breath.

French shouted back an ambiguous reply which, had he been a layman, could doubtless have been interpreted to mean: "Mind your own business." Here was no question of bringing the church into ridicule or disfavor; no vexing decision regarding gown and bands bred irresolution or timidity!

Settling his spectacles firmly on his nose, and hooking the lantern over his left arm, he was already letting himself down the concave side of the dry ditch, by the aid of a tangle of may-pop and morning-glory vines. The ascent on the other side was more sloping and far less difficult.

Ten minutes later Hilliard heard a sharp halloo. He ran up out of the bottom in the direction of the island, as fast as he could. French, on the farther side of the gulch, was swinging his lantern frantically in one hand. In the other he held out something which made Hilliard's knees tremble under him. It was a little blue sunbonnet.

The two men gazed at each other across the width of the gulch, trembling, and absolutely incapable of speech; the lanterns shook in their nerveless hands.

Then Hilliard scrambled down and over, — he never knew how. "I found it," said the parson in a whisper, "just here where I stand. I thought I saw in the trailing vines, broken here and there, evidences that something had fallen over into the gully. The fall was doubtless softened by the mass of vines. But — but it does not seem possible, does it, that she could have climbed up on this side?"

"No," Hilliard whispered back. They were both too awestruck to speak aloud. "Some animal, a wild-cat, or a cougar, must have brought the bonnet here in his mouth and dropped it."

He shuddered, not daring to examine the little bonnet too closely, lest he should find it sprinkled with blood.

The ridge, or knoll, was almost naked within its encircling, green-draped, empty moat. A few clumps of shinn-oak, covered with feather-vines in full bloom, grew here and there, dotting the barren ground with dark, white-starred masses. Hilliard walked to these, one after another, with his companion silent at his elbow, throwing the light carefully in every direction. He felt surer and surer in his own mind that the child had been torn to pieces in the bottom. He felt a sickening dread at the thought of beginning the search there again. Even as this terror shook him, he stooped by a little motte of shinn-oak to pull aside a curtain of feather-vine. Well, there she lay, her round baby-cheeks scratched and torn by the briars, her yellow hair matted with sticks and leaves, her clothes in tatters, but alive! And as rosy, and as sound asleep as if lapped in her cradle at home, or rocked on her mother's breast. A long trail of the feather-vine lying across her forehead, crowned her with its white silken blossoms.

Hilliard stooped with a sob and lifted her in his arms. He stumbled blindly across the island, French carrying the lanterns. They struck by chance the exact spot where the little one had toiled up the slope, holding on by the vines, and leaving fragments of her dress fluttering from the briars.

It was only when, with great difficulty, they had succeeded in getting their treasure-trove and themselves across the gulch — little Margaret sleeping profoundly during the transit — that Hilliard remembered anything, or anybody else.

"For God's sake, Mr. French," he panted, "get the pistol out of my hip-pocket and fire it off. Twice. Can you do it?"

"I reckon so," returned the Reverend David with a click in his throat almost as sharp as the click of the trigger. Two shots broke the stillness in rapid succession.

"Do you think, Roy," asked French, with his finger on the hammer, "do you think it would be amiss to fire off the other barrels?"

"God bless you, David, no!" shouted Hilliard, beside himself with excitement.

David emptied the other four barrels. Far-off answering shots were heard in different directions. They moved on as rapidly as possible, leaving the bottom to the left and heading toward the Parsonses' home. In less than a quarter of an hour a volley of shots seemed to indicate that the other members of the searching-party were now all together. These were answered by French from the reloaded pistol. In less than a quarter of an hour the dancing glimmer of lanterns advancing through the trees was descried. Hilliard paused. "Take her to him," he said huskily, placing the child in the preacher's arms. "I can't."

And he hung back, overcome and half ashamed

of his own emotion, until he saw Red Parsons
stoop with a mighty groan that shook his tall form
from head to foot, and take his baby-girl from
David's arms.

Not a word had been uttered. Bud attempted a
cheer, but it died feebly in his throat.

"Let us pray," said Mr. French, with quiet
dignity. He dropped upon his knees.

It was a strangely solemn scene, and one not
soon to be forgotten by those present, — the dark
woods stretching away sombre and silent, the dark
sky, darker for the faint streak of dawn under
the eastern horizon, the smoky lanterns dimly illuminating the kneeling figures, and touching with
almost unearthly brightness the flowing hair of
the child asleep on her father's breast, the fervent
upturned face of the servant of God, the clear
voice rising on the wandering night wind!

"Parson," said Green Parsons, when they arose
from their knees, "I 'm a Methodist born, an' a
Methodist I 'll die. But *ef* I wa'n't a Methodist,
I 'd jine *you*, an' what 's mo', by jing! I 'd be
dipped!"

"Lord, Red," he added solemnly a little later,
as they tramped together homeward, "supposen
me an' you had n't of made up! Supposen the
Devil had kep' me away from you endurin' of
this fiery trial!"

Red pressed his lips to little Margaret's forehead. "By the Lord's he'p, Green," he said,
looking at his twin with wet eyes, "we ain't never
goin' to qua'l ag'in."

"Amen," said Bagley, just behind them.

Croft, with Bud and Patty, had sped on ahead with the good news. When the remainder of the party reached the house, which was all alight and all astir with rejoicing, Hilliard and Bagley turned aside into the stable under pretense of saddling some horses, in order not to be present at the meeting between husband and wife.

When Abner and David, with Green Parsons, came out, their faces shone as if they had been standing in the glory of the Divine Presence. The party mounted, and began the homeward ride in silence. Only when they halted at the cross-road where they were to separate and go their several ways, Green Parsons opened his lips to say soberly: "Boys — beggin' of your pardon, Parson French! I have helt in as long as I can. Ef I don't holler, I'll bust wide open!" With this he gave vent to a succession of wild whoops which fairly shook the post-oak rough and aroused every bird and beast within reach. The others, even David himself, joined heartily in the unique expression of thanksgiving.

"Do you not think, Mr. Hilliard," said Mr. French as they rode on together, "would it not be well for us to ride by Mrs. Ransome's house and let Miss Ransome know that her namesake has been found, and is alive and well?" He had lost his tone of authority, and spoke with stammering timidity.

"Why, yes," said Hilliard, surprised at himself for not having thought of this.

She came flying down to the gate at the sound of their approach. "Oh, thank God! Thank God! And God bless you both!" she cried, with a rush of happy tears, when she had heard the story told by Hilliard. He was watching the lighted window while he spoke, and the figure behind the curtain which he surmised was Helen's.

"Thank Mr. French, Margaret," he replied. "If it had not been for him, she would not have been found. Or she would have been found too late."

"Do not believe him, Miss Ransome," said the preacher nervously, already turning his horse's head. "I was but his lieutenant."

They rode on. They were both beginning to feel, at last, the strain of the night's fatigue and apprehension; the chill dawn made them shiver. For the day was breaking, the stars had quite paled, and there was a yellow glimmer in the east.

"Mr. Hilliard," demanded the clergyman abruptly, as they turned into Hilliard's prairie, "can you tell me whether Miss Ransome's affections are engaged?"

The shock of the question made Hilliard almost reel in his saddle. The manly directness and the homely simplicity of it stirred him, but a queer dog-in-the-manger feeling at the same time shook him, and shook him hard. But he replied at once, with unaffected warmth, "She is heart-free. Of that I am absolutely certain. Margaret Ransome is beyond my poor praise, Mr. French; but

I can at least say that the man who wins her will be fortunate among men. She is as dear to me as if she were my own sister. And I wish you success with all my heart, David."

French grasped the proffered hand and shook it eagerly. What he might have said in reply, however, was checked by a horrified exclamation from his companion.

The latter had reined in his horse, and was looking down with dilated eyes upon the wreck of his pool. The dam had been destroyed, the loosened stones and earth were piled upon each side of the wide opening through which the water had escaped, leaving the tank empty, except for a muddy little pond in the bottom. The covered ditch leading from the underground spring had been laid open, and the pipe torn up; the twisted and disjointed fragments were found afterward in the creek bed.

The cattle had already discovered their loss, and were huddled dejectedly over against the trampled edge of the basin. As if in mockery, and as a last taunt, a strand of barbed wire had been stretched across the cleft in the dam, with a pair of nippers swinging to it.

Hilliard's square jaws worked convulsively; his birth-mark, which French had never noticed before, blazed out; then it faded slowly. Mastering himself with a quick inward struggle, he gathered up his bridle-reins. "The baby, or the dam, eh, David?" he said; and his smile made David's heart leap.

XI

MEASURING THE ROAD

ONE day in December, young Joe Wyatt stopped at Hilliard's gate. He wore an embarrassed air, and avoided looking at the master of the house, who came out, hailing him with the genial Mesquit Creek salutation: "Hello, young Joe. 'Light, and come in."

"No," said young Joe, threshing the toe of his boot with his quirt. "I ain't got time; I jest stopped by to pass the time o' day, an' to fetch you a message from Gran'pap."

The destruction of Hilliard's Pool was now an old story. Its direct result had been the death of numbers of the cattle which had watered there, among them several of his own.

"Shall you rebuild the dam?" Mr. French had asked him that October morning, as they turned their horses' heads homeward, after surveying the ruin.

"No," he had made answer. "I cannot rebuild it. My hands are full. It will be all I can do to get my cotton picked, and ginned, and ready for market. Besides," he added wearily, "it would be no use. Whoever destroyed it this time would destroy it again." He had sedulously refrained from any inquiry into the matter. "I cannot afford to know who did it," he said to Margaret Ransome, and it did not escape him that she drew a long breath as of relief. There was a shame-facedness about certain men when he met them, which disturbed him, the recollection of which he dismissed from his mind as speedily as possible. Young Joe's uneasiness now sent a flush over Hilliard's cheek. But he laid a friendly hand on the horse's neck and said gayly: "Does the old man want to beat me shooting jack-rabbits?" The elder Wyatt's conviction that he could "outshoot creation" was one of his amiable weaknesses, and many such a challenge had Hilliard received and accepted in times past.

"Worse 'n that," snickered young Joe, his dis-comfort vanishing before his host's frank smile. "He wants you to he'p him measure the Peleg road."

"Whew!" Hilliard thrust his hands in his pockets and puckered his lips into a shrill whistle. "All right," he laughed. "When?"

"To-morrow. Th' ole man 'll stop by for you about sun-up."

After a little more talk, young Joe galloped off, and Hilliard went out to his cotton-pens, where Manuel and Juan were loading a wagon for the gin. The flocky snow-white crop was all in. A few belated bolls only dotted the dry fields; the sheltered pens were filled to bursting.

Down by the creek, the Red Parsons boys and the Green Parsons girls, all under the self-constituted supervision of Bud, were thrashing down and gathering the pecans, — easily the largest and the finest on the creek. Their boisterous shouts and shrill laughter rang on the gusty norther which was blowing up, big end foremost.

Hilliard had a comfortable sense of freedom, after his year's hard labor, which went far toward counterbalancing his loss of popularity, — so galling to him in the beginning. He had, so it seemed to himself, recovered his equilibrium at the moment of his severest trial, — the wanton cutting of his dam. In truth, however, he had been settling, as it were, for some time before that event; the waters of his soul, shaken and muddied by the painful change in his outer condition, had been gradually clearing, and the ugly sediment of egotism and arrogance had gone to the bottom. He did not realize it himself, but he had been bettered and strengthened by the isolation in which he had been compelled to live. His exuberant nature had been a little sobered, but his grasp on himself, and consequently on others, would henceforth be firmer. A certain charming joyousness of manner had given place to a sedate self-restraint, destined to be equally winning in the days to come.

It must not go unrecorded that those friends who had remained stanch throughout his dark hours had had no small share in sustaining and strengthening his oftentimes troubled soul.

Nothing of all this shaped itself in his brain, as he lent a hand with the loading. But he did feel once more that life was good. The cotton, ginned and baled at the Skipton Gin, and the pecans gathered and barreled, he proposed to haul both to W—— himself. Only this year there would be a train of wagons instead of two.

"You shall dance in the wagon-yard at W—— next week, Manuel," he said, looking up at the old Mexican from the trace-chain he was fastening. Manuel's leathery face remained impassive, but there was a twinkle in his eyes. "Si, señor, si, si!" he said, curling the long lash of his whip over the back of his mules.

The wagon rolled out through the lot gate. Hilliard's first load of cotton was off to the gin.

The next morning, the dull rumble of Mr. Wyatt's heavy wagon-wheels heralded his approach long before sunrise. Hilliard, buttoned to the ears in his overcoat, went out to meet him, laughing a little to himself, and wondering what was in the wind.

For Uncle Joe's road-measuring was not a mere question of rods and miles, not a cut and dried counting up and setting down of the quips and quiddities of a neighborhood highway. It was an important and solemn function in itself, its result being each time a shifting of sign-posts and a general befogging of the public mind as to (official) distances. But the real significance of the ceremony — which took place at irregular intervals, sometimes as seldom as once a year, usually about once in a quarter — was that it indicated some profound agitation in Mr. Wyatt's own mind, as, for example, whether Johnny Giles, being a Republican, was entitled to vote for Justice of the Peace in Crouch's Precinct? How was Daniel let down into the den of lions? Is there any better rifle, lock stock and barrel, than the Winchester? etc., etc.

It was Mr. Wyatt's custom, whenever such vital questions disturbed his inner being, to summon one, or at the most two, of his fellow-citizens to assist him in measuring the Peleg road — from Peleg Church to the Skipton Junction. During the progress of this rite, the problem, whatever it was, was satisfactorily settled.

Uncle Joe, who on this occasion was alone, reined up his horses at sight of Hilliard, and held out his hand with a heartiness which had in it no such undercurrent of uneasiness as had accompanied young Joe's conscience-shamed greeting the day before. "Hop in, Roy," he said wheezily, "we'll medjure from here to the cross-road first, an' take t' other end as we come back. Tie her on."

He reached under the seat, and produced a white cotton rag, which his companion proceeded to tie, gravely, on a spoke of the left hind wheel. Then he seated himself beside the driver, but with his back to the horses, note-book and pencil in hand; Uncle Joe touched up his team, the ponderous wagon lurched forward, and the operation began.

The primitive method of measuring a road in vogue on Mesquit Creek consisted in first spanning the outer circumferences of a wagon wheel; afterward, by means of a white rag fastened to one of the spokes, its revolutions were noted and counted; these aggregated turns of the slowly revolving wheel giving, accordingly as the teller was more or less attentive, a more or less accurate admeasurement of the distance traveled over.

In the heat of the discussions which occupied Uncle Joe and his assistants, the miles on Peleg road varied in length from season to season. The women said it was aggravating never to be able to lay your hands on a milestone when you wanted it! To the men, these perennial shufflings, progressive and retrogressive, of the sign-posts were so many pleasant reminders of past controversies.

Hilliard had counted and set down several hundred turns of the white rag. He began to wonder why he had been asked. Mr. Wyatt, muffled in his blanket overcoat and knitted comforter, had not opened his lips except to remonstrate with his off horse, a fine colt hardly broken to harness. The norther had spent its force during the night, but had left the air tingling with a suggestion of sleet or snow. The low-hung gray sky was dotted from time to time by arrow-shaped strings of wild geese speeding southward, and honking

ominously. A forlorn jack-rabbit crossed the
road with a flying leap, and hustled away, scatter-
ing the dry leaves under the bare post-oaks; Mr.
Wyatt made a cross with his toe in the bottom of
the wagon, and spat in it. "Five hundred and
forty-one — two — three — four — five," counted
Hilliard monotonously.

"Roy!" The voice broke the silence so unexpectedly that he started and skipped a couple of
hundred. "Seven hundred and forty-six, forty-
seven, forty-eight. Yes, sir?"

"This here settle*ment* has got itse'f into a
durned mess, endurin' of the last six mont's."

"— Forty-nine. Seven hundred and fifty-one —
two. Has it?"

"Yes, it has. An' what's mo', it's goin' plum
to the devil, lessn somebody has got main strenk
enough to hold it back."

Hilliard's blood stirred a little, but he counted
calmly on. "Fifty-seven — eight — nine."

"The boys, leas'ways some of 'em, is gittin'
tired o' follerin a'ter Deerford. I don't take no
stock in him myse'f, al*though*, I'm boun' to say,
I was took by his sort o' dashin' way for a while.
I — I ain't goin' to tech on the subjec' of yo'
water-tank, Roy "—

"Eight hundred and ninety-nine," jerked Hilliard. "No, Mr. Wyatt, we will not speak of
that, if you please."

"Well, there's them that I know of, that's
mighty sorry they ever lent a hand in that busi-

ness, that's all! Now, the boys wants you to
come forrard ag'in an' take a-holt. They've been
quarrelin' with Deerford, an' they've been quarrelin' 'mongs' themselves. An' they've settled
on you to straighten 'em all out. Fer God's sake,
take a-holt, Roy. You kin lead the settle*ment*
onct mo', an' if you want to, by jing, I believe
you kin lead the whole county!"

"Stop the team a minute, Uncle Joe." Hilliard jumped down and picked up a baby squirrel
which was lying in the rutty road. One of its
forefeet hung limp and helpless; it looked at him
with suffering eyes, and cowered trembling in
his palm. He thrust it into his breast pocket.
"Well?" he said, leaning against the wheel. He
could not deny that the draught held to his lips
was tempting. A swift vision of himself surrounded as in times past with a ring of admiring
faces shot into his mind. "Well?" he repeated,
smiling up into the kindly old face looking down
at him.

"Well," echoed Mr. Wyatt anxiously.
"There's the leadership of Crouch's Settle*ment*
an' the county. All you've got to do is to pick
it up. The boys has got a big raid laid off for
Monday night. Clean acrost the county, onto
Colbrook's Ranch. They're startin' at nine
o'clock Monday night from Blackbird Gully.
You meet 'em there" —

"Mr. Wyatt," interrupted the young man, "if
I met the boys at Blackbird Gully, it would be

to do my best to keep them from any more unlaw-
ful fence-cutting."

"Then stay away!" returned Mr. Wyatt
quickly. "God Almighty could n't keep 'em from
wire-cuttin' now! It 's what they live on mostly.
That 's what they 're after you for. Ef you want
to lead 'em, you 've got to lead 'em where they
want to go." His voice had risen to a querulous
shriek.

Hilliard put his foot on the hub of the wheel
and sprang back into the wagon. "Drive on,
Mr. Wyatt," he said composedly. "Let us get
through with the measuring. I don't want the
leadership of Crouch's Settlement at any such
price."

Mr. Wyatt broke down suddenly. "I knowed
you would n't," he said in a dejected tone. "I
said I 'd ack as a trustee betwix' you an' them fool
boys. But I knowed you would n't go back on
yo' convincements an' yo' principles which is ag'inst
onlawful performances."

"Thank you, Uncle Joe," said Hilliard heartily.

"You 'll be mo' onpopular than ever, I 'm
afeard, Roy." The old man sighed as he picked
up the reins. "D—n Deerford, anyhow."

"Never mind, Uncle Joe. I have a few friends
left in the Settlement, eh? We will say no more
about it. Where did we leave off? Oh. Twelve
hundred and sixty-one — two — three."

"D—n Deerford, anyhow," repeated Mr. Wyatt, with increased gusto. "Are you goin' to the candy-pullin' at Mis' Crouch's Sat'day night?" he presently asked.

"Yes." Hilliard's thoughts, busy — and sombre — a moment before over his own semi-isolation, and the troubles which he believed were in store for the neighborhood, took another and a pleasanter tack. He had been looking forward for a week to this Christmas Eve frolic, where he knew he should meet Helen Wingate. His opportunities for seeing her were becoming more and more rare. He had again and abruptly ceased his visits to Mrs. Ransome's house. Jack had pointedly turned a cold shoulder upon him in full view of all his small world at Peleg Church, with Deerford standing by. It was a petty insult, and one that he could not in justice to his own manhood openly resent. But he could not present himself again in the house where the lad was master.

Margaret's eyes were troubled, and Helen's downcast, when he looked over at them, sitting on the women's benches in the church, from his own place among the men. The two girls no longer joined in the time-honored Sunday afternoon homeward race, but waited and rode quietly away, accompanied by Jack and Deerford. Deerford, hovering incessantly like a beautiful evil spirit about the neighborhood, seemed determined to cut his rival off from all communication with his kind. If Hilliard went to Crouch's after his mail, Deerford, seated on the fence with his adherents gloat-

ing admiration in his face, defied him with a swift
glance to enter the circle, or to draw away one of
its members.   If he rode to Skipton or Rassler,
he found Deerford there before him, as free of
every respectable office and counting-room in the
place as he was of low dive and common bar-
room.   If he galloped along the Branch road at
night, or in the early morning, in the hope of
catching a glimpse of Helen, he met Deerford
riding also, or walking with the light springy step
peculiar to him, shouldering his rifle, or swinging
his slender cane.   And the studied and exquisite
politeness of his enemy, for such he no longer
hesitated to name him to himself, made it impossible for him to come to honest blows with him, as
he longed to do.

"If he would only give me a chance, so that
I could measure paces with him!" he raged inwardly, aware at the same time that the only
weapons fit for this combat were those hammered
on the same anvil and taken from the same nail
as Deerford's own.

Meantime, as already remarked, his inner
strength grew, his youthful vanity was transmuted
into manly self-respect, his self-control became
at length so perfect that he could look into Deerford's face with a smile as inscrutable as his own,
and without a touch of color to throw the birth-
mark on his cheek into telltale relief.

"He will be there Christmas Eve, also," he
mused.   "But let him!   Helen will be there,

too!" Then aloud, "Two thousand and eight — nine" —

His reckoning was hardly up to the mark. But Mr. Wyatt was not critical; his thoughts, too, had been far a-field. "Them mile-posts is plum out of place," he remarked, when they finally halted and turned at the Skipton cross - road. "They'll all have to be changed ag'in."

"I reckon yo' convincements an' principles is right, Roy," he said ruefully, at parting. "But I mistrus' you'll be mighty onpopular with the boys. An' I be durn ef Deerford ain't gallopin' 'em straight to the devil."

Christmas Eve closed in clear and cold. The twigs and branches of the trees were still cased in the sleet which had fallen the day before; the moonlight made them glitter like so many crystal wands. There were icicles depending from the eaves of Crouch's front porch, and the well-bucket on the stone cover of the well was incrusted with several layers of ice. The still night air under the pecan-trees and among the saplings across the road was foggy with the breath of many horses. These champed their bridle-bits, or munched corn from feed-troughs behind the wagons drawn up in line.

The front door of the house stood wide open; a fan-shaped glow streamed from it into the crisp darkness outside. Every stick of furniture had been removed from the single large living-room;

chairs were brought in between the dances, but only for the older women; it was considered almost disgraceful for a girl to sit down as long as a fiddle scraped.

A medley of bedding, sleeping babies, groceries, and other odds and ends, including Uncle Sam's candle-box, strewed the floor of the upper room, and was heaped upon the stairs. A fire of misshapen but rich mesquit roots and stumps roared in the ample fireplace. In a corner of the hearth, Johnny Giles, weak in political principles, but sound as to catgut and rosin, was fiddling adorably; he had a heavenly smile on his lean face, and minded not that the nail keg on which he sat had but the suggestion of a cover. Billy Crouch was threading the big double quadrille with a radiant look; he was not dancing, but giving his soft little hands to his guests in rapturous greeting, and reminding one and all that supper would soon be ready. In fact, Mrs. Crouch, with Mrs. Wyatt and the Mrs. Parsons, was in the kitchen, which was set well back in the yard, frying chicken, boiling the candy, and setting the sillabubs to cool, in the torch-lit back-yard.

Hilliard made his way directly to Margaret Ransome. "I have been looking for you," she said, standing up with him for the dance; "I was beginning to fear you might not come."

"Oh no!" he returned, looking over at Helen who was just stepping into place with Jack Ransome. He thought he had never seen her look so beautiful. She wore a gown of soft white woolen stuff; a wreath of bamboo berries with their dark green glistening leaves crowned her hair. There was no constraint in the face she turned toward her partner; she smiled on him with frank friendliness; he bent over her, smiling back; and Hilliard noticed that for the first time in many weeks the lad's eyes were limpid and his speech clear. "How well Jack looks!" he cried involuntarily.

Margaret's eyes sparkled. "Does he not!" she exclaimed fondly. Many a time afterward, both recalled the boy as he looked that night in his dark blue white-embroidered woolen blouse, his tasseled boots drawn up over his trousers, and the scarlet silk Mexican banda, or sash, knotted around his waist.

"Does he not!" cried Margaret again. Margaret herself looked like some graceful tropical bird, flashing in and out among the dancers in her crimson dress, with great clusters of red-haws on her bosom and in her blue-black braids of hair.

"I wanted to tell you," she said, poising lightly again by her partner, "that Helen is leaving the day after to-morrow, for home. Yes," for Hilliard had uttered an exclamation of surprise and dismay, "she has received letters calling her back at once. We are much distressed, for she had promised, you know, to stay with us until spring. You must speak to her as soon as you can," she concluded significantly, "for we shall go home early. We came with Mrs. Red in her wagon."

"If I had not been sure you would be here," she resumed, when a figure of the quadrille brought them again to their places, "I would have come over to tell you, even if I had had to make it a night ride." She smiled at him kindly.

"How good you are to me, Margaret," he said softly. But he was scarcely aware of what he was saying. His whole soul was filled with one desire, one determination, — to get a moment's speech with Helen. He approached her as soon as the fiddler, with a flourish of his bow, gave the order, "Seat your ladies," — the signal, not for sitting down, but for a laughing interchange of partners.

"Will you put this on, Miss Helen," he said boldly; he handed her a woolen shawl which he had caught up from the stair, "and come out on the porch for a breath of air?" The pretext was flimsy enough, but it served. She took his arm without hesitation, and they stepped out upon the porch. "I hear that you are going away," he began, in a low agitated tone, when they had taken a turn or two up and down the small gallery. "I had intended — Under different circumstances, I should not, at this time, say what I am about to say " — he paused, feeling her hand tremble on his arm. "But, you surely understand why I cannot let you go away without telling you — oh, Helen, you know that I love you! Wait, I do not ask any confession, any pledge from you, or any answer even, now. I only ask you if I may come to you, at your own home, in the course of a few months, and there, — and then " — He paused again; the long-repressed feeling threatened to burst all bounds; he recovered control of himself with difficulty. At length he asked quietly, "May I come, Helen?"

"Yes," the answer came almost in a whisper. Under the many eyes which were following them curiously, or sympathetically, Hilliard dared do no more than touch quickly and furtively with his own the ungloved hand on his arm. The touch thrilled them both, with the sweetness of a first caress. To Hilliard it was the seal of a betrothal to be kept sacred so long as life should warm his veins.

"I do not know why I am called home," Helen said presently. "My mother's letter was strangely reticent. I fear something is wrong, although she reassures me as to her own health. For some reasons, I am glad to go — to get away " — a slight shiver ran through her frame. "But, I am much troubled at leaving Mrs. Ransome and Margaret. Oh, Mr. Hilliard, Roy," her voice sank to a tremulous whisper, "can you do nothing to rescue Jack Ransome from — if you only knew! — if you could but understand! " —

"I do. I do!" said Hilliard tenderly. "And I promise you, by my love " —

"Miss Helen," said Jack, appearing in the doorway, "where are you? Oh!" he looked with pretended surprise at Hilliard. "Are n't you afraid to trust yourself out there with — ah, allow me to protect you!"

"Miss Wingate," said Hilliard calmly, ignoring the speaker, "will you go in now? I will claim my dance, if you are not too fatigued." She lifted her pale proud face to his, and laid her hand frankly in his outstretched palm. Then, unfastening a spray of bamboo-berries from her wreath, she gave it to him with a smile, and swept. haughtily past Ransome, without so much as a glance in his direction, into the house.

Here something unusual was taking place. The guests were all pressed back against the wall, leaving an open place on the bare floor. Hilliard, attending Helen, pushed forward to the front row, where he found himself for the first time that evening in close proximity to Deerford's own particular gang. Even through the glow of hope and happiness which enveloped him like a rosy cloud he could not but observe the added disfavor with which some of these men eyed him. He remembered Uncle Joe's prophecy! He shrugged his shoulders and smiled. What did their hatred or their goodwill matter at any time? And now! What does a king care for the fretful grinding of the dust beneath his throne? For a time, elbow to elbow with his detractors, he saw nothing but the blissful dreams which floated before his inner vision. But the silence around him finally aroused him. He looked up.

Johnny Giles, with his head laid low on his fiddle-neck, was playing — not one of the gay, rattling tunes to which Crouch's Settlement joyed to foot

it, but a soft dreamy melody which filled the room
like a supernatural whisper; even the leap of the
yellow flames could be heard above it, and the
quick breathing of the men and women, who leaned
forward, listening, and gazing with fascinated eyes
at Deerford.

Deerford had stepped without warning into the
middle of the room; the company at a significant
wave of his hand had fallen back. Giles as if
under a spell had drawn his bow gently across the
strings of his wonderful violin.

And Deerford was dancing!

No one present had ever seen anything like it.
His feet made no more than a whispering sound on
the floor, though clad in the regulation boots. His
lithe body swayed first to one side and then to the
other with a stealthy cat-like grace; his arms were
slowly outstretched, with the slender white fingers
curved inward to the palms of his hands; his eyelids were lowered until only a line of light gleamed
through the dark lashes; the swaying motion became slower and slower until it ceased, and the
slender figure stood motionless, yet instinct with
unrest. Then bounding rapidly forward, he
crouched with his shoulders drawn together until
his head nearly touched the floor, — "like a cougar
smellin' blood" Bagley declared afterward, — and
springing backward, he resumed his rhythmic un-
dulatory movements. His eyes suddenly opened
wide, emitting flashes of living flame from their
dilated pupils — or so it seemed to the spell-bound

circle about him; his lips were curved in an inscrutable smile.

The hilt of the little dagger in his belt, catching
the firelight, glittered like a diamond spark.

Hilliard's first feeling was one of supreme disgust. To this succeeded, in spite of himself, wonder and admiration; for the performance and the
performer were alike weirdly and strangely beautiful. Then, without warning, he found himself
struggling with a memory — or, not a memory, but
one of those unaccountable suggestions which had
stirred several times of late below the threshold of
consciousness and tugged like half-drowned creatures for recognition. He seemed to feel rather
than see, hovering above the oscillating figure before him, a small lightly clad child, with a crown of
roses on its sunny head, swaying and smiling and
tossing its little hands.

He drew a long breath as the vision faded. The
music at the same moment died away into something like an involuntary moan. Deerford stopped;
his arms dropped heavily, his eyes closed as if
overcome with languor, his yellow curls quivered,
as if blown by some mysterious wind.

There was an interval of dazed silence, then the
men rushed upon him with a shout of savage delight, lifted him to their shoulders, and bore him
out into the moonlight. He submitted to their
boisterous greetings, seemingly as impassive as an
oriental god, on his improvised throne. But as he
passed Hilliard, he glanced down at him and Helen,

who were standing close together, and a malignant scowl darkened his brow.

In a few moments, a gay medley of song and laughter floated out from the kitchen, where the hero of the evening and his followers were at supper.

Meantime great platters of molasses candy had been set on the tables out in the yard, and the young folk were already dabbing their palms and fingers with butter and flour preparatory to attacking the red-hot, sticky mass.

Hilliard lent a hand here, with Margaret and Helen. The scene remained graven on his memory, and often came back to him in after years. The moon was just dropping behind the sombre line of woods skirting Crouch's field, the wind had risen, and a few clouds were gathering and scurrying across the sky. The ice-clad branches of the pecan-trees rattled in the fitful gusts that whipped around the corner of the house, and flared to and fro the smoky torches on their stands. The cold was intense, but no one seemed to mind. The yard was filled with brightly-clad figures which flitted to and fro; there were bursts of loud laughter, cries of pain, affected or real, around the fiery platters, shrill remonstrances from those who were getting too little of the contents, shouts of dismay from those who had got too much; weavings of arms and hands over and under the yellow ropes that quickly became cold and brittle in the night air. And above all the joyous tumult the sound of Johnny Giles's dance-tunes within! Hilliard, laughing into

the laughing faces of Helen and Margaret who
"pulled" with him, had quite forgotten Deerford,
until looking up from the amber-colored loop flung
toward him by Helen, he saw him pass stealthily,
as if wishing to escape for once from his noisy companions, across the yard toward the front gate, and
disappear in the darkness.

A little later, Hilliard helped Red Parsons harness his horses, and assisted the two girls, with
Mrs. Red and all her brood — from Bud to little
Margaret — into the wagon, and watched them
drive off. He pressed Helen's hand at parting.
"I will ride over to Skipton with you, Monday,"
he said significantly.

When he reëntered the house, he noted with
some surprise that although Deerford had gone
Jack had remained, and was among the dancers.
He himself stepped off a reel with Lorena Crouch,
who, secretly adoring him, was so dazzled by this
unexpected and un-hoped-for honor, that she
stumbled over her own feet, trod on her partner's
toes, and suffered agony in trying to find something to say. He smiled at her kindly, as he
handed her in at the kitchen door, and bade her
good-night. "He's wo'th a million o' caperin'
monkeys, Roy Hilliard is," remarked Mrs. Crouch,
dropping a well-floured chicken-leg into the frying-
pan.

Lorena retired into a corner to wipe the tears of
gladness from her eyes. "And Miss Helen is a
plum an—an—gel," she sobbed irrelevantly to
herself.

Meantime, the object of her worship was cantering homeward, glad to be alone at last with the thoughts of his assured happiness.

It was long past midnight; the moon had gone down, and the gathering clouds had quite obscured the stars, when Hector, dropping into a swift walk, began to descend the sloping bank which led to the creek bed in front of Hilliard's house; he stumbled a little, and his rider, aroused from a pleasant reverie, lifted his head. He became instantly alert. His watch dog, Bruce, was barking furiously and with the peculiar intonation which said as plainly as words to his master's ear that a stranger was somewhere about. Reining up his horse, he sat motionless, straining his eyes forward in the darkness. He could dimly descry the low irregular outlines of the house beyond the rise of the opposite bank, against the sullen sky. There was no one on the premises, he knew, Manuel and Juan having gone to Skipton that afternoon with a load of loose cotton, not to return until the next day. The challenging bark of the dog continued. Hilliard threw himself from the saddle, leaving the well-trained horse standing unfastened, and ran across the dry creek bank and up the opposite slope. A tiny flash of light — in summer-time it might have been the bluish sparkle of a firefly — shone for an instant somewhere between the dark masses of house and stable, danced about fitfully, and disappeared. He crept cautiously and noiselessly to the front gate; it was unlatched, open. He slipped in, expecting to be greeted at once by Bruce's caressing whine, for the barking had ceased abruptly; his finger was on the trigger of his pistol.

At the corner of the porch, he stepped upon a soft yielding mass, which he divined instantly to be the still quivering body of his dog. At the same moment, a sheet of flame ran like heat-lightning over one of the larger cotton-pens in the rear of the stable-yard. It died down, smouldered red, and shot up again.

Hilliard leaped with a single bound past the burning cotton, and gripped the shoulder of a man who was loping swiftly across the lot, with his knees bent, and his head to the ground. At the touch, Deerford stood upright, whirled, and closed silently with his pursuer. The assault was so sudden that Hilliard had no chance, had he been so minded, to use his pistol. Neither could Deerford draw back his arm for a deadly thrust, as he endeavored to do. Hilliard's iron grasp was on his wrist; the bones of his forearm cracked, the dagger, dripping with Bruce's life-blood, dropped to the ground. He made a feint of yielding, and as his antagonist stepped back, he sprang upon him, grappling him in a close embrace, fairly twining his lithe slender body around his foe, and trying to strangle him with his long fingers. For a moment Hilliard was powerless; then, with an effort he wrenched himself free, and twisting his hand in Deerford's collar, he forced him inch by inch back upon his knees. He felt the convulsive rattle in the throat against his knuckles. He could see by the glare of the burning cotton the figure writhing helpless at his knee, with the head fallen backward, the blue eyes starting from their sockets.

Suddenly his grasp relaxed; he bent hurriedly, and laid his hand over Deerford's heart; he caught the limp hands in his own and chafed them anxiously. The vision had reappeared with startling clearness, and hovered above the backward bent head — the lightly-clad form of a little child, rose-wreathed, dancing and clapping its hands.

"*Allan!*" he had heard himself whisper as in a dream.

No audible word had been spoken during the brief struggle. The prostrate man arose to his feet, panting and trembling. Hilliard stooped mechanically, picked up the bloody dagger, and handed it to him. They stood staring at each other, the one with dazed eyes, as if he had hardly regained consciousness; the other, with a strange unnatural feeling of helplessness.

In one instant, however, the color flowed back into Deerford's pale cheeks; he lifted his head and shook his shoulders slightly; the light mocking expression returned to his eyes. "Come!" he cried gayly, "it is high time we were putting out that fire." He ran toward the burning pen, and, running, he pulled off his heavy overcoat.

The cotton, partly protected by the rails of

which the open pen was built, and crusted with
sleet and ice, had burned but slowly. It was only
at the moment when Deerford approached it that
the flames, eating into the dry fleece underneath,
began to blaze up fiercely. He climbed up the
sides of the pen, graceful in this as in everything
he did — threw the overcoat upon the mounting
flames, and began tearing off the top rails. These
fell smoking at Hilliard's feet before he had recovered himself sufficiently to lend assistance.
His hands were scorched and Deerford's wrists
badly blistered when the fire, after a short but
sharp tussle, was finally extinguished. He felt
painfully the grotesqueness of the situation, when
they two stood facing each other again, in a darkness faintly illuminated by a pile of smouldering
rails.

"Mr. Deerford," he began, stiffly and awkwardly, "I " —

Deerford interrupted him. "Oh," he said airily,
"without knowing exactly what you are about to
say, Mr. Hilliard, I will risk the remark that you
cannot very well thank me for helping you put out
a fire which I myself kindled! "

"At least I can thank you for the remark, Mr.
Deerford," said Hilliard grimly. "And now " —

"And now you will thank me if I will stand
not on the order of my going, but go at once," he
interrupted again quickly. "You are quite right.
I will relieve you of my presence immediately.
But one thing more, if you will permit me. And
that is " —

A tongue of flame broke out on the charred rail at his feet; it brought his face into full relief as he leaned forward. He was smiling contemptuously.

"And that is, Mr. Hilliard, that you have won the game very cheaply. A few pounds of cotton, a burnt rail or two, a worthless watch dog " —

"What do you mean?" said Hilliard, stirred by the tone to a frenzied desire to seize the man again by the throat.

"What do I mean! Could anything be clearer, if only one chose to comprehend? You tell the story — eloquently, as becomes a fledgling of the law — at Crouch's, to-morrow. A midnight attempt to destroy your property by fire, your own magnanimous conduct, generosity *versus* villainy, and the gaping, imbecile, unlicked cubs will hurrah at your heels, as they now do at mine. Victory number one. You pour the tale — with romantic additions — into the ears of the fair Helen; she drops like the heroine of Troy into the arms of her Paris. Victory number two. The fair Helen " —

"You scoundrel!" cried Hilliard, choking with rage, "if you dare to take Miss Wingate's name again upon your evil lips, I will shoot you, like the dog that you are!"

"I have finished," said Deerford imperturbably. "Only I repeat that you have purchased these important victories at a very low price."

There was an undercurrent of anxiety in his

voice which cooler senses would have detected. Hilliard was too much shaken to note it. He fell an easy prey to the ruse.

"I shall not mention this particular piece of rascality, if that is what you are driving at," he said angrily.

"You are a man of your word," responded Deerford quickly, "and I hold you to this promise."

"I see no reason why I should keep faith with a rogue," returned Hilliard with growing impatience; "nevertheless, you are at liberty, so far as I am concerned, to hold your supremacy — wherever you can. I warn you, however, to keep out of my way after this. Now go — while you may."

Deerford's tongue for once seemed to have lost its readiness. He turned and walked slowly across the lot toward the back gate, where his horse was stamping fretfully.

"Mr. Deerford!" Hilliard's voice arrested him. "Your overcoat I see is ruined. The night is very cold. Will you allow me to offer you one of mine?"

"No, I thank you. A rapid ride homeward will keep me warm. Good-night, Mr. Hilliard."

"Good-night."

Both men had dropped unconsciously into the courteous speech and tone of ordinary intercourse.

"All this is past belief," Hilliard mused, standing stock still, and listening to the flying hoof-beats on the hard road. "But I can understand him, complex as he is, better than I can understand myself. I know why he hates me; I can partly see why his hatred goes far enough to wish to burn my property. But I? Well, I suppose I am a quixotic fool! Did a man, caught red-handed, as it were, ever before dictate and receive terms in such easy fashion!" He laughed under his breath. "Well; and can I not afford everything — anything — now!" he exclaimed, after a pause, "now that Helen is really mine!"

He drew water from the well, and dashed it over the half-consumed cotton-pen, as a last precaution, and extinguished the still burning rails. Then whistling for Hector, he walked out toward the front gate. At the corner of the porch he stooped to draw the stiffening body of his dog out of the path. "Poor faithful Bruce," he muttered, tears filling his eyes. "Worthless!" — the expression, unnoted at the time, recurred to him all at once — "worthless! Why did I not strangle the lying villain when I had the chance!" he cried in a fury. "Poor devil," he added, softening again, "let him go. He does not know — yet — how much he has lost!"

XII

IN PELEG CHURCH

THE grotesqueness of the situation struck him more forcibly still the following Monday, when he found himself riding to Skipton beside the open wagonette driven by Deerford. Nothing in the handsome face turned from time to time in his direction betrayed the faintest recollection of the scene through which they had so recently passed. The bright unembarrassed greeting of his avowed enemy threw Hilliard himself into momentary confusion, and he colored up to the eyes when Margaret demanded merrily, "Why, what have you been doing, since we saw you, Mr. Hilliard? You look as if you were hiding a crime!"

"I am!" he laughed, really amused at the reach of this random shot.

Deerford, who was handing Helen to her place on the back seat of the wagonette, laughed also, easily and audaciously, with a malicious side glance at his foe.

The drive seemed very short through the woodland and across the dry prairie strewn with the bleached bones of dead cattle. The fences cut by Hilliard in June had never been restored; the cedar posts with the rusted wire trailing from them still dotted the wind-swept plateau. He glanced at one of these, overthrown and lying near a certain bend in the road, then his eyes instinctively sought those of Deerford; they seemed utterly vacant of rancor, or acknowledgment.

Helen maintained during the drive the curious reserve habitual to her in Deerford's presence. But this no longer disturbed Hilliard, sure at last of his own place in her heart; he talked but little himself, but feasted his eyes in rapturous content on her graceful figure and her lovely face, rosy with the whipping of the north wind. Margaret, too, was silent and seemingly oppressed by some secret anxiety. Deerford chattered incessantly, urging the horses to a furious speed the while, yet handling them with a skill and grace which provoked even Hilliard's unwilling admiration.

They stopped near the outskirts of the little town of Skipton, at Mrs. Temperance Holloway's Tavern, a queer-looking house, half-log, half-box, the more substantial part dating from earlier times, when Pap Holloway had to fort himself against Comanche Indians. Aunt Tempy herself, a fat, comfortable-looking old body, came out to meet them. "'Light. 'Light. Git right down an' come in," she cried. "You 've got oodles o' time. The stage don't start for haff 'n hour. Howdy, Margaret. Howdy, Roy."

"How are you, Aunt Tempy?" said Hilliard heartily, "and how is Mr. Holloway?"

"Oh, pap's a-movin'. An' yaller-dog poor, ez common." She laughed, and waddled back to the house, shooing them all before her like a motherly hen. Deerford stopped in the gallery to give some directions about the horses; Margaret was borne off to an inner room to convey particular instructions concerning some yeast Mrs. Ransome had sent over to Mrs. Holloway. Hilliard found himself alone with Helen for one moment in the small prim tavern parlor. The unexpectedness of this good fortune deprived him of speech. He could only gaze with dumb craving into the violet eyes lifted to his.

"Is it really true?" he breathed at length. "Tell me that I am not dreaming, Helen! Helen! I am to come to you in the spring? I am to woo you in your own home, and win you, my beautiful darling? Forgive me, forgive me, if I say too much!"

"In the early spring," she corrected, smiling shyly.

He seized her hand and pressed it ardently. "And, until then? Until then, my Helen?"

"You will hear from me through Margaret," she returned. He had been hoping for encouragement to write to her, and longing for her promise to answer his letters. She divined his disappointment. "I think we can trust each other, even if we do not hear at all from each other," she said quickly. In her heart she feared that Deerford, if he knew that letters were exchanged between

herself and her lover — and what letters were
sacred in Billy's candle-box! — that Deerford
might work mischief. Hilliard dared not urge
his petition. Instead, he resolved within himself
to see her before the early spring! He said as
much, hurriedly, for he heard footsteps and voices
in the hall outside. "I will be glad," she said
frankly. "And, oh Roy," she added, with great
earnestness, "remember your pledge to save Jack,
if you can — *from him*."

"I will remember everything," he said. There
was no time for further speech, or for private
leave-taking. Mrs. Holloway burst in with the
announcement that the stage was coming. Hilliard
folded Helen's wraps around her and followed her,
with the others, to the gate. The lumbering big-
bodied stage had already swung up; the staid
elderly couple, man and wife, in whose company
she was to make the homeward journey were already seated within, together with two or three
other passengers.

As the vehicle started with a jerk and rolled
away, the driver executing an uncertain tune on
his battered horn, Hilliard turned to Margaret,
who leaned over the low fence, looking after it
with streaming eyes. He would have liked to
take her in his arms! They seemed to bring her
so near to him, those tears shed over Helen's departure. "It is more than that," she confessed,
in answer to his burst of sympathy. "I shall
miss her sadly. I can hardly imagine the passing

days, the house, myself, without her dear presence.
But "— she glanced around, and seeing that they
were quite alone in the bare little yard, she went
on. "It is foolish, perhaps, to put the feeling
into words. But I have had lately, I know not
why, a sense of impending danger, a presentiment
of coming evil. Oh, I know well enough what
you would say! that these forebodings generally
have no significance at all, and that in this case
they are but prophecies of the loneliness and heart-
ache I shall surely feel. My reason tells me you
are right, but something deeper than reason warns
me that some terrible calamity is hovering over
Helen — something, perhaps, that will befall her
on this journey."

He laughed outright. "If that were true," he
said meaningly, "do you not think *I* would be
overwhelmed with forebodings?"

"You have spoken to her, then?" she asked
quickly. "And she has shown you her heart? I
guessed as much from what she herself told me.
God bless you, Roy, my friend, my brother! You
have made a noble choice — and so has she!"
She smiled as she added the last words, putting
out her hand and looking bravely in his face. If
she had grown a shade paler, he was too blinded
by his own happiness to perceive it.

"I will tell you all about it — about us, at the
first opportunity," he said, clasping her hand.
"So you see that your apprehensions cannot mean
anything. But I do not wonder that you are sad!

Where can Deerford be with the wagonette?
Shall I " —

"Oh," she interposed, "I am not going back
home just yet. I am to do some shopping for my
mother. And Bud Parsons is to drive me home.
He brought over Mr. Deerford's horse. I would
not go back with *him* — for worlds!"

"Where is Jack?" asked Hilliard, who had
not heard the last half-whispered remark.

"He stayed at home with mother. I — I think
Jack is coming back to himself, Roy. He has
been different this last day or two. A little silent
and gloomy, perhaps, but gentle and affectionate.
Oh, more like he was before — more like the dear
old Jack, Roy."

Her lip quivered and she turned away her head.

"Oh, Jack will come out all right, Margaret,
don't worry," he said with conviction. "And I
do not think Deerford will linger here — now."

"I suppose he will follow Helen," Margaret
sighed. "You are not afraid of his influence upon
her?" She asked the question involuntarily.

He lifted his head proudly. "She has given
me her word," he said with simple earnestness.

Margaret clenched her hands nervously under
her cloak. "I wish he could realize as I do," she
thought, "what a spell-like sway Deerford has
over her. But I dare not say more, now!"

He walked with her to the plaza of the town,
and left her at the entrance of one of the squatty
stores. The open square was filled with wagons,

mud-bespattered hacks, and saddle-horses. Among the last, hitched to a post, he recognized Jack Ransome's Black Prince, which Deerford usually rode. Deerford himself was sitting on the curb of the town-well with a knot of countrymen around him. As Hilliard passed the group, he heard one of the men in a burst of enthusiasm urging the young stranger to allow his name to be "put up" as a candidate for governor of the State!

That night, sitting alone before his crackling mesquit fire, he heard the signal-shot that announced the gathering in Blackbird Gully of Deerford and his gang. He remembered for one moment the big raid, whose leadership Uncle Joe had offered him, on the part of the "boys." He smiled disdainfully; his eyes went back to the dancing flames, and his thoughts to Helen! Helen!

Sometime, toward daylight, it began to rain. The clouds had been accumulating for weeks, and all that day and the next, and a part of the next, — which was Thursday, — the heavens seemed not to weary an instant of pouring forth their garnered and repressed floods, or the earth, parched by more than six months of continuous drought, of receiving them.

The creek, long before a patch of blue sky overhead announced a truce, was roaring and seething between its banks, and where the land was low, swelling far beyond them. Hilliard congratulated himself and Manuel that the last wagon-load of cotton had gone to the Skipton gin, and the whole crop, ginned and baled, awaited transportation under shelter there.

Late Thursday afternoon, he rode over to Crouch's Well. He told himself that he was expecting a letter from Mrs. Blackmore, as indeed he was, but in his secret soul he thought it conceivable that Helen might have sent him a line from the nearest post-office on her route. He measured her impatience by his own, and he did not believe that she would hold to her resolution of not writing. He could not afford not to get this letter at the first moment possible. It was necessary to swim his horse across Mesquit. This was accomplished at the expense only of a dripping mane and tail for Hector.

At Crouch's he found but a handful of men. These, seated stoically on the wet fence-rails, were fortifying themselves against the cold by draughts from individual whiskey-flasks, or requisitions upon the joint-stock jug, which stood ready, uncorked, upon the edge of the horse-trough. Among the loiterers were Deerford and Jack Ransome. The subject of conversation at the moment was evidently an uncomfortable one, for Hilliard noted an open anxiety on their faces. The topic, whatever it was, was dropped at his approach. "Where's your horse, Jack?" demanded Tom Roper, by way of bridging over the awkward silence.

"I did not ride over," replied Jack sullenly.

Hilliard saw at once that he had been drinking
again. "I came over in the Skipton mail-hack,
and I am going back in the Rassler mail. It will
be along pretty soon, I reckon. Unless they are
stalled in the mud somewhere."

"Or gone sailing down Blackhaw Creek," suggested Waldrup facetiously.

Hilliard passed on into the house, and stood
looking feverishly on while Billy rummaged in the
candle-box for his mail. There was a package of
flower-seed, a pair of spurs, a letter from Aunt
Amanda, and a couple of magazines. Hilliard
took them, telling himself severely that this was
all that he had looked for, but he wondered if
Billy in his anxiety to get back to the "boys,"
had not overlooked Helen's letter!

"The boys has got themselves into a peck o'
trouble this time, I'm afeard, Roy," said Billy,
pushing the post-office back under the bed with
his foot.

"Have they? How?"

"I dunno exactly. Seems like they had a
scrimmage som'ers last night. This here wire-
cuttin' has gone too fer, anyhow. I wisht to God
you'd take a-holt ag'in, Roy! Why, the post-office
is regular busted. The boys don't keer nothin'
'bout politics any more. The gover'mint at Austin, an' the United States Senate can set yander
an' do what they durn please, an' Crouch's Settlement goes postin' on its downward way, an' don't
even try to stop 'em! What do you think young

Joe Wyatt said this mornin'? Said he did n't give a damn *what they done about the revenoo!*"

Billy delivered himself of these gloomy reflections in a low tone, and with sundry uneasy glances toward the half-open door. His round face was clouded, the corners of his mouth drooped. He looked like a grieved infant.

"Oh," said Hilliard, more cheerfully than he felt, "don't fret, Billy. The boys will come around."

When he came out of the house, he saw that Jack was standing near the well, alone, and somewhat apart from his fellows. He went over to him deliberately. "Jack," he said, but without offering his hand, which he feared might be refused, "I wish you would come over to-morrow and see me. I have got a brand new rifle which I would like you to try."

Jack looked at him, his face assuming a dogged expression, but made no answer.

"For the sake of old times, Jack!" Hilliard persisted. "Come with me now. You have n't your horse, but we will ride and tie, as we have done many a time," he added gayly.

"Let me alone, d—n you!" shouted the lad, shaking the friendly hand from his shoulder; "if you don't, I know how to make you."

"Very well, sir," Hilliard said curtly, turning away, "I promise to let you well alone from this time forward."

"I 've a good notion to go after him and lick

him yet," Ransome blustered, watching Hilliard as he mounted and rode slowly off.

"Bully for you, Jack! Bully for you!" laughed one of the men, winking broadly at his companions. " 'a little game-cock like you can do up a dozen yellow-legged Domineckers like Miss Mary-Ann Hilliard, yonder!"

"I'll do it!" cried Jack, delighted, and he started running down the wet road.

"Don't forget to-night's business, Jack!" Deerford called after him.

He stopped a second and looked back over his shoulder. "All right!" he cried; "I'll attend to it," and ran on, shouting Hilliard's name.

"How will the boy get home?" Roper asked, frowning a little, "he's half drunk."

"Oh," replied Deerford carelessly, "the mail-hack from Rassler will pick him up on the road, if he does not come back here. Trust the Lord to take care of a fool and a drunkard."

Hearing himself called, Hilliard drew up and waited near the turn of the road. "Did you want me?" he asked when Jack came up, stumbling and panting; his young face was red and swollen, his brown eyes were bloodshot.

"Yes, I want you," he said in a threatening tone. "You can't buy me, Mr. Leroy Hilliard. D—n your new rifle."

"Oh, come, Jack." Hilliard smiled in spite of himself. "You don't mean that."

Jack looked up at him stupidly. He knitted

his brows doubtfully; the anger suddenly vanished from his face; he burst into a gay boyish laugh. "I reckon I don't mean it," he chuckled; "but if I don't, I swear I don't know what I've come prancing through the mud after you for!"

He looked down at his muddy boots and laughed again.

"Well, now that you are here," Hilliard said, dismounting, and taking the bridle over his arm, "come on home with me." A swift backward glance showed him the expectant group at Crouch's.

"No," returned Jack, drawing away, "I can't. I have some business to attend to to-night — in Skipton. But I'll walk a little way with you — and if that gang of loafers don't like it, they can lump it, that's all," he muttered between his teeth.

They turned around a knoll which hid them completely from the view of the men they had left, and passed on into the post-oak rough. Neither spoke; the short winter day was drawing to a close. The heavy clouds lying about the horizon showed that the rain was not yet over. The woods were so still that the sucking sound of their booted feet on the soaked ground came echoing back through the trees. They had tramped along for over a mile in silence, and had reached the by-road which led to Hilliard's place, when Jack stopped.

"Are you tired, Jack?" asked Hilliard kindly. He had refrained from speech, fearful of changing the boy's wayward mood. "Get into the saddle. I am glad of a chance to stretch my legs."

"No." Jack's voice sounded wistful in the falling gloom. "I am not going home with you, Roy. I — I — can't. I've got business" —

"What business?" urged Hilliard. "Let it wait until to-morrow. Your lounge is waiting for you, and some uncut magazines, and your pipe; you haven't smoked that pipe for an age, you young rascal! Come, boy; it's just the night for a snug doze by the fire. If you think Mrs. Ransome and Margaret will be anxious, I will send Manuel over ᴜᴜ let them know where you are. Or I will go on home with you now," he added, striving not to appear too anxious. A wave of tender feeling swept over him. He felt half-tempted to seize the boy by force, throw him on the horse, and keep him a prisoner until his tempter should have left the neighborhood.

"No! No! I tell you! Let me alone. I know my own affairs better than you do."

The older man was silent, seeing the uselessness of pleading any longer. "Anyway," he reflected, "he will not have to cross the creek alone, for the Rassler mail must be along in a few moments."

"All right, Jack," he said aloud, "but you must come over soon, and try that rifle."

"Yes, I will," Jack returned, his good humor bubbling up again. "And, I say, Roy, old fellow, you'll shake hands once more, won't you?"

"Shake hands! Of course!" He did more. Moved by an irresistible impulse, he threw his arm around the lad's shoulders and clasped him closely.

He could not be sure, but he thought that a sob shook the breast against his own. "You young rascal!" he repeated, laughing to cover his own unexpected emotion, "don't you ever dare to snub me again — in public!"

"I — I won't," whispered the boy.

Hilliard mounted and rode away reluctantly, turning his head from time to time, though the darkness soon hid the motionless figure behind him from sight.

When he had disappeared, Jack walked rapidly back about a quarter of a mile, and turned into a travel-beaten, wheel-rifted road, which bore off to the left. He was completely sobered by the chill air, and he made his way along through the unbroken gloom like one familiar with his course.

Abner Croft had that day dug a grave for old Mrs. Barry, who lived several miles back of Crouch's Well, near Bethesda Church. The heavy rain had made the task a difficult one, for the Bethesda graveyard was on level ground, and it was the work of hours to keep the grave emptied of water, and get it sufficiently deep to allow the funeral to take place. The body was borne to its last resting-place just at nightfall, and when Abner had filled in the dripping earth and patted the muddy mound into shape with his spade, it was too dark for the mourning relatives to distinguish each other's faces. The last funeral hymn — the wailing farewell to the dead — arose and floated

weirdly away into the night. The singers groped
their way through the wet bushes to their wagons,
or their saddle-horses, and departed. It was a
part of the neighborhood etiquette for Abner to
wait until everybody had gone, before gathering
up his "tools" and leaving the dead alone under
the open sky.

He waited, therefore, keeping company with
old Mrs. Barry to the last. In his determination
to overcome his instinctive terror of the dead, he
forced himself to stay longer than was necessary;
then shouldering his pick and spade, he trudged
off afoot, chill to the bone. He never rode any
of the horses he raised, even to break them. He
respected a horse too much, he said, to force that
noble animal to carry a poor human sinner like
himself!

It was towards nine o'clock when he found himself in the neighborhood of Peleg Church on his
homeward journey. A few scattered drops of
rain were falling, and the wind, blowing in heavy
whirling gusts, presaged one of those violent clear-
ing-up storms peculiar to the region. He stopped
in the narrow path and reflected, shifting his
grave-digging implements from the right shoulder
to the left. "It was all I could do to swim the
creek by daylight and keep clear of floating tim-
ber. Maybe she 's run down some since, and
maybe she ain't. Anyhow I 'm not going to resk
it, al*though* I 'm the best swimmer and the best
diver in the Settlement. Old Ma'am Croft won't

be expectin' me, considering of the weather. I reckon I'd better put in at Peleg Church — until moonrise, howsomever."

He walked on a few hundred yards and struck into the beaten road to the church. A little later, he pushed open the door, which was never fastened, stepped in and pushed it to again, shoving against it with the toe of his boot the stone which served as a drag.

"The darkness is cert'ny biled down in here," he muttered, feeling his way with outstretched hands along the aisle to the pulpit. He ascended the steps, and laying his spade and pick on the preacher's bench, he faced about. The wooden shutter of the window directly opposite the pulpit had been wrenched from its fastenings by the tempest, and hung loosely from one hinge; it swayed and creaked in the blasts of wind which swept around the corner of the building. The rain dashed in spurts through the un-paned casement. Across the oblong square, not of light, but of lesser darkness, the limb of a pecan-tree outside seesawed, beating the low eaves with a dismal sound. Above this, Abner could hear the boom of the creek lashing its banks at No-Bottom Pool.

"Even Brother French couldn't do much dippin' in Peleg Pool now," he mused aloud, leaning his elbows on the edge of the box pulpit. "But he'd cert'ny resk it, ef he thought God called him to do it." Abner's admiration of the Reverend

David since the night of the search for Red Parsons's child had been well-nigh as boundless as
that he accorded Hilliard. "An' the Lord 'd
b'ar him up. Yes, the Lord 'd b'ar him up!"
he continued, with solemn conviction, "less'n he
dash his foot aginst a rock. My bretheren, 't ain't
always the weak an' po' in body that's weak an'
po' in sperret," he went on, exhorting imaginary
hearers. "There's them settin' in the amen
corner now, under the droppin's of this here pul-
pit that has the strenk of Brother Joe Wyatt's
black bull Peter, an' the livers of chickens. Jedge
not less'n ye be jedged, bretheren. I've got bull-
strenk myself to dig a well, er a grave; I've got
strenk to raise a house, er swim a creek, an' yit
God knows I'm tremblin' this minute, an' I'm
preachin' to you because I'm plum skeered, re-
memberin' of the graves I've dug, an' the corpses
I've kivered up out yander in Peleg Church
graveyard! I kin see Mr. Ransome's headstone
a-shinin' whenever it lightens!" His voice, fighting against the rain and hail that beat the roof,
and the wind that shrieked around the corners,
filled the empty church with echoes. He closed
his eyes and steadied himself with his hands resting on the big Bible. "Pray for me, my bretheren, an' ast the good Lord to he'p me git ole
Satan under my feet."

As he uttered the last words, the storm suddenly
abated; the rain ceased, easing off in a light patter
that ran like a child's footsteps over the shingles;

the wind dropped; on the instant a watery moon-
beam stole in through the window. Croft felt a
corresponding calm descend upon his own soul;
his terrors vanished. He leaned forward, still
clasping the Bible. "The congergation," he said,
"will now sing the forty-fo'th hymn, beginnin': —

> ' Am I a soldier of the cross,
> A follerer of the Lamb ? '

Brother Green Parsons will please raise the tune."
Abner's voice was clear, sweet, and sonorous; he
always sat on a back bench in Peleg among the
confessed sinners, but he never failed to join in
the singing. He cleared his throat and opened
his lips. Before a note had issued from them, the
rasping of the drag-stone on the floor gave warning that some one was pushing open the door from
the outside. He dropped to his knees, quaking
with fright. "Suppose the Lord is mad with me
because I have dast to preach in Peleg pul-*pit*
without a license!" he groaned inwardly. "Sup-
pos'n He has sent ole Satan to drag me out'n the
pul-*pit* by the hair o' my head! Lord ha' mercy!
I didn't mean no disrespec'! Lord " —

Whoever, or whatever it was, was now stepping
across the threshold. There was a moment of
silence, then a stumble. "Oh, damn it!" Abner
breathed once more. He recognized the voice instantly, as belonging to Jack Ransome. His relief
was for one moment as paralyzing as his terror
had been. Then he opened his lips again — this
time to call out a friendly greeting to a water-

bound neighbor. But his keen ear caught the
sound of horses' feet beating the slushy road
softly. The drag grated again on the floor, and
Jack's light halloo rang out, evidently from the
threshold of the door. There was an immediate
answering halloo, and very soon the tread of entering feet. Uncertainty and curiosity kept Abner
silent. He was squatted on the pulpit floor with
his head crouched low. So far he had not even
tried to look out.

"Is that you, Jack?" He recognized this voice
also. It was Deerford's.

As he spoke, the newcomer, now within the
church, scraped a match, and through a crack in
the pulpit wall Croft saw him walk over to a table
which stood in a corner, shading the tiny flame
with his hand, and light one of the pulpit candles
which stood there in their flat tin candlesticks.

"What are they up to? Some devil*mint*, I'll
be bound," thought Abner, with his eye to the
crack. "Anyhow, I won't speak, onless they find
me."

He observed that the door remained open. The
moonlight was losing its watery pallor and becoming clear and white; the wind reached the corner
where the table stood, only in light puffs which
blew the yellow flame of the tallow-candle gently
to and fro. Ransome had seated himself sidewise
on a bench; his broad-brimmed hat was pushed
back from his forehead; he had a distinctly sulky
look on his comely face. Deerford leaned against

the wall with his hands thrust into the pockets of his overcoat, looking at him with the air of a master.

"Where is your horse?" he asked. "How did you get here?"

"I walked," said Jack laconically; "that 's how."

"What the devil did you walk for?" demanded Deerford. "I thought you were to go home in the Rassler mail-hack, and ride over, as usual."

"You know why as well as I do, by G—d. I have told you that I will never straddle one of my horses again, — your horses, I mean. I 'd rather walk a thousand miles than back one of them."

"Pshaw, Jack, what a d—d young fool you are!"

"I know I 'm a fool, and I 'm a tired, wet, hungry fool to boot. I 've been tramping the woods ever since I left Crouch's, — when I was n't standing under a tree, praying God Almighty to strike me dead with lightning!"

"How did you and Hilliard make it?" Deerford broke in curiously.

"None of your d—d business! Give me some whiskey, if you 've got any."

Deerford took a flask from his pocket and handed it to him. From the other pocket he drew a fresh pack of playing-cards, and began tearing off the wrapping. "It is time the others were here," he remarked, crumpling the paper in his hand.

"The others?" Jack took a long pull at the flask, then rested it half-empty on his knee. "They are not coming." He looked at his companion with ill-concealed triumph, as he spoke.

"Not coming!" echoed Deerford. "Why?"

"Why!" Jack laughed disagreeably. "Principally because you've got all any of them have to lose, already!"

"If any man dares to hint that I have been cheating," cried Deerford hotly, "I'll" —

"Don't overheat yourself, Mr. Deerford," sneered Jack, the fiery draught mounting to his head. "You play fair enough — I reckon. But you have extra—or—di—nary *luck*. That's all! You own pretty near everything on Mesquit Creek, in the way of land and horses. You ought to be satisfied!"

"How do you know they are not coming?" asked Deerford, ignoring the offense of words and manner.

"Roper and Waldrup and young Joe told me themselves to-day at Crouch's. The balance of 'em sent me word. I came myself only because you happen to be my guest," continued the lad, with an air of sullen pride.

Deerford uttered an exclamation of disdain; he dropped the cards back into his pocket.

"Maybe you don't believe what I say!" said Jack defiantly. "I don't care whether you believe it or not. You've raked in everything I own in the world. I haven't even got a horse to

ride here to play cards with you in Peleg Church!
Even the whiskey I am drinking belongs to you!"
He laughed a little bitterly, and handed the flask
with an exaggerated bow to Deerford, who slipped
it mechanically into his breast pocket.

"If you think it is any pleasanter for me to
come, under the circumstances, than it is for the
other boys, you are mightily mistaken. We've
played with you three times a week for the last
six months. You've run us all to the ground, —
every one of us! The others can drop you. I
can't!" .

"Don't be a fool, Jack Ransome," said Deerford roughly. "What do you suppose I want
with the raw-boned knock-kneed plough-horses of
Crouch's Settlement? I'd like to see the figure
they'd cut in Kentucky!" He laughed contemptuously. "And I don't want land that is too poor
to grow jimson weeds, either! I shall take your
brown filly, because she has carried the woman I
love. By the way, I have not mentioned, have I,
that I am leaving for home in a few days? And
I may keep an acre or two, here and there, out of
Roper's and Wyatt's bottom-land. Helen may
want to come out one of these days and spend a
summer, and I may build her a cottage somewhere
on the creek. But you may rest easy about the
rest of your stuff. And so may the others."

"Ah!" sneered Jack. "Is it possible! Why,
you are almost as generous as — as Hilliard!"

"Let Hilliard alone," retorted Deerford. "He

is worth the whole clod-hopping ill-mannered pack
of you!"

"You are pretty late finding it out!"

"Perhaps I am. And I hate him; but he is a
gentleman, and that cannot be said of anybody
else in this settlement."

"Yes, he is a gentleman!" cried Jack coolly.
"And gentleman enough to do what you could not
do to save your soul from hell, and that is to win
Helen Wingate!"

"That is not true," said Deerford, looking at
him steadily; but the bantering sneer was gone
out of his voice.

"It is true. I heard her myself tell Margaret.
Poor Margaret," he whimpered, breaking down at
his own mention of her name. "The filly is hers,
and I've gambled it away. Poor Margaret! Poor
mother!"

"Helen Wingate cares nothing for Hilliard,"
persisted Deerford, coming close up to him, and
speaking between his teeth.

"Helen Wingate is engaged to Leroy Hilliard."

"You lie!" shouted Deerford, his face livid in
the pale light of the candle.

Without another word Jack leaped up and
sprang upon him. Abner saw the two men clinch.
Holding each other in a close embrace, they struggled violently and silently. They backed against
the table, jarring it; the candlestick rolled to the
floor and the light went out, leaving the place in
total darkness. Abner rose to his feet and stared

over the pulpit in the direction of the combat. There was a shuffling of heavily-booted feet on the floor, an intermingling of quick, hard breathing, then an indistinguishable mass appeared in the shaft of moonlight near the open door, swayed to and fro on the threshold, lurched forward, and rolled down the steps. Abner slipped noiselessly from his place of concealment and crept a few paces down the aisle. Inarticulate cries of rage floated in from where the men, locked together, still fought like a pair of wild beasts on the muddy sod outside. He ran back to the pulpit for his grave-tools and shoved them under the pulpit-floor, where he had often left them before; then he made his way to the window. He climbed, by the aid of a bench, to the high sill and dropped to the ground without. There he stooped and crawled along the soggy ground to the corner of the church, and crouched, staring and trembling, under the still dripping eaves.

XIII

THE RED BANDA

JACK RANSOME'S absences from home had been so frequent of late that his failure to return Thursday night occasioned distress and anxiety there, but no surprise. The skies by Friday morning had cleared, and a crisp tingling breeze had succeeded to the stormy norther and the languid dying wind of the night before; the sunshine lay chill and sparkling over the leaf-strewn sod. It was a day to rejoice in. Deerford, sitting before a roaring fire in the cosy sitting-room at Mrs. Ransome's, glanced up from his newspaper from time to time, through the window and out to the road, as if he expected some one. Each time his eyes rested with a strained look on the silhouetted branch of an althea which tapped the window-pane like a warning finger. There were dark rings under his eyes, — an unwonted sign of weariness with him, and he shifted his body occasionally to a more restful position in the easy-chair. But his voice was clear and untouched by fatigue, as he demanded of Margaret Ransome whether her brother had yet returned.

She had just entered the room, and she stood

looking at him quietly a moment before answering.
"No," she said, "he has not. I thought — at
least I hoped — you might know something of him."
It cost her much to say this. It was the first time
she had ever, in Deerford's presence, seemed to
acknowledge the change in Jack's habits. But
Helen's departure had left her suddenly without
support in this affliction. The few days during
which the lad had appeared disposed to return to
his former gentleness and sobriety had unnerved
her for this new strain. She saw her mother —
aged and broken by grief and mortification — now
suffering keenly, and she had nerved herself after
a sleepless night to seek information at the hands
of the man she both despised and feared.

"I came in myself about half past eleven o'clock
last night." This she knew to be true; she had
been looking and listening for Jack, and had stolen
out to the stable at the sound of the opening lot-
gate. "I supposed he was here before me. I
have not been in his room this morning."

She turned away, but came back and rested her
hand on the edge of the mantel. "He started
from here yesterday, on foot, — leaving Diana,
strange to say, in the stable, — intending to catch
the Skipton mail-hack at the cross-road. Did
you see him at Crouch's?"

"Why, yes," he answered, standing up. "He
was there. He came in the Skipton mail, and
said he would ride back in the mail from Rassler.
He left word for the hack to pick him up on the

road. When I saw him last, he was walking down the road with Mr. Hilliard."

"With Mr. Hilliard! Oh, thank you, Mr. Deerford. Then I am sure he is safe." A look of intense relief crossed her face. She left the room, and he presently heard her humming a gay tune — one of Helen's songs — as she moved about the house.

His dinner was served, as it generally was, on the rare occasions when Jack was absent without him, in the sitting-room, where he continued to lounge away the day. Toward sunset, a noise in the yard drew him to the window, and thence to the front gallery. Margaret was leading Diana, saddled and bridled, to the gate. "Can I be of any service, Miss Ransome?" he asked, descending the steps and walking out to meet her.

"No," she said curtly. Then, as if ashamed of her tone, she added, "I am about riding over to Mr. Hilliard's to see if Jack is there. It is not like Roy — Mr. Hilliard — to allow mother to suffer such anxiety. He should have sent us some word. Of course I know Jack is all right, but mother " —

"Oh," cried Deerford, springing forward and taking the bridle from her. "Why did you not tell me! Why did I not think of it myself!" His voice was genuinely self - reproachful. "I will go myself, at once. And if by any mischance I should not find Jack there, I am sure Hilliard can tell me where he is. Just the time to get my hat and overcoat, and saddle Black Prince."

He dashed into the house and then into the stable, and soon reappeared, leading Jack's splendid saddle-horse by the bridle. "You never could have crossed the creek, Miss Margaret," he said, as he put his foot in the stirrup. "I had to swim it last night. Tell Mrs. Ransome that I am sure Jack is safely housed at Hilliard's, and that I will fetch him home as soon as Black Prince can take me there and back again."

Margaret had never seen him mount this horse before without a pang of resentment. He had appropriated it to his own use almost from the day of his arrival on Mesquit Creek, Jack yielding it to him with enthusiasm. Now she watched him ride off upon it with a blessing and a heartfelt prayer for his safety.

In less than an hour he returned — alone — the horse's glossy coat white with the foam of speed, and his mane and tail wet from breasting the creek. Deerford looked slightly concerned. He did not dismount, but sat in the saddle awaiting Margaret at the gate. "He is not there," he said, bending down and speaking in a low voice as she approached. "Hilliard says he left him in the Skipton road about dark — when he himself turned off homeward. He was waiting for the Rassler mail. I think it quite likely that he went on to Skipton in the mail-hack, and that I will find him there. I am going on at once. You may look for us some time before nine o'clock."

He struck his spurs into Black Prince's side and galloped off without waiting for an answer. "Oh," he said, riding back, "I forgot to say that Hilliard has business which will take him to Rassler to-morrow. I told him to look for Jack there, in case he should not turn up in Skipton."

"Thank you, Mr. Deerford," returned Margaret. She went back to her mother, outwardly cheerful, but filled with inward worry. She recalled the hints dropped by Jack more than once lately, of some vague plan for his future. "I am going to quit this settlement, Margaret," he had said to her only the day before, "and try my luck somewhere else. I think anything and any place would be better than this." She had responded gayly at the time; now, she remembered, or seemed to remember, that his eyes had turned to her wistfully as he spoke, and that he had choked down something like a sob. She said nothing of all this to Mrs. Ransome, but it made her own heart so heavy that by the time Deerford got back it was well-nigh bursting. Both women ran out to the gate in the moonlight.

"There is only one horse," Margaret said quietly. "It is Black Prince, and Jack is not riding him. I know the difference in his gait when — But don't worry, mother, darling; I am sure " — The words of cheer stuck in her throat. She looked up at the rider, who had checked his horse near them; his face was wan and set in the clear moonlight.

"Jack is not in Skipton now, Mrs. Ransome," he cried, "but I think I know where our young gentleman is!" He had dismounted, and was unbuckling the saddle-girth. He was silent so long that Margaret pushed open the gate and came out.

"What is it?" she demanded hoarsely, catching his arm. "What do you know? What has happened to Jack? Tell me. Tell me the truth at once."

Deerford's laugh was somewhat forced. "There is no cause for alarm, Miss Ransome," he said. "At least, the matter does not seem serious to a rover like myself! You have doubtless heard Jack talking lately about going away. I confess I thought it but idle talk, myself, but I — I hear that he has really gone. He is, I am sure, waiting for me somewhere, intending to join me on the road. You know that I am going in a few days" —

"Yes, yes, that is it! Mother, do you hear what Mr. Deerford is saying?" She ran back to Mrs. Ransome and repeated his words.

"You must not blame the boy, Mrs. Ransome," he said, coming forward. His voice had not quite regained its easy assurance; he stammered a little and turned his face away as he went on. "He feared you might oppose his going, and so did not say good-by. But when I — I join him" —

"Oh, he will write!" cried Margaret. "Dear Jack! That is it! I am sure that is it." She was sobbing hysterically; Mrs. Ransome, now the more composed of the two, led her into the house, where together they wept thankful tears, and together prayed for the absent boy.

Margaret came into the sitting-room after her mother had dropped asleep. She and Deerford sat long over the dying embers of the fire. She had never before been so near to liking him. His mocking humor was quite subdued. He had a gentle and at times even an appealing look which was wholly new to him. He seemed very young, somehow. Her heart was strangely moved. "If I could only help him!" she thought, all her soul yearning over him. She led him, tactfully, to speak about himself, his inner and outer life, feeling for the first time that she was beginning to know him, and to understand his influence over Jack.

"I fear that I have not been the best companion for Jack," he sighed at last, "or for myself, either! But try and remember, Miss Ransome — Margaret — that " — He paused a moment, staring steadily into the fire, and went on. "I do not recollect my father. My mother has never made a secret of the fact that she loves me more than she loves her other children. She has always preferred me above them, God knows why! for I have given her little but trouble! I have been over-indulged, always. I have had more money to spend than is good for any young man. I have never been thwarted in anything in my life. And I — well, I have not turned out a brilliant success.

And it is a charming thing, is it not, to hear a man who has made ducks and drakes of his life, and who will probably continue to do so until he, or somebody else, blows his brains out — it is truly charming for him to sit down and whine like a woman, to a woman!" He jumped up as he uttered the last words, with a sudden return to his usual reckless manner, and pushed back his chair, yawning significantly.

His attitude forbade any further reference to the subject. Margaret arose at once and put out her hand. "And you will send him back to us soon? He will be homesick enough by the time he meets you, poor boy! He has never been long away from mother and me. You are quite, quite sure that he is waiting for you, somewhere?"

"Quite sure. Good-night," Deerford said, with a solemnity which jarred upon her. He was picking up the books and newspapers scattered about the table, and did not observe her proffered hand. She opened her lips to speak again, but only a half-dissatisfied sigh escaped them. He held the door open for her. "I know that Jack is all right," he said, smiling brightly at her, as she passed out.

The weather the next day continued fine. Mrs. Ransome, almost reassured as to her boy, fretted a little at the non-appearance of Abner Croft, who had promised to come and "knock up" some shelves for her pantry. For Abner had developed quite a genius for home carpentering, and nothing

pleased him so much as to put in a whole day at
Mrs. Ransome's, puttering about under her directions, following Margaret the while with the tail
of his eye. "It is outrageous in Abner not to
come. He promised to fix those pantry shelves,
and to make your flower-boxes, Margaret," the
old lady said, frowning over her spectacles and
gazing up the deserted road. "I am afraid Abner
is shiftless."

"No, he is not, mother," cried Margaret. She
turned her face, glowing with the cold, from the
honeysuckle, blown down by Thursday night's
storm, which she was tying to its trellis. "I
cannot let you abuse Abner. He is one of my
friends. But I will see him at church to-morrow
and take him to task for you. Perhaps his mother
is sick."

Deerford remained in his room all day, as he
often did, keeping out of the way of the Saturday
bustle, he laughingly explained.

About nightfall, old Manuel, the Mexican, came
over, bringing a note to Margaret from Hilliard.
Jack had not been in Rassler. Was he at home?
If not, he, Hilliard, would come over at once.
Otherwise, the Reverend David French being his
guest, he would wait until the next day. Could
he accompany her home from church? He wished
particularly to speak with her.

Margaret sent him a line in reply, saying that
Jack had not come home, but they had every
reason to believe him to be out of harm's way,

and that he would be with them in a few days.
She, too, had something special to say, but would
reserve everything until their homeward ride the
next afternoon. Would he kindly say to Mr.
French that her mother wished to see him before
he left the neighborhood? "Try and not blame
Jack, Roy," she concluded.

The congregation at Peleg Church Sunday morning was unwontedly large. It was New Year's
Day, and the great hamper in the wagons, the
coffee-pots, and the kettles and sauce-pans for
warming-over purposes, testified to the universal
decision, that since New Year's Day had fallen on
a Sunday, and since Brother French was "up for a
preach," the Settlement might as well celebrate on
the grounds.

Little David had become a mighty favorite in
the Settlement. The women loved him for his
gentleness, and his (apparent) need of red flannel,
horehound syrup, and mullein strengthener. The
men respected his mingled sternness and indulgent
humanity. His very name tickled the ear of the
Bible-reading community. When Elder Whipple,
in one of his powerful tirades, from Peleg pulpit,
against Old Satan, described himself as a panoplied
Joshua, with a shield and a two-handled sword,
and his esteemed Episcopal brother, then absent
in the flesh, as a little shepherd with sling and
pebble, an irrepressible murmur of enthusiasm
ran over the church, and Red Parsons in the amen

corner shouted at the top of his lungs: "Glory to God for the child of Jesse, an' for his sling, an' for the content*ments* ther'of!'"

And Bagley responded "Amen."

Several huge brush-heaps were piled here and there on the slope, and behind the church, ready to be lighted after the first sermon. The men, when these had been gathered, stood about in groups, as usual, discussing neighborhood affairs.

Deerford had come early, riding, not Jack Ransome's Black Prince, but Margaret's Diana. He moved from group to group, dropping a word here and there, restless, alert, and handsome. If there was any diminution of his power or popularity, it did not appear; the younger men especially seemed to be more than ever under the magnetic spell of his presence. There were a couple of strangers present,— steady, quiet-looking men,— who finally noted the constant recurrence of Jack Ransome's name in the talk. Their indifferent questions drew the whole matter to a head. By the time Hilliard arrived, in company with the preacher, nearly everybody on the grounds, men and women, knew that Jack had disappeared, leaving no trace of himself anywhere; that he was last seen in company with Leroy Hilliard late Thursday afternoon; that he and Hilliard, between whom there had been bad blood for some time, had had an open quarrel; that there was every reason to suspect foul play on Hilliard's part; that, finally, if Jack Ransome had been

hurt or put out of the way — no one finished this
sentence. The buzz of excitement was rising beyond restraint; Hilliard's friends were protesting
in loud and angry amazement against the implied
suspicion, and freely offering to "lick the sash-
lights" out of his detractors. At sight of him,
calm, frank-looking, and manly, there was a sudden hushed silence. It was already time for the
service to begin. In a few moments everybody
was in place within the church.

A fire roared in the rock chimney; the smaller
children, in a huge semicircle, were roasting
around the hearth like so many rosy crab-apples,
turning first one side and then another to the yellow blaze. Every bench was full, and all faces
were turned gravely toward the pulpit. But the
uprisings and downsittings, by this time tolerably
familiar to the people, were performed mechanically, lacking a certain fervor which usually accompanied them. Mr. French, sensitive to the
least spiritual change, knew that the thoughts of
his apparent listeners were elsewhere. He felt
the swift quiver which passed over them when
Margaret Ransome, a little belated by having
waited for Bud Parsons, came in with her small
escort and sat down near the door. He also felt
the undercurrent which drew toward the place
where Hilliard sat, absorbed and unconscious, with
his arms folded across his breast, and his dark
earnest eyes uplifted to the preacher's own.

David had an overwhelming desire to shorten

his sermon, whose text, taken from one of the Psalms for the day, — "And he shall be like a tree planted by the water-side," — had come to him as he rode up to the church and glanced down at an enormous pecan-tree standing on the edge of the pool at the foot of the slope. But even while his mind leaped painfully forward with this intention, he caught sight of Margaret Ransome's serene face; he looked from her to Hilliard; his equilibrium was instantly restored, and as he preached, he compelled the disturbed atmosphere around him into momentary calm.

When the sermon was concluded, the congregation poured out; the brush-fires were lighted, the coffee-pots were set to boil, coals were raked under and piled over the skillets, and for a time there was only a joyous and friendly bustle around the outspread table-cloths. But the men ate hurriedly and withdrew to their own side of the church grounds. Hilliard, who stood somewhat apart with Red and Green Parsons; the Reverend David, who, according to his custom, was pacing up and down the slope, alone, meditating his afternoon sermon; and Margaret Ransome, surrounded by a knot of women near one of the bonfires — these three were by this time the only adult persons present who were unaware of the wild conjectures concerning Jack Ransome's disappearance, and of the fast-gathering suspicions against Leroy Hilliard.

"Mother is well, thank you, Mrs. Crouch,"

Margaret said, in answer to an inquiry, "but she did not feel quite like driving over this morning."

At this moment Mrs. Kinchley came hurrying up. She was a kindly but heedless old body, and at the mere sight of her face puckered into insistent curiosity, alarm spread through the group. Mrs. Wyatt laid a hand on her arm, and tried to drag her away before she could open her mouth, but she shook herself free. "Margaret Ransome!" she demanded breathlessly, "ye don't believe it, do ye? Ye dassent believe it! 'T ain't true! 'T ain't true!"

"What? Believe what, Mrs. Kinchley?" asked Margaret, trembling a little without knowing why.

"Yo' new log-cabin quilt, Mrs. Kinchley," interposed Mrs. Red Parsons volubly, "is the prettiest quilt in the " —

"Believe what, Mrs. Kinchley?" persisted Margaret.

Mrs. Kinchley was too frightened to take advantage of any loophole of escape. "Thet Roy Hilliard hez murdered Jack," she gasped.

Every particle of color forsook poor Margaret's cheeks. She swayed forward with closed eyes; half a dozen women sprang to her assistance. But she stood suddenly erect. "Jack!" she whispered. "Hilliard! No," she cried, her voice gaining strength and ringing proudly out, "I do not believe it. Jack is no more dead than I am. And as to Leroy Hilliard, how can anybody *dare* to accuse him of *any* crime!"

"I knowed it! I knowed it, Margaret," said Lorena Crouch boldly. "I knowed you would n't believe it. Mr. Hilliard is a an-an-gel." She melted suddenly into tears.

"Mrs. Parsons," said Margaret earnestly, "what does all this mean? I do not understand. We are not uneasy about Jack. What is it all about? Please tell me."

Mrs. Parsons told her in a few words what was being said concerning Jack's absence. "I don't *know* who started the lie, Margaret," she concluded, "although I think I could give a pretty fair guess. But I'd take my Bible-oath that th' ain't a woman in Crouch's Settle*ment* as 'd believe Roy Hilliard has teched a hair o' Jack Ransome's head, not ef a million o' caperin' mule-ear rabbits swore to it!"

"Believe it!" echoed Margaret scornfully. "If there is any one on these grounds who wants to know what *I* think of such a monstrous story, I will show him!" She quitted the women and walked rapidly over to where Hilliard stood. It was an unheard-of thing for an unmarried woman to cross the invisible but rigid line of demarcation between the women's or family side of the church-yard and the men's lounging place until after the second sermon. Everybody, therefore, turned open-mouthed at this flagrant violation of etiquette. There were some men present who expected nothing less than a scathing denunciation of the supposed assassin from the lips of his victim's sister. These pressed forward to listen; others held back, apprehensive of they knew not what; all were only the more bewildered when she put out her hand and spoke a few cordial but commonplace words of greeting in a clear unembarrassed tone. Only the women understood her action.

Hilliard, himself surprised at the unwonted demonstration, returned her hand-clasp a little confusedly, but said with a smile, dropping his voice: "You will ' shake ' Bud Parsons in my favor after church, I trust, Miss Margaret? "

"Yes," she smiled back. "He accepted my invitation, indeed, on that condition only. He has other aspirations — I think in the direction of Lorena Crouch."

They stood chatting unreservedly a little longer, then she recrossed the boundary and walked quietly down the slope toward the baptizing-pool. A touch on her arm startled her. She whirled about and found herself face to face with Abner Croft.

"Don't run, Miss Margaret," he said humbly. "I ain't goin' to hurt you. Don't be afeard."

"Why, Abner — Mr. Croft! " she cried, shocked no less at his appearance than at his words, "what do you mean? Why should I be afraid! What is the matter? Have you been sick? "

His eyes were sunken, his face was hollow and drawn, the hands, folded in front of him, trembled painfully, his clothes were disordered, as if hastily thrown on.

"I've been in bed, an' out'n my senses ever sence — ever sence last Thursday night." He spoke in a husky whisper. "I never come to myse'f ontell this mornin'. Ole Ma'am Croft says I've been dee-lirious an' cuttin' up like somebody plum crazy. God knows how I got home, I don't!"

He drew her still further apart from curious ears, and began speaking in low and rapid tones, without gesture, and standing perfectly still. Mrs. Green Parsons, who could see Margaret's face plainly from where she was sitting with her cronies, saw her shrink back with wild, terrified eyes, and throw up her hands, as if in shocked protest.

"Abner Croft is plum cracked," she remarked. "The Lord only knows what odd-come-short of a tale he's tellin' Margaret Ransome. Sompn 'bout ghosts or sperrits, like he tells the childern, I reckon. Anyhow, it'll take her mind offn Jack. She's oneasy about that boy, for all she knows wher' he is. He ought to be ashamed of hisse'f, runnin' off like the prodigal son, to feed on husks an' swine!"

Croft was now urging Margaret to do something from which she shrank, troubled and pained. "You say you don't think anything has happened to him, Miss Margaret. But ef it had! *Ef it has!*" he pleaded despairingly.

"Oh, Abner, I am sure he is safe. Mr. Deerford says he is, and I know he would not deceive me — in this. Don't ask me, Mr. Croft; I can-

not. I cannot. It seems almost sacrilegious —
wicked!" she exclaimed, trying to turn away from
him. But in spite of her conviction that the poor
creature's mind had been unhinged by fever and
exposure, she felt something like a cold hand
clutching at her heart and arresting its motion.

"Never mind, Miss Margaret," he said gently.
"Just you go up to the church an' set down inside.
That 'll be better, anyhow. I 'll get Mr. Hilliard.
He loves Jack nigh as much as you do."

"No, no, Abner! I will do it. Give it to me.
It can do no harm. Where did you get this?"
she whispered tremulously, taking something from
him and slipping it under her jacket.

"I come by yo' house, an' I seen it on the sofa,
an' I ast Mrs. Ransome for it. I did n't tell her
what I wanted with it. She humored me, because
she thought jest what you are thinkin' now, Miss
Margaret, that I 'm sort o' crazy, an' don't know
what I am doin'. But I swear to God " —

"Never mind, Abner," interrupted Margaret,
shivering, "tell me exactly what you want me to
do."

A few words sufficed for this; then the two
walked together toward the creek.

"I 'll summons ever'body to come," he said solemnly.

The water had fallen a little; an up-thrown line
of débris on the slope showed where the flood had
been, but the great pool was still nearly level with
the steep banks. It had a sullen and angry look,

and deserved the reputation — long accorded it by
common report — of being the most dangerous
water-hole on Mesquit Creek. The outward curve
of the banks on either side made it a long oval in
shape; the water swirling in at the upper end,
near which the baptizings at ordinary times took
place, bubbled and foamed for a few feet, then fell
suddenly still. The shadows of the leafless trees
overhanging it lay motionless and jet black upon
its smooth mirror-like surface; the great pecan-
tree which had suggested the text of the morning's
sermon jutted out over the water, twisting its
gnarled roots about the high point of land upon
which it stood; a hackberry partly uprooted had
fallen some distance below, the rough trunk reaching out like a rustic bridge about midway of the
pool; one broken fork stood upright near the end;
another, thrust downward into the water, had in-
tercepted and held a floating network of dead
leaves, grass, and twigs, that clung to it, and
swayed gently to and fro, wreathed about with
yellowish foam. At the lower neck of the oval
the water scurried out noisily, rippling over unseen rocks.

Margaret, guided by Croft, approached the
pool, and stepped upon the projecting point at the
foot of the pecan-tree. She had regained her
composure, though her eyes were downcast, and
her face was deadly pale.

There were others besides Mrs. Red who had
observed with surprise the prolonged talk between

the grave-digger and Miss Ransome, and when these saw her turn with him in the direction of the creek, they followed almost instinctively; others again hurried after them, under the impression that something was happening at the pool. Abner had no need to summon the congregation. In a few moments nearly everybody present had crowded to the creek bank and stood there with necks craned forward, silently expectant. Deerford was among the first to press to the front; he looked around eagerly, but the swift glance showed him only the girl poised on the gnarled root, — a slender, graceful young figure, with her arms hanging quietly and her white face turned toward the western sky. He stepped into the rear circle and resumed his interrupted conversation with Roper.

The crowd was already beginning to melt and flow back toward the church, for the hour for the second sermon was approaching, when those standing nearest Margaret saw her take from her bosom and unfurl a long crimson streamer. It was Jack Ransome's Mexican banda, — the tasseled silk sash which he had worn so constantly during these last weeks. He had tossed it over a chair Thursday morning just before he left home.

Many of the spectators wondered what it was. Some recognized it instantly, and a suppressed whisper ran from mouth to mouth: "*Jack Ransome's banda!*"

Margaret turned her face appealingly to some one in the crowd, faltered visibly, then, leaning

forward, steadying herself with a hand on the
tree-trunk, she dropped the fluttering piece of silk
on the bosom of the pool.

"What a fantastic, conspicuous thing for Margaret Ransome to do!" thought Hilliard, slightly
disgusted. "And how unlike her !" But for the
life of him, he could not help bending over and
gazing with a sort of fascination at the line of
scarlet which had begun to float slowly and softly
down the pool. An unseen eddy whirled it toward
the bank, and swept it out again, dancing and
quivering like a weird thing; it paused, steadied
itself, and drifted on, still more slowly. A ray of
sunlight, striking it as it moved forward stretched
out to its full length, heightened its intense color;
it looked like a long red tongue. As it neared
the fallen hackberry log, it stopped with one end
puffed out — a tiny bellying sail. Then, as if
seized from below by some invisible hand, it was
drawn slowly downward, inch by inch, until it
disappeared. The onlookers, who had regarded
the whole thing as a bit of child's play, a girl's
caprice, broke into laughing exclamations as the
black water closed over the last shred of fringe.

At the same moment, a man, coatless, bareheaded, and in his stocking feet, darted out of the
crowd, leaped upon the fallen hackberry, ran
lightly along it to the upright fork, and stood
silhouetted an instant against the sky; then, raising
his arms high above his head and dipping forward,
he plunged into the pool.

The consternation on the bank was extreme; men and women ran distractedly back and forth, uttering excited, incoherent cries. "Who is it?" "He's drowning himself!" "It's Abner Croft!" "Ab's the best diver in the Settlement!" "He's plum crazy!" "Watch for him when he comes up!" "He'll never come up! He's drowned hisse'f on purpose!"

Several men had already thrown off their coats and boots and stood ready to grasp the drowning man as soon as he should rise to the surface. One or two, Hilliard among them, were in the act of springing in after him, when he appeared — almost in the exact spot where he had gone down. He held a pocket knife between his teeth. He looked up, shaking the water out of his shaggy hair and treading water gently with his feet. He took the knife from his mouth and called out: "Stand back ever'body. I'm all right. I know what I'm doin'. Mr. Hilliard, you go over yander an' git her out'n the way." Hilliard stared at him with uncomprehending amazement as he sank again out of sight.

All commotion ceased. The people stood as if turned to stone; there was a breathless silence broken only by the refrain of a hymn which came floating down from the church, where some mother was putting her baby to sleep: —

"And we'll cross over Jordan,
Over deep, deep Jordan;
We will cross over Jordan
To the city — of — Rest!"

A man was making his way through the dense human ring, — a lithe, light figure that sped up the slope, but so stealthily that no one heeded or heard the fall of his booted foot on the turf. He looked back several times, turning a livid face over his shoulder, but without pausing. He drew a pistol from his hip-pocket as he ran. Some small boys, heaping brush surreptitiously on a bonfire behind the church, saw him leap upon a horse, — Jack Ransome's fleet filly, Diana, — and ride furiously away, digging his spurs into her sides. But they were too absorbed in their forbidden pastime to notice whether he took the right or left fork of the road.

It seemed as if Croft would never rise again! A handful of bubbles danced on the water, and little waves riffled across the pool in widening circles and lashed the banks. The suspense was painful, the wonder too acute for half-formed conjecture to grow into suspicion. At length his dark head appeared once more, and he began swimming slowly towards the shore, breathing hoarsely.

"*My God!*" Hilliard shouted. Bagley jumped down from the log where he was standing. "Get Margaret Ransome out of the way, Amos. For God's sake, quick, man, quick!"

For the swimmer was pushing something before him, something formless, ghastly, horrible.

Hilliard himself reached the poor girl as she tottered forward with a piteous, inarticulate cry.

He carried her, fainting, in his arms, to the church, and gave her into tender, motherly hands. Then he hurried back to the creek, accompanied by Mr. French, already in his robes, and prepared for the afternoon sermon.

They had dragged the swollen and disfigured corpse from the pool, and laid it upon the trampled ground. Abner, dripping, and shivering in the keen north wind, was standing beside it. He had not uttered a word since he had brought Jack Ransome's body up from the treacherous depths of No-Bottom Pool. The men ringed about him stared in speechless horror, now at him, now at the awful thing at his feet; the women, drawn apart, were weeping aloud.

As they drew near, Hilliard took off his coat and threw it over Abner's shoulders; the minister hesitated a second, then, removing his gown, knelt and spread it reverently over the corpse, covering the poor face with its glassy staring eyes and hideous open mouth.

XIV

THE LAW

ABNER CROFT'S teeth were chattering, but less from cold than from terror; he cast an appealing glance around, shrinking away from the dead body and into himself. All the strength and spirit which had sustained him throughout the extraordinary scene at the pool seemed to have gone out of him. He looked exhausted, and pitifully weak and old. A dazed expression crossed his face when he felt the warm coat thrown over his bent shoulders and drawn gently across his breast. But the light touch of Hilliard's hand on his own was like a galvanic shock. He straightened himself instantly, lifted his head, and stepped quietly forward to his former place beside the drowned lad.

All heads were reverently uncovered.

"Poor Jack! Poor boy!" said Mr. Crouch, breaking the silence which followed Mr. French's short but impressive prayer. "He must of got drownded las' Thursday night tryin' to cross the creek, a'ter he lef' the post-office, an' been washed down here."

"Poor Jack! To think of him layin' there, an' his banda findin' him!" remarked Waldrup.

It now seemed strange that no one among those who had seen the sash floating on the pool should have remembered the superstition, well known to Crouch's Settlement, that something a drowned person has worn in life, if cast on the water, will find his body, though he were lying twenty fathoms deep below!

"Seemed like that banda knowed he was drownded" — began Green Parsons.

"Jack Ransome wa'n't drownded," interrupted Croft, in a loud clear voice.

"What do you mean, Ab?"

"I said so from the first!"

"So did I!"

"For God's sake, man, what do you mean?"

"It's murder, that's what it is!"

"Choke him, ef he won't tell!"

"Hang him! Hang him! He's in cahoot with the devil, anyhow."

"Gentle*men!*" said Uncle Joe Wyatt, stepping forward, and taking his place beside Hilliard and the well-digger, neither of whom had stirred under this hail of angry menace, "gentle*men*, I'm the oldest man here present, I reckin, an' I take it on myse'f to say ther' shell be no lynchin's an' no defyin' of the law. Ther''s been enough o' law-breakin' an' too much already in this Settle*ment*. I've knowed Jack Ransome ever sence he was born, an' I've knowed Abner Croft — well-diggin', grave-diggin', house-raisin', an' horse-raisin' — a matter o' twelve year. I take this here case

in my own han's. I ain't afeard but what I'll
have backin', ef I need it." He glanced significantly at the Parsons twins, Mr. French, and Bagley, who had closed up behind Hilliard. "I order
silence in this crowd, ontell Abner Croft has had
a hearin'." He spoke with a quiet dignity which
commanded instant obedience.

"Now, Abner," he concluded, "you tell yo'
tale. Nobody dassent to tech you."

"I'm not afeard," Abner said calmly.

He began his story without preliminary. He
related how he himself had taken refuge in the
church, just before the wind and rain storm on
Thursday night. He confessed his fear lest the
sheeted dead in Peleg churchyard should rise
from the graves into which he had lowered them,
and dance gibbering around him. His voice faltered a little when he repeated what he could remember of his sermon, — for which he asked God
and Mr. French here present to forgive him. He
told how Jack Ransome, and a little later another
man, had come into the church and lighted one of
the church candles. He passed over the pack of
cards and the whiskey-flask, remembering Margaret Ransome, and slurred over the words which
led to the quarrel. There were but few among
his listeners, however, who could not conjecture
what these words were. "Jack jumped at his
throat," he continued, "an' they clinched, an'
backed, an' knocked over the candle. It was
pretty dark in the church, but the moon was

bright as day outside, an' I saw 'em plain enough, wrastlin' together, an' I heard 'em pantin', over an' above the roarin' of the creek. Jack was the heaviest, but *he* looked like he was made out'n steel. They kep' on wrastlin' an' pantin' an' not sayin' a livin' word, an' then they staggered-like an' rolled out'n the door. I run an' jumped th'oo the window. I wanted to git out'n the way before they come back, because I knowed they would be crazy-mad to think I had heard what they said. The moon was bright as day, an' I dassent to move. I scrooched down by the corner of the church, behind that big stump, an' helt my breath an' watched 'em. They was gripped close in each other's arms, an' first down on the ground, an' then up " —

"Who was the man?" interrupted some one in the crowd, unable to stand the suspense any longer.

But Abner, absorbed in his own narration, went on, with his eyes fixed on Mr. Wyatt's face. "They was both cussin' an' swearin' by this time, but I thought 't wa'n't no more 'n a tussle betwix' 'em, else I 'd ha' jumped in an' tried to part 'em. But all at once, I saw 'em both go down, an' roll over an' over. An' only one of 'em ever stood up any more." A dry sob shook the speaker's breast. "I saw the one that was up, stoopin' over, an' then he commenced to say: ' *Jack! Jack!* ' like that, in a whisper. ' *Jack! Jack!* ' Jack never groaned, nor nothin'. But I never dreamt he was dead! I scrooched still, and listened " —

"Who was the man?" broke in a dozen voices, hoarse with excitement.

He turned his head slowly. "Did n't I tell you?" he asked. "I thought I told you. It was Deerford!"

This time not a word was spoken; men clutched each other and gasped brokenly, as if awaking from a dream; a shiver of hysterical excitement ran through the group of women. "Go on, Abner," ordered the minister, lifting his hand in grave warning to those about him.

"He kept on standin' there — Deerford, I mean. My God A'mighty, he kept on standin' over Jack Ransome. I thought he would stand there ontell Jedgment Day! After a long time, he went around the church to where his horse was hitched; it was Jack Ransome's Black Prince, — I could n't see him, but I knowed him by the way he pawed the ground. I thought he was goin' to ride off an' leave Jack layin' there. But he went after his lariat an' his slicker. He had 'em both over his arm when he come back. He gathered Jack up an' carried him down to the creek; he stumbled onct or twict. I saw Jack's face over his shoulder; he did n't look like he was dead! I waited, an' waited; an' then I crope along the slope todes the creek to see what they was at. Jack was layin' on the ground. The moon was bright as day. He was pilin' some rocks in the slicker. I seen him wrop 'em up an' fasten the slicker to Jack with the lariat. An' then I seen him straddlin' the hackberry log, hitchin' hisse'f

along with Jack in his arms. An' I heard a splash.
I reckin I must of run. But I don't know how I
got away, ner I don't recollect anything more
ontell I come to myself in bed, at home, this mornin'. I thought at first I had just been dreamin'.
But when I come clean to my senses, I remembered. I jumped up, an' I run ever' step of the
way to Mr. Hilliard's to tell him. But he was
gone to Peleg Church; then I run on to Mrs. Ransome's, to tell Miss Margaret, but she was gone to
Peleg, too. I got Jack's banda, because I knowed
it would find him, ef he was layin' in No-Bottom
Hole. *Ef* he was layin' there! I did n't know
but what he might of come to life, or — or sompn!
I begged Miss Margaret to throw the banda in,
because 't would n't work lessen somebody that he
loved throwed — it — in!'"

The last words dragged themselves out in a faint
whisper; the speaker's eyes closed, his head fell
forward on his breast, and he sank, unconscious,
to the ground beside Jack Ransome's corpse.

Hilliard lifted him in his arms, as he had lifted
Margaret. As he did so, he displaced the black
robe which covered the dead body. Mr. Crouch
uttered a quick exclamation, dropped to his knees
and rose again, with something in his hand. He
held it up. It was Allan Deerford's little dagger,
and he had drawn it from Jack's heart, where it
had been buried up to the hilt.

The sight of it broke the spell of horror which
had paralyzed the throng during the latter part of

Abner's story. A howl of rage shook the air.
"Murderer!" "Scoundrel!" "Where is he?"
"Here!" "No, he is not!" "He was beside me
one minute ago!" "Run him down!" "String
him to the first tree!"

Many were positive that Deerford had been present when Croft had begun his narration. Several had spoken with him just before the diver
arose the second time to the surface of the pool.
But others began vaguely to recall that they had
seen him edging his way through the crowd, and
walking rapidly up the slope, toward the church.
When it finally became apparent that he had escaped, there was a hurried mounting of horses for
the pursuit, and the look on the grim faces of the
men who sat in their saddles, holding a brief consultation before starting, boded ill for the assassin.

Hilliard was among these, but he could hardly
steady his nerves sufficiently to bear his part in the
council. His breast was still shaken with the sobs
which he had not tried to repress. He could see,
at the foot of the slope, Amos Bagley and Billy
Crouch busy over the dead lad, — trying to com-
pose the stiffened limbs, closing the staring eyes,
and removing the mud and leaves from the matted
hair. Some women near by had spread a wagon-
cover on the ground to serve as a winding-sheet.
From the church came the echo of smothered cries,
and Margaret's low, unconscious moans; above
these, Granny Tatum's cracked voice chanting
weirdly: —

" Death an' jedgment, Lord, are thine.
          Save us Jesus,
               Save us ! "

All this came to his outer senses like the dim
and shadowy sights and sounds of a dream. What
he really saw was a boyish face turned to his, in
the solemn twilight of the forest; what he really
heard was a young voice eagerly asking: "Won't
you shake hands with me once more, Roy? "

"How could I have been so blind? I, who know
Deerford so well! Why did I not carry the lad
with me by force, if need were! Or, why did I
not stay with him! Oh, what is friendship worth,
if it means no more than this! I can never forgive myself. But I *can* help to avenge you, dear,
dear Jack! " These thoughts, which tormented his
brain now, followed him unceasingly for many a
long day after.

He gathered up his bridle at the word of command from Roper, and dashed forward. But the
men had not had time to separate into the different squads agreed upon for the various directions
of the chase, when a heavy trampling of horses'
feet resounded about them; a loud ringing Halt!
echoed in their ears, and they found themselves
confronted by a body of armed horsemen. The
foremost man was instantly recognized by nearly
all present. It was Morris Pattison, the sheriff
of the county.

With the thought of Deerford uppermost in
their minds, they crowded eagerly about him.

"Have you caught him?" "Where is he?"
"Th' ain't a jail in the State strong enough to
keep us offn him, Morris!"

"Who are you talking about?" demanded the
sheriff, frowning. "Caught who?"

"God Almighty! Don't you know?" cried
Roper, forgetting that it had not been an hour
since poor Jack Ransome's body was taken from
its watery grave. He explained hastily. "Deerford is riding the fastest horse in the county," he
concluded, "and he has an hour's start. But he
can't ride forever. And we can't stand here forever, wasting time, either. Ride up, boys! Ride
up. You'll come along with your posse, Morris?"

"Wait one minute, gentlemen," said Pattison
gravely. He set his teeth together and glanced
over his shoulder at his men, among whom rode
the two quiet-looking strangers who had appeared
at the church that morning. "I have come here
on special business of my own — for the county.
I have warrants with me to arrest, for wanton
destruction of private property, arson, and murder, the following persons here present, to wit:
Allan Deerford, Thomas Roper, Joseph Wyatt,
Junior, Jesse Waldrup, Green Parsons, Jack
Ransome, Samuel Whitehead, Jack Tatum, Jonas
Clayton, and Peter Clayton."

During the reading, the older men and many
of the women came running up and stood listening, open-mouthed. The unexpected words fell
like a bombshell. At another time it is likely

that the men named in the sheriff's notice — all
of whom, except Deerford and his victim, were
mounted on fresh horses and armed in one way or
another — would have attempted flight or resist-
ance. But the awful sight they had just witnessed,
the awful story they had just heard, and the terrified sense of participation which Deerford's immediate followers had in his misdeeds, guiltless
though they were of Ransome's death, paralyzed
them into silent submission.

Green Parsons alone made open protest.
"Look-a-here, Morris Pattison," he said earnestly,
pushing his horse forward to where the sheriff sat,
"I ain't never cut a strand o' bob-wire, ner rode
a foot on a raid. I did give them boys some encourage*ment* in the beginnin', by goin' to Blackbird Gully an' hurrahin' 'em off by night. God
forgive me for it! I'm willin' to pay a find.
I'm willin' to die, ef die I must. But I swear to
God I'll blow my brains out befo' I'll spend a
night in jail!"

"Don't talk that-a-way, Green!" cried Red,
leaning over from his own horse and throwing his
arms around his twin. "I'm goin' long o' you.
Ef you lay in jail, I'll lay in jail too. Shucks!
What does jail matter, ef yo' conscience is clar,
an' yo' sperrit free! Wa'n't Peter in jail?
Wa'n't Paul in jail?"

He spoke cheerfully, but the tears were streaming down his face.

The women, huddled together, were wailing

and weeping. The prisoners, with hanging heads, waited under guard while Pattison made arrangements with Hilliard for the immediate pursuit and capture of Deerford. Then they moved slowly off in the direction of Rassler, Red Parsons fairly holding his half-crazed brother upon his horse.

"The jedgment of the Lord has fell on Peleg Church," moaned Uncle Joe Wyatt, lifting his trembling hands heavenward. "The jedgment of the Lord on the congregation of Peleg, on the elders, an' on the children ther'of!"

XV

PREPARATION

On Monday afternoon the mortal part of Jack Ransome was laid to rest in the wind-swept Peleg graveyard, beside his father, and in full view of the spot where he met his tragic death.

Hilliard and French conducted Margaret Ransome to her home, where the grief-stricken mother awaited her. They left her at the gate. "No, do not come in," she said, "you can do nothing more for us, now. You must go on at once to Abner. Thank him for us, and give him our dear love. But for him our agony would have been greater even than it now is."

But little more than twenty-four hours had passed since she had given Hilliard loyal greeting in the face of Peleg congregation; it seemed impossible to associate the wan, wraith-like creature before him with the vivid blooming girl he had then looked upon!

Both men remained silent, loath to say the parting word. "God bless you, dear," the preacher said at length, the caressing word slipping unaware from his lips.

Her hands, resting on the low fence-pickets,

trembled; she bowed her head upon them, and burst into a passion of tears. "Oh Jack! Jack!" she sobbed. "You were not wicked, whatever they may say. And you loved us! Oh, you loved us!"

"Listen, dear." David's voice was inexpressibly tender. "You must not add these painful thoughts to your natural grief. Jack was not wicked. His feet were caught in a snare, and he stumbled — that was all. Do you think God has not infinite pity and infinite pardon for all His creatures, and particularly for all His young creatures?"

"Oh, yes, I know," she cried. "But if only he had not gone out on that last raid! If I had tried harder to keep him at home! They told me that the sheriff said" —

"Margaret," — Mr. French had taken her hands and held them folded close in both his own, — "listen. Jack did not fire a shot that night; he even tried to dissuade the others. I know. I talked with them all at Rassler last night. I have been over to the ranch where the fight took place, this morning, and seen the ranchmen. Jack was not with the raiders at the time of the serious trouble."

Hilliard stared at him with undisguised amazement. He must have been almost literally in the saddle for nearly twenty-four hours. His own heart throbbed with a remorseful pang. "And I? I have done nothing, but grieve with her," he thought, almost envious of the cry of heartbroken rapture which broke from her at David's last words.

The two men turned their horses into the by-path that led in the direction of Abner Croft's cabin, and rode on, silent for some time, now side by side, now one following the other when the path narrowed between encroaching trees.

The story of the night-carousals in Peleg Church was now known to everybody; the card-playing, the dicing, the betting, the dram-drinking, and profane singing and shouting there, these three or four months past; Deerford's almost diabolical influence over the reckless gang, his gradual absorption of their property, the refusal of all but young Ransome to attend the last rendezvous, — all this was added to the horror of the lad's final, lonely struggle for his life on the moonlighted slope. The knowledge hung like a pall over the hitherto respectable and self-respecting community, where the arrests of Sunday had left foreboding and terror. The falling darkness and the brooding stillness of the wood brought it all so vividly to Hilliard's mind that he started violently and uttered an exclamation when French spurred his horse alongside to ask, "Has anything been heard of Deerford, yet?"

"Yes, and no," he replied. "The filly, Diana, has been brought in. She was found about twenty-two miles below, broken-winded, wandering about loose. Two or three persons had seen her and her rider in the early part of last night. But we have as yet no reliable information. I do not myself think he will be easily captured. He is quick and clear-headed, and will manage to give his present pursuers the slip. Of course telegrams with full description of his personal appearance will be sent from the nearest telegraph station, and rewards will be offered. It is only a question of time. But in my opinion it will take time. And that brings me to " —

"I wonder that he did not leave at once. It would have been a very easy matter before the homicide was discovered," interrupted French.

"I think I know him well enough not to be surprised at his lingering. Even if he had known there was a witness of the deed, which of course he did not suspect, he still might have stayed. His reckless bravado is extraordinary." A vision of the midnight scene on his own premises rose in the speaker's mind. "Besides, he could in any event count on the theory of death by drowning."

"But the knife?"

"Even there, unless the body should be found immediately, which was unlikely, he was comparatively safe. For Jack had often worn the dagger in his belt. Poor boy!" He was silent a moment. "I was about to say," he went on, "that I wish to ask your advice with regard to my own immediate plans. Standing over that boy's dead body, yesterday, I vowed vengeance on his murderer. I then and there determined to follow

Deerford to the end of the world, if it should be necessary, and bring him to justice. This is what I wish to do. I confess that the man is my own personal enemy, and this perhaps adds weight to my feeling in the matter. But I also loved Jack Ransome. I love his mother and sister as if they were my own. For such they have ever been to me since I came a stranger to a strange land. On the other hand, I foresee a hard fight for those poor fellows who are doubtless lying to-night in the jail at Rassler. I know better than any lawyer there can possibly know, just how they have been tempted and misled. I have studied the whole situation. I know the ranchmen. I think I may say if I were to appear in the defense of our boys, I could be of service to them. This will take weeks, perhaps months, and in the mean time, Deerford, who has abundant means, will certainly leave the country."

The minister was silent a long time. Finally he said, "I cannot make the decision for you, Roy. I can say, leave the word ' vengeance ' alone; but I believe that feeling to be a mistaken one which would withhold justice from a criminal, with the idea that God will bring about his punishment in some mysterious way of his own. Human laws are necessary wherever human nature, with all its varied phases of light and darkness, holds sway. Otherwise, we should have unimaginable chaos. Deerford ought and must suffer the just penalty of his crime. But my heart aches with yours for those poor lads — for lads the most of them are — over yonder. Public feeling is very strong against them. I saw that for myself last night. They will need friends. They will need you! But — I feel incompetent to decide the question. Ask Margaret Ransome. She can tell you what you ought to do. And she will tell you."

"You are right, David," Hilliard cried. "I will see her early to-morrow morning."

A few moments more brought the riders to the little isolated cabin they sought. It stood in a sheltered hollow under the lee of a shelving ridge. Red firelight gleamed through the cracks of the window-shutter, and at the loud barking of a yard-dog the door was cautiously opened.

"It is I, Mrs. Croft, Leroy Hilliard. Mr. French is with me," Hilliard called out reassuringly. There was a quick exclamation within. The door swung wide and the little bent woman whom he judged to be Abner's mother came hurrying out.

"'Light an' come in, both of ye," she said anxiously, "else that child 'll be gettin' up."

"How is he, Mrs. Croft? " Hilliard asked, following her into the house.

Abner himself answered from the bed where he was lying. "Oh, I 'm all right, Mr. Hilliard — 'specially now! " The look of pleasure on his gaunt face deepened as the two men approached and shook hands with him. "It beats reason, yo' comin' to see me!" he said, "onless " — his eyes clouded — "onless you 've come to tell me I done wrong ?"

"Not a bit of it, Abner," cried French heartily. "We came to see how you are, and whether we can do anything for you. Everybody in the Settlement is saying fine things about you, and Miss Margaret Ransome sends you her own and her mother's love."

"*Me !* Ever'body sayin' — Miss Margaret sends — shucks, parson! You know I ain't fitten " — His throat swelled and two great tears gathered on his eyelashes and rolled slowly down his cheeks. "Ole Ma'am Croft is a master-hand with fever," he said, with an artful attempt at a smile; "but she 's give me so much biled-root stuff that I 'm a plum baby."

The fever which had followed the swoon of the day before was quite gone. It had left him weak, but he was eager to talk. Hilliard looked apprehensively at the mother, who stood at the foot of the bed. "Let him talk it out," she said, nodding her head wisely. "It won't hurt him now. An' it 'll keep him from wearyin'."

Abner went over the story as he had already told it at Peleg, but more in detail. When he came to the finding of Jack's body, they listened with breathless interest. "I knowed nobody would believe me about the — the killing, unless I could prove it. I know that most folks thinks I 'm sort o' crazy! And I knowed nobody would dive into that No-Bottom Hole but me. I was sure-cer-

tain that Jack Ransome's banda would find him,"
he said, "an' it did. It went right down to where
he was a-layin' on his back, with the pile of rocks
tied up in that slicker, holdin' him down. The
banda was floatin'-like jest over him, about a
foot from his face, when I dove the first time. I
did n't see it at first — nor nothin' else, except a
sort o' yaller light all around — an' that tree-fork,
standin' up black as tar aside of me. Then I saw
the banda, an' I felt around ontell I teched sompn
soft. I knowed that was *him*. I tried to cut that
lariat around his waist. But I could n't. I
thought I'd die whenever I teched him! I quit,
but seem-like he looked at me out'n his pore eyes,
a-beggin' me to try onct mo'. It was awful, Mr.
French. I had to come up to breathe. An' I
did n't nowise intend to go down the second time.
But there was Miss Margaret by the pecan-tree
wher' I put her myse'f. The sight of her give me
strenk to dive ag'in, an' I helt tight a-holt to the
thought of her, whilst I sawed the rope in two,
an' felt him risin' up ag'inst me, like as if he had
come alive, only cold an' clammy."

Mrs. Croft's entrance with a bowl of chicken
broth for the invalid, and two steaming cups of
coffee for her guests, put an end to the gruesome
recital. "Ole Ma'am Croft is a master-hand at
cookin'," he remarked, smiling at her proudly.

"Indeed she is, Abner!" cried French, lifting
his nose from the emptied cup.

After a little more friendly talk, they took their

leave. "Mr. French!" Croft called, as they reached the door. The minister returned to the bedside.

"You know I 've been out'n my senses, parson?"

"Yes."

"An' had fever, an' dee-lirium?"

"Yes. But now" —

"Well. I 've dreamp a heap o' things, an' seen a heap o' sights, sence last Thursday. An' I 'm sech a everlastin' fool that I can't edzackly make out what I 've dreamp an' what I have n't."

"Don't let that trouble you, Abner. You are all right now."

"Maybe, parson, maybe, but I 'd like to be plum sure in my mind whether I dreamp it, or whether you said" —

"Oh," interrupted the parson with sudden comprehension, "yes, Abner. Every man, woman, and child in the Settlement is anxious to take your hand. And Miss Margaret and her mother send you their thanks and their dear love."

Abner was silent a moment, then he said solemnly, "I reckin I 'll tromp many a long mile yet, an' throw up many spadeful of dirt, an' maybe find many a spring o' well water. But ef the Lord wants to take me now, I 'm ready to go. An' I don't ast Him for no better heaven than I 'm in right now!"

Hilliard sought Margaret the next morning and begged advice and counsel of her. "I come to you at the suggestion of David French," he concluded. "I wonder that I did not think of it myself, as the only thing to do. But I seem to have been a laggard in many things." He smiled a little sadly.

She gave him a quick look, then dropped her eyes. "You — you wish to defend those men, after — after all?" she questioned, with some wonder in her voice.

"After they have so persistently — misunderstood me, you mean? Oh, yes. That cannot now affect my feeling in the matter. It was only a part of the whole strange, mad, sad business" — he faltered, and both fell silent.

"Roy, I wonder if you know" — she began wistfully.

He laid his hand on hers. "I know what you would say, Margaret. Yes, Margaret. I do know now, that for a few hours I stood accused, under nearly every man's breath in the Settlement, of the murder of that dear boy. I know that, in the blackest hour of my life, when I did not even dream of the chasm near which I stood, you came to me before them all, looking confidence into my face with your sweet eyes, and clasping my branded hand in yours! God bless you for it, Margaret, dear, dear Margaret!"

His voice trembled with emotion. She turned away her head, not daring to trust her face under his eyes. Her heart beat wildly at this sweet praise. It was only with an inward loyal cry of *Helen! Helen!* that she steadied herself.

"Then, Roy," she said, with quiet decision, "your duty, it seems to me, is quite plain. Leave the pursuit of — Deerford " — she could hardly frame her lips to utter the name — "to others. What will it avail to my mother and me if he is caught and brought to justice? It will not restore our darling to us. But these anxious and desolated homes around us! Oh, I know but too well what it means to agonize as the mothers and sisters of these poor lads are doing! Save those lads, Roy, if you can. They were led astray, just as Jack was. I will feel — we will feel — that whatever you do for them, you will be doing for him."

Here tears came and compelled her to cease speaking.

"Then I take it upon myself, as a solemn engagement," he said, lifting his hand as if under oath, "and afterward "—

"Let afterward take care of itself," she interrupted quickly.

He told her about his last parting with Jack, and what now seemed like a sad premonition in the boy's good-by. She in her turn related the strange conversation she had had with Deerford in the very room where they now sat, while his murdered victim lay hidden under the dark waters of Peleg Pool.

"I know now that there was meaning in the tone with which he repeated my own words: ' Jack will be waiting for me somewhere,' " she shuddered. "Strange to say, it was the only time I

ever liked or trusted him. Had Helen been
here " —

Hilliard started. Helen had been utterly
crowded out of his mind by the rapidly succeeding
events of the past two days. Now a rush of feeling overwhelmed him at the mere mention of her
name. Margaret, with quick intuition, divined
this, and quietly turned the talk in her direction,
speaking of her in words to suit the fondest lover.

"Have you written to her about — Jack? " he
asked at length, rising to go.

"Not yet. When I do, I shall tell her all you
have been to us, and what you propose to do for
Jack's companions."

"Thank you, Margaret," he said, lifting her
hand to his lips.

He made arrangements in Skipton the same day
for sending his cotton-crop to market, and on the
following Thursday he went over to Rassler to be
present at the preliminary examination of the
fence-cutters. He found, as French had intimated,
public feeling very strong against these men, and
for the first time he learned the particulars of the
affair which had caused their arrest. They had
set out from Blackbird Gully with the avowed
intention of cutting, for the third time, the fences
on a ranch about eleven miles from Crouch's Well.
The ranch was not one of those which had lately
been opened in the county. It was a small one,
long established and of undisputed title. Its
owner, Colbrook, was a respected and well-known

citizen. Hearing of the projected raid, — for the reckless gang had boasted openly of their design, — he had armed his cowboys and laborers, and posted them at different points about the place. It appeared, according to the statement of the prisoners, that almost at the last moment, when nearing the ranch, Jack Ransome, for some reason, had "backed out;" he and Deerford had had some hot words, and Jack, as young Joe Wyatt said, had "sulled," and remained alone at a cross-road half a mile from the ranch.

The others, riding forward, had dismounted, and were in the act of cutting the wire fence, when they were attacked by Colbrook himself, the ranch owner, at the head of half a dozen armed men. In the hurried scrimmage which ensued, one of Colbrook's men was killed outright, and another mortally wounded. Deerford galloped off with his followers, leading them in pure devilment quite around the dwelling-house and lots, even stopping to set fire with his own hands to an outbuilding and some ricks of hay. This at least was the story.

The preliminary examination was conducted in the presence of a large crowd of townspeople, and of representative men from both settlements; those from Colbrook's angry and threatening, the Crouch's Well faction anxious and dejected. The court-house several times during the progress of the examination threatened to become a battle-ground.

Green Parsons was discharged, there being no evidence whatever against him; the others, with the exception of Tom Roper and young Joe Wyatt, were released on bail. Roper and young Joe were remanded to jail, there to await trial.

Hilliard immediately offered his services to defend each and all of the accused, thereby bringing upon himself much obloquy.

The cutting of wire fences, when these first invaded the county and stretched their feelers about, regardless of public or private rights, had unquestionably been a popular movement. Many of the best citizens had, like Hilliard himself, taken part in an open crusade against injustice, thereby bringing about not only an abatement of the wrongs wittingly or unwittingly committed, but forcing the State legislation on the subject which finally restored harmony.

But it was not long, in other neighborhoods besides Crouch's, before wire-cutting became a cloak for wanton mischief, disorderly gatherings, and at length for unbridled license.

This section of the country is law-abiding to an almost astonishing degree. The fence-cutters soon fell under a ban almost as severe as that decreed against the poaching fence-builders themselves. The Crouch Settlement gang, in particular, came in for a really undue share of denunciation. Wild tales, many of them exaggerated, were told of their midnight raids; the unholy roistering in Peleg Church, unsuspected by the more respectable inhabitants of the Settlement, — all this was known in Rassler. Deerford's charm of manner and his personal magnetism among men saved him for a time from reproach; even he had fallen into disrepute, and his name, coupled with those of his boon companions, Ransome, Roper, and young Joe Wyatt, was everywhere branded with shame.

The story of the lawless assault upon Colbrook's ranch came as a fitting climax. It spread like wildfire through the county. A meeting was held in the town of Rassler two days afterward, and resolutions passed, declaring the good name of the county at stake, and urging the authorities to take immediate steps toward the arrest of the perpetrators of this and similar crimes.

The prisoners, brought in and lodged in the jail at Rassler, were regarded with indignant horror; the killing of young Ransome seemed in some way a part and parcel of their wrongdoing. The judge was loudly censured for having admitted any of them to bail, and Hilliard's offer to defend them was past belief.

For, according to the well-known axiom that home folks are the last to recognize either the distinction or the dishonor of their own, Hilliard's course during the past six months — almost unnoticed by his neighborhood — had provoked much favorable comment in and around the county-seat.

"I think you are in for it again, Roy," said Amos Bagley, approaching him after the prelimi-

nary examination, with the buzz of surprise at
Hilliard's action still ringing in his ears.

"I think I am," he replied quietly, "but I also
think I am right."

"Amen!" said Bagley.

The young lawyer realized that a hard task lay
before him; the absolute confidence reposed in
him by his clients and their families was both a
spur and a clog, stimulating him, but adding to
his painful anxiety.

"You could ha' knocked me down with a feather,
when Roy Hilliard come forrard to take them
boys' case after the way he's been treated," observed Green Parsons.

"Shucks!" replied Red proudly, "he ain't got
nothin' little about *him!* An' he'll pull 'em
th'oo."

"It'll pretty near shake his soul-case to pieces
to do it," said Johnny Giles decidedly, "for they
are in a bad row of stumps."

"Well," broke in Billy Crouch, "the United
States Gover'mint ought to pay Roy Hilliard out'n
the Treasure at Washin'ton for undertakin' of the
business. For if anybody can save Crouch's post-
office, it's him."

"Why, what is the matter with the post-office,
Billy?" demanded Bagley.

"Matter!" exclaimed Billy indignantly. "Th'
ain't a stamp been licked, ner a dinner got, at
Crouch's Well, sence them boys was arrested!"

"According to your own showing, Tom," Roper's older brother Dan, who had come up from W——— to "stand by" him, remarked grimly at the conclusion of the private consultation between Hilliard and the two young prisoners in the jail, "you are not *worth* keeping out of the penitentiary."

"I thought I had found that out, myself," Tom returned humbly, "but if Roy Hilliard thinks I am, I'll live up to it the balance of my life, penitentiary or no penitentiary; so help me, God."

Young Joe, who had the woe-begone face of a lost child, said nothing, but clung fast to the hand Hilliard held out to him at parting.

The case was set for the first week in February. Hilliard spent the intervening time in preparation. When he was not shut up in the room he had taken at the Rassler Hotel, writing briefs, consulting authorities, or pacing back and forth mentally shaping his course, he was riding indefatigably about the country, looking up testimony, but chiefly combating personally the bitter prejudice against his clients. On several of these expeditions he was accompanied by the Reverend David French.

"You are killing yourself, Roy," the latter said one day, toward the end of January; "you look haggard and ill. I shall be heartily glad for your sake, as well as for the others, when it is all over."

"It is my first case!" Hilliard returned, smiling; "but it is far more than that, David, as you know," he added gravely.

"Yes, I know. I saw Uncle Joe Wyatt last night. I believe the old man will die of grief and mortification if young Joe suffers further disgrace."

Hilliard sighed wearily and a little dejectedly.

"Nothing has been heard of Deerford, I suppose?" French continued.

His companion looked up quickly. "He was in my mind as you spoke — naturally enough, I admit. I have just learned through a private source that he has been seen in the vicinity of his home in Kentucky. By the boldness with which he showed himself on at least one occasion lately, I judge he considers himself safe, for the moment, from pursuit. I know, in fact, how he undervalues the common intelligence of our people here! As soon as this trial is over, I shall follow him there — or to the end of the world, as I have already said."

"You doubtless know that Mrs. Ransome is very ill?"

"Yes. I have stopped there whenever it has been possible for me to do so. Poor Margaret, she is very desolate and alone!"

"If she will but give me the right to shield her, as far as a mortal man may, from further care!" said David fervently.

And again Hilliard confessed to himself an unreasonable pang!

XVI

THE TRIAL

The day of the trial dawned clear and bright; a stout norther blew lustily, whirling the dust along the country roads, whipping across the public square at Rassler, and shrieking noisily around the stone court-house. Long before sunrise every available space in the square was crowded with vehicles and their teams — buggies, buck-boards, carts, wagons, hacks; a compact and serried line of saddle-horses nosed the court-house fence; the wagon and cotton yards were thronged with cowboys, teamsters, and drovers, who had spent the night there, sleeping on the bare ground, or swapping stories around the camp-fires. The stores were early filled with women and children, but except for a fitful business in apples and candy, there was but little trading; the men, lounging in the wagons, congregated about the town well, or gathered in corners, were discussing the chances, pro and con, of the wire-cutters.

Out in Crouch's Settlement, every house, except Mrs. Ransome's, had been closed and left tenantless somewhere between midnight and dawn; their habitants had parked their wagons and horses on the edge of the town in Rassler, just beyond the new little Episcopal church; they themselves waited mute and apparently stolid and unfeeling, around the closed doors of the court-house, or under the spiked wall of the ugly squat jail.

When Hilliard entered the court-room, it was already filled almost to suffocation. Bagley, who accompanied him, carrying an armful of law books, noted with some surprise that he shook hands with Colbrook near the door, and nodded pleasantly at his old enemy Jellson a little farther down the aisle. A suppressed murmur ran through the Settlement people, who sat in a solid phalanx near the judge's dais, at sight of their champion; it communicated itself to those near them and for a second "*Hilliard! Hilliard!*" rang in loud whispers through the room. It seemed to Bagley's keen perception that a certain note of extreme animosity had dropped out of the cry since he had last heard it in the same place. He had little time for such mental comment, however, for the judge, a dignified, elderly man, had taken his seat; Walworth, the prosecuting attorney, was hurrying in. Behind him, headed by the deputy-sheriff, came the twelve jurors accepted and sworn the day before. A few moments later the prisoners filed in, marshaled by Pattison, the sheriff, and his men. The crowd was so great that scarcely any one present was aware of their entrance until they stood before the judge's seat, awkwardly awaiting further orders. Their appearance sent

a thrill through the spectators. There were eight
of them, all told; they looked like mere boys. Not
one of them, in fact, was over twenty-two years
of age; several were under twenty. Roper and
young Joe Wyatt were pale and thin from their
short confinement in the jail; the young faces
were all pitifully solemn and terror-struck. The
loud sobs that burst forth at sight of them were
not all from the Mesquit Creek women, who were
their mothers and sisters and sweethearts; every
woman's heart there ached for them. But with
these sobs were mingled hisses and whispered
menaces.

"Silence in the court!" thundered the judge.
The prisoners were conducted to their seats and
the business of the trial, begun the day before,
proceeded.

Had Hilliard been more experienced, he would
doubtless have used more freely his privilege of
challenging the jurors presented, when the case
was first called. Even the confident Billy Crouch
quaked when he saw among the chosen twelve two
men from the very heart of Colbrook's Settlement.

But the novice showed unquestionable ability in
his management of the case; his handling of the
various witnesses was extremely skillful, albeit
somewhat unusual. The appearance, for the defense, of the cowboy supposed to have been mortally wounded on the night of the Colbrook raid,
proved a dramatic surprise. He testified that he
had stood elbow to elbow with his comrade who

was actually killed. The same man, he declared,
fired both fatal shots; to the best of his knowledge
that man was the leader of the Crouch Settlement
gang. He was a tall, slight man, with light, curly
hair, riding a large black horse. Witness was
positive about the light, curly hair, because the
moonlight fell directly on the man's face; he was
bareheaded; his hat was on the pommel of his
saddle. Witness would know the man again if he
saw him. He was not among the prisoners here
present.

A vigorous cross-examination failed to shake
the wounded cowboy's testimony.

A number of witnesses were immediately brought
forward by the State. The exultation which had
leaped up in the breasts of the Settlement folk
died down again into deep despondency. When
the sitting closed for the day, and the boys trooped
off between the sheriff and his deputy, to the jail,
and the jurors marched out under guard and across
the square to the Rassler Hotel to supper, and the
crowd gradually melted out of the dim court-room,
the general feeling was, that although Hilliard
had done his level best in a manly and straightfor-
ward way, his case was as good as lost.

About two o'clock the next day the State rested
its case, and the prosecuting attorney began his
speech. Walworth was a large man, of commanding presence, great experience, and with a keen,
biting tongue. His speech was a scathing denunciation. The youthful prisoners fairly ducked

their heads as the lash of sarcasm and invective curled around their shoulders. The whole story of their misdeeds was rehearsed, with the coloring such a man knew how to give it. Not only the culprits, but the entire Settlement fell under his castigation; they dropped their eyes and went white with shame and helpless indignation. The "youthful and over-confident antagonist" of the prosecuting attorney came in for his share of ridicule and satirical advice; the "champion whose budding wings had barely sprouted, yet who aspired not only to fly, but to carry with him in his dizzy flight — not one man like the Genie of the Arabian Nights, but eight! and these eight weighted with a burden of crime!"

It was really a masterly discourse of its kind, backed up by cool and logical argument. The listeners would have burst into loud and enthusiastic applause had they dared.

When Hilliard rose to reply, the contrast was so striking as to produce a momentary reaction in his favor. He was as pale, and almost as haggard, as Roper himself; the thin line on his left cheek was scarlet; the dark curls tossed back from his brow looked unkempt. Many in the audience were for the first time aware of his youth. There was a hush of intense expectation as he began to speak.

With the exception of the fatal shot, or shots, fired that night at Colbrook's, he frankly admitted at the outset of his carefully prepared speech nearly everything as charged in the indictments, and he was then proceeding to lay out his argument, when he suddenly found himself floundering; a mist swam before his eyes, a cold sweat broke on his forehead, his tongue was dry, his sentences became rough and jerky. He glanced at the stolid faces of the jurors, and from them to the accused, leaning forward with parted lips, and staring, blood-shot eyes. Then he turned and looked out over the vast sea of heads, in reality seeing no one except Walworth with his large self-satisfied smile, and but faintly hearing the sound of his own words, which continued to drop automatically from his lips.

"The jig is up," muttered the older Roper between his teeth, ramming his hands in his trousers pocket, as if by so doing he could force down the lump in his throat.

Hilliard's roving eyes had finally lighted upon Granny Tatum, who sat near a window, with her white old head upon her breast. Beside her, with the wrinkled old hands held in her own strong young grasp, stood Margaret Ransome. The girl looked pale and wan in her mourning garments, but her face was calm and her eyes were full on his, expectant, trusting, confident.

He stopped deliberately, gathering himself together as if for a spring. Then facing about again, he opened his lips — how it happened he never could explain, but it came rushing forth, that fervid and passionate appeal to the jury which he had determined not to make! It was old-fashioned, this throwing of argument to the winds, this torrent of fiery, pathetic, tender, homely entreaty — invocation — importunity; this skillful play upon those chords which have their roots under the hearthstones of the beggar and the king alike; this wide sweep of the arm which infolds the bruised hearts of all motherhood and all fatherhood! It was primitive, it was old-fashioned, it was obsolete! But it was a genuine and unpremeditated cry, and it found an echo in the soul of every man and woman who heard it.

The judge's voice silenced all exclamation, but in the hush which followed, "the roof of the co'tehouse," Red Parsons afterward affirmed, "riz and fairly stood on eend, and angels, as it were, was seen ascendin' and descendin'!"

Nobody listened to Walworth's short concluding summing-up of the case, or to the judge's charge to the jury, which was delivered in a slightly husky voice.

The jury managed for form's sake to stay out about ten minutes.

Hilliard heard the verdict, "Not guilty," as in a dream, and far away, some thousands of miles off, as it seemed to him, he saw Uncle Joe Wyatt lift his trembling arms in thankfulness above his gray head, and in a radiant cloud pricked with shooting specks of black, farther away still, Margaret Ransome's beautiful face floated, floated; then a sudden darkness overtook him.

"Margaret!" he murmured, drifting back to consciousness. "Where is Margaret?" he demanded faintly, opening his eyes into the disturbed faces of French and Bagley.

"Miss Ransome has gone," returned the former, still vigorously chafing his wrists. "She went as soon as she saw you beginning to revive. She had left her mother in the care of Mrs. Croft. Abner came in from Crouch's with her and accompanied her back. She is very anxious about her mother."

The court-room was empty. Hilliard had been carried into a small office adjoining, whence he could hear his own name tossed aloft from the surging crowd in the square. "They would like to carry you around on their shoulders in a triumphal procession," smiled French, assisting him to his feet. "But as I happen to know that you have eaten nothing for twenty-four hours, I shall rush you across to the hotel, instead."

He left him there with strict injunctions to the motherly landlady to see him fed and looked after, and walked on, out to the open lot beyond St. Mark's, where the Crouch Settlement people were encamped. There, according to Bagley's report, "he stood the wire-cutters, that *was*, up in a row in the middle of Peleg Church congregation, and gave 'em such a soul-rakin', heart-searchin', spirit-poundin', gizzard-reachin' sermon as none of 'em ever listened to before. They fairly wallowed in the dust. To tell the truth, I wallowed myself!"

A fortnight later, Hilliard bade Margaret Ransome and her mother good-by. Mrs. Ransome, feeble and worn and much changed, was at length able to sit up for an hour or two during the forenoons. "I shall go first to Kentucky," he said, "and afterward to Carolina, to see my family."

"Helen is not in Kentucky," Margaret hastened to say. "She has gone south with her mother, who is in failing health. They are visiting some friends — she does not mention their names — on a plantation in Louisiana. They have been there some time. I will give you her address."

He glanced at the slip of paper before laying it in his pocket-book: "*Eastwood Plantation, near St. Denis, Louisiana.*"

"You will tell Helen — everything," she said, following him out to the gate. "My mother's dangerous illness has kept me from writing anything more than the mere fact that Jack — has been taken from us. I thought, I hoped, she might have heard the story from others, or seen it in the newspapers. But she has not — at least she had not when she wrote. Oh, Roy, you will be gentle with his memory!"

His answering look was enough! He had said nothing to her of his intentions with regard to Deerford. But she had easily divined that his journey to Kentucky meant Deerford first of all, then Helen.

"I beg you to be careful," she urged. "As I have already said, it can give us no comfort to see *him* brought to punishment, and if in attempting it you should fall into danger, think what that would mean to me — to us!"

"I will be careful," he returned, much moved.

"Then, good-by, Roy. God reward you for the happiness you have brought to this sorrowing neighborhood by your defense of those poor lads! God be with you on your journey. And God speed you in your wooing, dear Roy!"

That night he sat dreaming before the fire which glowed on his hearth. His packing was done, his last instructions given to Manuel; and Abner Croft, who was to drive him over to Skipton the next morning, had already gone to bed. A well-known voice brought him to his feet and upon the porch. "Is that you, David?" he called gladly. "I was half expecting you. Come in! come in!"

Mr. French seated himself, on entering, in the armchair reserved for him. He seemed thoughtful and preoccupied; he had removed his spectacles and sat staring absently at his friend with his beautiful short-sighted eyes.

"I come from Margaret — Miss Ransome, Roy," he said at length, "and you know the hope which I have been cherishing — foolishly, perhaps — these many months. Well, that hope is at an end. The happiness I have so ardently craved is not for me!"

"Oh!" cried Hilliard, starting forward, his

genuine regret and sympathy for his friend mingled with an odd sense of relief.

David's lifted hand and averted face checked further words. "Let us not talk of it — now," he said. But he presently asked, without turning his head, "Are you sure — pardon me, Roy — are you sure that you yourself have not a place in her heart?"

"I! Oh, no. Margaret certainly looks upon me as a sort of older brother, that is all. And she knows that I love another woman."

David's pale lips moved; they really framed the words, "Blind and foolish!" But he remained silent; and Hilliard ventured to add lightly, "You too will find some one more yielding. There are other women."

"There is no other woman for me," David said sternly; "no woman in all the wide world for me, now or ever, save Margaret Ransome!"

XVII

EASTWOOD PLANTATION

On his journey, Hilliard spent one night at a famous old hotel in the heart of the French quarter of New Orleans. He forced himself for the sake of long-cherished dreams to take outward note of his quaint surroundings, but though scenes and sounds returned to him later, with that vividness which proves that the mind is a sensitized plate, receiving and holding impressions without as much as saying "By your leave" to the master within, yet at the time he was too eager and excited to consciously see and hear. He was early at the train the next morning, and waited for some time about the station before the cars were unlocked. When he found himself actually moving — toward Helen! — he sank back in his seat with a sigh, and compelled his impatient thoughts to momentary soberness.

He glanced from the window at the sodded levee guarding the great yellow river and lined with shipping; at the forest of tapering masts and wide-mouthed steamer chimneys overtopped here and there by the ungainly bulk of grain elevators. As the rushing train sped on, he eyed with interest which at another time would have been keen enough, the widespread sugar plantations, where the faint green of young cane lay like a film over the rich dark soil, and the plantation-houses, with their outlying negro cabins, rose-hedged and tree-embowered.

After each preoccupied glance, his eyes came back involuntarily to the slip of paper he held in his hand: "*Eastwood Plantation, near St. Denis.*" He was stealing one day, half a day, an hour, from self-imposed duty to give to love! "To see her, to hear her murmur my name but once, and then — Kentucky and Deerford!" he said over and over to himself.

The two hours' run to St. Denis, a small town on the railroad, was nearly at an end when he felt a touch on his shoulder. He looked up hastily. "I beg your pardon," said an elderly man, who was standing in the aisle and bending over him, "I beg your pardon, sir, but is your name Hilliard?"

"Yes," he replied, surprised. "My name is Hilliard, Leroy Hilliard."

"The son of Leroy Hilliard of South Carolina? Ah, I thought so! One could not easily be mistaken in those features. My name is Milgrove. I knew your father well, Mr. Hilliard."

Hilliard grasped the extended hand. "Sit down, Mr. Milgrove," he cried with sparkling eyes. "It is such a pleasure to meet any one who knew my father."

Milgrove sat down in the opposite seat. He

had grown pursy and portly; the hatchet face had
puffed out and the sharp nose was rounded to
a scarlet bulb at the end. Only the keen eyes
remained to suggest in the successful lawyer the
sometime lawyer's clerk. He rubbed his hands
with genuine pleasure; the sight of the young
man brought back a whiff of his own departed
youth. It also awakened his professional curiosity.

"Is your father living?" he asked.

"No," replied the younger man, with that deep
regret in his voice which always came with the
memory of his loss. "He was killed in one of
the last battles of the Civil War."

"Yes, yes, I remember now. General Hilliard
he had become; had he not? Yes, yes. And
your mother?"

Milgrove, remembering the beautiful Lilla Armstead, found himself wishing very much to know
something concerning her divorced husband's career. "Evidently Leroy Hilliard found another
woman to make him happy, as she found another
man! I wonder if it was a second ' perfect match '
for him also! At any rate, here is the son of Hilliard's second marriage," he thought, listening to
the young man's reply.

"My mother died while I was an infant," he
said, seeing in his mind's eye the short-waisted,
slim, pretty young creature, whose portrait in the
boudoir at home old Martha had encouraged him
to appropriate as his mother's. He could remember distinctly, he thought, standing by her knee

and looking up into her dark, tender eyes. Mrs. Blackmore had always assented silently with a sympathetic caress when he lisped these memories.

"I was brought up by my father's people," he added.

"Ah." The lawyer's interest in the younger Hilliard flagged a little. But he looked up courteously when the young stranger asked, "Where did you know my father, Mr. Milgrove, may I inquire?"

"Why, here!" he said, smiling; "he lived hereabout for several years."

"Indeed!" cried Hilliard joyfully. He was not at all surprised that he should never have heard this. Mrs. Blackmore had but rarely spoken to him of those years of his father's life which lay between her brother's college days and his own earliest recollection of him. But it seemed to him a good omen that he should be seeking Helen Wingate in the neighborhood where his father had once lived, and where he must have left many friends. A rush of questions came to his tongue, and Milgrove, suddenly mindful of deep waters into which he might plunge unaware, was saved possible embarrassment by the stopping of the train at the St. Denis station.

"Can I serve you in any way, Mr. Hilliard?" he asked as he was about stepping into the comfortable trap which awaited him. "At least you will allow me to offer you a seat in my carriage? Your luggage"—

"Thank you, Mr. Milgrove," replied Hilliard, accepting the invitation frankly. "I have no luggage except a small bag. I am here only for the day. If you will set me down at a livery stable I will be greatly obliged. I wish to hire a horse. I have lived so long in the West," he continued as they spun along the road to the village, "that I hardly know a horse except under the saddle. But this is a superb pair."

"You have friends in the neighborhood, then?" They were approaching a livery stable, whose sign swung out over the sidewalk.

"Yes. I am going to spend a few hours at Eastwood plantation. Do you know the place?"

Milgrove brought his horses up with a sudden jerk. "Eastwood!" he exclaimed sharply. "Oh, yes." He hastened to calm his voice. "Beautiful place, Eastwood. About twenty miles out. You might have gotten off nearer the place — at a flag station. However, I am glad to have met you, Mr. Hilliard. Call and see me before you leave, if you have time."

Hilliard shook his hand heartily. "I shall certainly see you again if possible," he said. "It is a rare privilege to meet any man who calls himself my father's friend."

Milgrove drove away slowly. "Friend? Well, I did like the poor devil," he muttered, as if apologizing to himself for misappropriation of the word. "But what in the name of the past can a Hilliard want at Eastwood!"

Hilliard, in the mean time, entered the wide doorway of the stable. A man lurking in an empty stall near the rear door came suddenly out.

"Hilliard!"

"Roper!"

Dan Roper, for it was he, drew the newcomer into a shadowy recess, looking around mysteriously as he did so. "How did you find out?" he asked in a low tone. "I 've got him as tight as a rat in a trap," he proceeded, too impatient to communicate his own news to await an answer. "He could n't get away now, not if he was greased."

"Who? What do you mean, Dan?" Hilliard demanded, though he surmised at once that Deerford was in question.

"In just four days after you pulled Tom through — if it had n't been for you, Leroy Hilliard, I believe that poor boy would be under ground by this time. He could n't have stood that jail — much less the penitentiary." Roper's dark eyes softened, and he gripped his companion's arm affectionately. "Inside of four days after that boy was free, I was in Kentucky, a deputy sheriff, with a warrant in my coat pocket for that cold-blooded villain's arrest. I spotted his hiding-place near X—— at once; or rather his loafing-place, for, by Jupiter! he was no more hiding than I am; not as much! He had been pretty careful at first, it seems; but he had come to think, I reckon, that there would be no further pursuit of him. Oh, I heard gay tales about him up there among his neighbors, I can tell you! Yet the dare-devil has friends there who would die for him. I moved cautiously, although, never having seen me, he would hardly have thought twice about Mr. Colston, even if he had met that horse-trader. Colston, you understand, is my name at present. But while I was kicking my heels around, waiting for requisition papers, he left X—— and came on here. Of course you know why he is here?" Roper suggested, with the fixed idea that Hilliard's business in St. Denis was the same as his own.

"Yes, I do know that," Hilliard replied. It seemed quite in keeping with Deerford's other reckless doings that he should have followed Helen Wingate at a time when his neck was in danger of the halter! "Well," continued Roper, "I followed him, of course. He has been here ten days."

"But why have you "—

"Waited so long? You may well ask! I haven't enjoyed it, I can assure you. I have been waiting for the proper papers to be signed and forwarded. I have them now, safe enough. Meantime, I have had him watched, night and day. I have a spy in his very house. He is making preparations to leave this country for Europe, and will probably try to get away from here to-night. He has not, so far as I can tell, the slightest suspicion that the law is at his heels. I have my net so drawn that he cannot slip through. By God, if he so much as tries, I will shoot him down like a dog! He led Tom into disgrace, and has done all he could to ruin his life, and he's got to pay for it. I didn't know Jack Ransome, poor fellow, but if there is any justice, Deerford shall swing for that murder, or rot in the penitentiary! I mean to take him back to Rassler, dead or alive! So help me, God!"

"You can count on my help, Roper. To tell the truth, I did not know he was here. I came on private business of my own, and intended to leave for Kentucky to-night, to run him down myself, if possible. But I am not surprised to find him hanging around here. Is there any one here with you from Texas?"

"No; but I have several first-class detectives in my service, who are keen for the reward offered."

"Have you seen Deerford yourself?"

"Yes; twice. Riding about after dark. He has not stirred abroad in the daytime. Now, here is what I propose to do" —

"One moment, Dan." Hilliard looked at his watch. "I am going — well, to be frank with you, I am on my way to see a lady."

"And you want to get that off your mind first, eh?" laughed Roper. "All right, old fellow. I've been there myself — frequently. Take your time. We have the day before us in any event."

"Then I will meet you here, say at three o'clock. Or I can postpone my visit until to-morrow?"

"No, no. Not the slightest need of that. I tell you I've *got* him. Tight as a rat in a trap.

One thing, though. Whatever happens, don't spoil my game."

He led out a horse himself, assuring Hilliard that it was the best one in the stable, where he seemed much at home, and saw to the saddling and bridling.

"Good luck!" he called at parting.

Hilliard made no inquiry concerning the road to Eastwood plantation, until he was well out of sight of the stable. He shrank from Roper's possible well-meaning but familiar comments. The countryman who directed him also volunteered the information that Eastwood was the finest plantation in the parish. It was owned, he said, by a bachelor, who sometimes had gay house-parties there. At the present moment it was occupied by some people from "up North, somewhere," who had rented it for the winter and spring.

He listened, not unwillingly, to the man's rambling talk, eager to catch some chance word concerning his lady-love, but he was obliged to ride on none the wiser as to her well-being or her plans, from this encounter.

The horse he rode was not Hector, as he kept telling himself, with a longing sweep of his thoughts to Mesquit Creek; but the livery hack bore him rapidly enough over the good country road. He passed several plantations, but for the last three or four miles of his journey his way lay through a rather lonely forest, where the giant oaks and the tall cypresses were draped in Spanish moss which waved mournfully in the wind, and where pools of dark, still water gleamed under the tangled underbrush. The broad, fanlike leaves of the palmetto were mirrored in the pools, and the trumpets of the scarlet creeper glowed against the sombre tree-trunks; semi-tropical birds flitted through the shadows; a purple gallinule sailed majestically across an open glade, delighting the horseman's eyes with the flash of his royal wings.

At the end of this bit of virgin wood Hilliard came unexpectedly upon Eastwood plantation. The wide wooden gate before which his horse stopped had been minutely described by the countryman. He was in the act of dismounting to unlatch it, when it swung open, and a bent old negro stood aside, hat in hand, to let him pass. He lifted his own hat in courteous greeting.

"God-a-mighty, Marse Roy, is dat you?" cried the old man, catching at the bridle-rein, and peering up in his face. "Wher' — wher' did you come from? Don't you recollec' Jerry, Marse Roy?"

But for his meeting with Milgrove, this salutation would have been startling to the newcomer.

"How do you do, Uncle," he said, reaching down and grasping Jerry's horny palm. "I think you must be taking me for my father, Leroy Hilliard?"

"Is *dat* it? You don't sesso, Marse Roy! Has you r'aly got a growd-up son? I mean, is you

Marse Roy's growd-up son?   Lord, you is de spit
o' Marse Roy!   Well, I *dee*clar!'"

The old man laughed foolishly, scratching his
bald head.   "An' wher' is Marse Roy, hisse'f?
Huccome he ain't come?'" he asked, stepping out
and gazing anxiously down the road, as if he expected to see his old master.   "Huccome you ain't
fotch him?'"

"My father is dead, Uncle.   He died many
years ago."

"*Daid!*   Marse Roy *daid!*   Den, Jerry, it's
time you was gwine, too!'"   He shook his head
mournfully, and tears started into his bleared
eyes.

"Where did you know my father, Jerry?'"   Hilliard asked eagerly.

"Wher' — wher' did I know Marse Roy?   God-
a-mighty!   On dis yer plantation, of co'se.   Huccome you don't know Marse Roy lived at Eas'wood
fo' de wah?   He was de bes' marster!   Lord,
Marse Roy has laid de lash on my back mo' times
dan I kin count!   Yah!   Yah!'"

"And where do you live, Uncle Jerry?'"   Hilliard took up his bridle reluctantly; he would
gladly have lingered on, listening to the old man's
talk about his father.

"Who, me?   Right here at Eas'wood, Marse
Roy.   I'm free now, but I jes' stays on."

"Then I will see you again."   He emptied his
pockets of change, which he poured into Jerry's
shaking palms, and rode on.

"Neenter tell *me*," chuckled Jerry, wagging his old head and chinking the coin. "Dey ain't but *one* Marse Roy, an' dat's him. Dat's his looks, an' dis is his ways."

Riding, as another Leroy Hilliard had done, many many years before him, along the winding road which led through the heart of the plantation, with the fields swarming with laborers on either hand; the Cherokee-rose hedges, glistening green in the sunlight, skirting the wide lanes; the sugar-house looming up idle and picturesque under the horizon — noting all these, the impatient lover came at length, by an abrupt turn, in view of the Eastwood plantation house. It was a stately mansion; the great square central building was surrounded with broad verandas upheld by white fluted columns, and flanked on either side by ample wings connected with it by airy pillared arcades. The smooth-shaven lawn in front was shaded by a few noble oaks, while the circular drive leading down to the carriage gates was arched over by thick, low-branched magnolias. Rose gardens, orange groves, and banana plantations stretched away from the lawn toward the rear of the house, and beyond these, the low roofs of the negro quarter showed above masses of greenery. Hilliard reined up his horse, uttering an exclamation of pure delight. Strangely enough, here, with his eyes actually dwelling upon the noble façade of the house where he was born, and upon the grassy

sweep of lawn where his infant feet had first
learned to walk, he was perplexed and disturbed
by none of those vague memories and intangible
hints which had so often puzzled him at other
times! He rode forward joyously.

"It is just the setting for her," he thought;
"the white palace of a fairy princess!"

He paused again, stricken for the first time by
the realization of what money could do. A picture
rose before him of his own little cabin in the wil-
derness, with its homely surroundings; how could
a woman used to such luxury as this consent to
share his poverty! The all-pervading sense of joy
which possessed him was dulled for a moment.
But only for a moment. "Oh, but I *know* her!"
he cried confidently under his breath.

He had already dismounted before the low gate
opening upon the lawn. A staid negro-man —
Samp, in fact, grown proper and pompous in the
service of the several dynasties which had ruled
at Eastwood — Samp came forward to meet the
visitor; he carried a pair of shears, and a tray
containing a heap of freshly-cut roses.

"Is Miss Wingate at home?" asked Hilliard.

Samp stared at him with rolling eyeballs, but
recovering himself, received his card with a por-
tentous bow. "Yes, sah. Miss Helen is in. Be
please to walk in, sah. You will find the ladies
in the summer-house."

He indicated with a sweep of his hand the large
arbor, draped with honeysuckle and multiflora
roses, to the left of the house.

"Shall I " — the visitor hesitated.

"Oh, yes, sah. Walk right to the summer-house. They ginerally receives mornin' company in the summer - house. They 's expectin' you, sah."

Hilliard wondered, not knowing that this was Samp's invariable formula of reception to all visitors.

"Margaret must have written," he thought, walking rapidly up the flower-bordered walk.

Samp, looking after him, allowed his surprise to appear in his well-schooled black face. "Ef dat ain't Marse Roy Hilliard," he muttered, relapsing into the patois of the quarter, "'t ain't nobody! What 's gwine to happen, I wonder!"

As he approached the summer-house, Hilliard heard the sound of several voices. He had so counted upon meeting Helen alone that he felt discomfited; he slackened his pace, glancing up at the house as if admiring its majestic proportions, but in reality to recover a little from his disappointment. When he stepped upon the threshold of the arbor, he saw that there were four persons within: two women, evidently mother and daughter, — and he remarked at a glance that both were very beautiful, — were seated on a low bench facing the entrance; between them sat a young man, apparently about twenty-two or three years of age, whose face seemed curiously familiar to him; the honeysuckle, thrusting its flowering branches through the green trellis-work, made a frame, as it were, for the three blond heads.   In front of this group, but with his back to the entrance, another man was standing.

Hilliard, realizing that these strangers were unaware of his presence, waited in embarrassed uncertainty for a second; then his slight movement toward retreat attracted the attention of the older woman.   She looked up; a spasm of terror contracted her fair features; she sprang to her feet with a piercing shriek.   The man standing before her whirled about, and Hilliard found himself face to face with Deerford.   He was not wholly unprepared for such a meeting; although he had left it out of his calculations as much as possible. But Deerford's surprise and consternation were unmistakable.   His face became ashen gray; he shot a quick glance over each shoulder, as if he were reckoning the chances of a successful dash for liberty.   Then, resuming his wonted air of careless indifference, he stepped up to the intruder.

Meanwhile, at a wave of his hand, the two bewildered young people were half-leading, half-carrying the older woman — now moaning hysterically — out of the arbor and toward the house.

Hilliard looked after them, painfully disturbed.

"What do you want here, may I inquire?" Deerford's voice, strangely harsh and strained, recalled him to himself.   He turned; the impulse was strong upon him, as he looked once more in the fair false face, to spring upon the murderer and rend him in pieces then and there.   But he controlled himself, remembering Roper's injunctions, and replied briefly: —

"I know of no reason why I should account to you for my presence here, Mr. Deerford."

"Since you are trespassing on my mother's premises"— began Deerford, with a sneer.

Hilliard's hat was off in an instant. "Oh, I beg your pardon," he said in genuine distress, forgetting everything except his own good-breeding. "I did not know that your mother occupied the house. I came to see Mrs. Wingate and her daughter, who, I heard, are visiting here."

A look of relief which did not escape Hilliard's eye passed over Deerford's face. It was succeeded by a flush of anger which he promptly controlled. "Mrs. and Miss Wingate are my mother's guests," he said; and he added, his own good-breeding also rising instinctively to the surface, "Will you walk into the house? I will have the ladies informed of your call."

In a brief flash, Hilliard saw his burning cotton pen and a white hand clutching a dagger; saw a slim form slipping from group to group in the grounds of Peleg Church, spreading insidious poison meant to blast his, Hilliard's, life; saw Jack Ransome's swollen, disfigured face upturned to the sunshine by Peleg Pool; saw — could it be that it was he, Hilliard, who stood here bandying compliments with such a man! His half-paralyzed lips opened; what he might have said he never himself knew; a window was thrown open. The cry, "*Allan! Allan!*" rang sharply on the air, and Deerford — the hunted look coming back to his face — darted past him and ran to the house.

Left alone, Hilliard sat down and dropped his head upon his hands.

"*Roy!*"

It was a whisper so soft that another's ears would not have heard it, but it penetrated his soul like the still small voice that sounded at Horeb. He sprang to his feet and clasped her in his arms. "*Helen, my Helen!*" was all that he could say for a time, now gazing rapturously at her lovely face, now drawing her to his breast in silent thanksgiving.

"Margaret told you where to find me?" she asked at length, drawing him to a seat beside her in the shaded stillness of the old summer-house. "Tell me of her — of all."

"Afterward," he said, jealous for the moment even of Margaret's name in this their first talk.

"Afterward we will speak of all that has happened there," he repeated half an hour later. He saw at once that she remained in ignorance of the manner of Ransome's death and of Deerford's flight. "I cannot tell her these terrible things now," he thought, summing up the case rapidly in his own mind. "I must leave Roper free to carry out his own plans. Besides, I will not mar the glory of this first meeting, which is love's, and love's only. Forgive me, Margaret, dear sister Margaret!"

Helen was speaking. "It has been very long in coming," she said, smiling gayly, "this ' early spring '!"

"Helen! my Helen! — but how is it that you are here," he asked, suddenly remembering, "visiting his — Mrs. Deerford?"

"Indeed it is not pleasant for me," she said gravely. "As I have told you, we have always lived near the Deerfords. My mother and Mrs. Deerford have been warm friends for many years, and although neither has told me in so many words, I know that they both cherish the hope that I may one day become Allan's wife. My mother has never been able to see him as he really is; and indeed, when he wishes he can be very winning. Lately, she has begun to realize that such a marriage is impossible for me. But she has been nervous and ill for some months, and when Mrs. Deerford, who formerly owned it, rented this house from its owner for the winter, and wrote, begging us to come and spend some weeks with her, I could not refuse. Mother so wished it, and Mrs. Deerford expressly stated that Allan would not be here. I am really fond of Mabel and of Paul. Allan came ten days ago. He is leaving, I believe, to-night. He is going abroad, and perhaps " —

"He is leaving to-night!" echoed Hilliard inquiringly, and with a quick contraction of the heart.

"Yes. So you will have nothing more to fear

from him," she smiled playfully. "But — but there is one thing I must tell you, Roy. I do not know why, but my mother, who is one of the gentlest and loveliest of women " —

"Of course!" interjected Hilliard, "since she is your mother."

"She — she has conceived for some reason a violent prejudice against you."

"Against me?" cried her lover, startled. "How can that possibly be? She has never even seen me."

"I know. But the few times I have ventured to speak of you since my return from Texas, she has been so agitated that I have been alarmed. She has forbidden me to mention your name again, and refuses to give me her reasons. Indeed, I now believe that it was in consequence of a reference to you in one of my letters, that I was recalled home."

"Impossible," said Hilliard again, "unless," — he paused in his dismayed reflections to say, "unless she objects to my poverty. This indeed " —

"No, no. You do not know her. That would never weigh an iota with her. But do not be troubled about this, Roy. I felt bound to tell you. But you have only to see her, and she will not only understand my feelings, but she will love you, too."

"Flatterer!" Hilliard's alarm subsided; and he basked again in the sunshine of love and hope. "And you will keep your promise, whatever comes?" he demanded, slipping upon her finger a thin circlet of gold, upon which hung, like a tear, a single great pearl.

"Whatever comes!" she whispered. She arose, for a shadow darkened the entrance. "Did you want me, Mabel?" she asked. "Come in. Miss Deerford, this is Mr. Hilliard."

Hilliard bowed. The young woman looked at him strangely. Her eyes were red and swollen. She was very pretty and graceful. "My mother begs you will come to her for a few moments in the library, Mr. Hilliard," she said timidly. "And, Helen, Mrs. Wingate has sent for you. She is in her room."

XVIII

MOTHER AND SON

HILLIARD responded to Mabel Deerford's greeting, outwardly courteous, but inwardly deeply anxious. Could it be possible that Mrs. Deerford knew of Allan's perilous situation, and was about to appeal to himself for help? He remembered her uncontrollable agitation at his sudden appearance in the arbor, and he thought, pityingly, that she must have mistaken him for one of those who were dogging her son's footsteps. He considered rapidly the propriety of excusing himself; and regretted, in spite of the joy of meeting Helen, that he had not waited, before seeking his betrothed, until the business of the arrest was well over. He felt acutely the pain and awkwardness of his own presence at Eastwood under the circumstances. But even as he debated the question he was moving mechanically toward the house between the two young women.

At the entrance of the wide hall he stopped and took Helen's hand in both his own. "You will see me again before I go? For one moment, at least?"

"Why! Are you going?" she exclaimed. "I

hoped you were going to stay until the evening. I want you to meet my mother. I have heard nothing, as yet, about Margaret and Mrs. Ransome, and poor dear Jack! Must you go? But I understand. It could not be pleasant for you, with Allan here."

"It is not that. Or rather, it is not that alone. I am compelled to return to St. Denis. I have pressing business there. But to-morrow I shall be free, and the next day, and the next," he continued, gazing into her lovely violet eyes, "until I start to Carolina to see my people. I shall see you — wherever you may arrange for our meetings. Not here, unless it be necessary. And when I go, I shall carry you away with me, never to part with you again while life lasts!"

Helen blushed, but did not avert her face. Mabel Deerford had stepped back upon the veranda.

"May I?" he persisted.

"Perhaps," she returned. There was a ring of consent in her voice.

"Then, if I should have to leave the house without seeing you again, good-by — until to-morrow."

"Until to-morrow, Roy." The clasped hands parted reluctantly. She ran on up the broad stairway. Miss Deerford came forward; he followed her into the library, where she left him, closing the door behind her.

The room presented almost the same appearance as when Henry Armstead first brought his bride

into it, neary sixty years earlier. The furniture
which Lilla remembered as a little girl, the claw-
footed tables and chairs, the great mahogany sofa
with its carved rolling ends and high back, the
footstools with their faded embroidery, even the
low lounge drawn into the bay window, and the
long triple mirror over the mantel — all these remained, sold with the house by Francis Deerford,
who was glad to rid himself of all associations
with Eastwood. Only the old portraits were gone
from the walls; and the modern trifles scattered
about alone suggested the later occupants.

Mrs. Deerford was sitting on the sofa; Allan,
leaning against an angle of the bay window, stood
looking down at her. His face was pale, and distorted by some emotion which had come into it
since he had quitted the summer-house.

Lilla Deerford, in her close-fitting black gown,
was still a slender, graceful, and very beautiful
woman. Her abundant blond hair had not darkened perceptibly. Certain lines on her forehead
gave it an expression not familiar to it in earlier
days, but her blue eyes were full and lovely, and
her lips were almost as red and smiling as Lilla
Armstead's had been. There was hardly a trace
on her fair countenance of the storm at that moment raging within her soul. She raised her eyes
as Hilliard paused, standing before her; a look
which the elder Hilliard would have recognized
came into her face — the set, hard look which presaged a mortal combat.

"Pray be seated," she said, with formal politeness.

He acknowledged the invitation with a slight bend of the head, but remained standing.

"By what right do you call yourself Leroy Hilliard?" she demanded abruptly.

Hilliard felt and resented something in her voice beyond its imperiousness, but he replied quietly, smiling a little, "By the best possible right, madam, — the right of a son to his father's name."

"You are twenty-seven years old?"

"I am," he said, ceasing now to wonder; the woman's mind was plainly unbalanced.

"You do not remember your mother? No? Did Leroy Hilliard never speak to you of your mother?"

"No," he stammered, flushing scarlet. "My father was killed when I was very young. He" —

"That is enough."

Something in the manner of the interruption enraged him; the birth-mark flamed into his cheek, his eyes flashed. He threw up his head and demanded haughtily, "You ask me by what right I bear my father's name, Mrs. Deerford. May I ask by what right you put these questions?"

Her folded hands trembled on her lap; he saw the glitter of diamonds on her slender fingers as they twisted themselves together. Deerford, who had not uttered a word, bent over her and said something in an undertone. Hilliard's senses, sharpened by rage and suspicion, heard him dis-

tinctly: "Do not tell him. Surely you need not
tell him — after all these years."

"By what right do you question me, madam?"
he repeated, raising his voice and drawing a step
nearer.

"By the best possible right. I am your mother!"

The answer leaped from her pale lips and rang
through the room. Hilliard staggered back, his
senses reeling under the blow. But in a second
he had recovered himself. He looked at her pityingly. "If you will permit me, Mrs. Deerford, I
will take my leave. I understand," he continued,
turning to Deerford, who was regarding him curiously. "I have learned, since coming to this part
of the country, that my father lived at one time
here, at Eastwood. It is possible that your mother
may have known him. Some unpleasant memory
connected with him doubtless has " —

"Your name is not Hilliard. Leroy Hilliard
was not your father. Your father was Francis
Deerford. Your name is Francis Armstead Deerford. And I am your mother."

This time Hilliard tottered and would have
fallen, but for Deerford's arm. He stared at the
rigid form on the sofa with wide, terrified eyes.
"*Francis Deerford!*" he whispered, "*Francis
Deerford!*" The name came echoing up from
the depths of his consciousness like a cry from the
grave. Yes, he knew it! He heard himself called
by it, indifferently, sternly, harshly, tenderly.

"*Aunt Pau-line.*" His lips just framed the syllables.

Mrs. Deerford threw up her arms wildly. "Ah," she cried. "He remembers! He remembers!" There was an echo of mother-love in her voice; she started forward as if to spring to his breast.

He stooped and caught her wrists in his vise-like grasp. He would have liked to bend them backward, as he had once bent Deerford's, until the slender bones cracked. He forced her to her seat. "Tell me what you mean — woman! The truth! The truth! — if a Deerford can tell the truth!"

His face was close to hers, his brown eyes scorching her blue ones.

The momentary tenderness vanished from her face. She lifted her head and returned his furious gaze with eyes as hard and as cold as steel. He released his grasp and stepped back, breathing heavily.

"The truth? Yes, I will tell you. Listen, Francis Deerford. You shall hear all the truth." She rose to her full height and stood before him with folded arms, tragically beautiful while she told the story.

She told it from the very beginning, sparing no detail of her own misery or of Leroy Hilliard's brutality. Allan Deerford, who had known nothing of this episode in his mother's life, listened, amazed and horrified, at the torrent of words

which poured impassioned from her lips.   Hilliard
— the discarded and hitherto forgotten Francis
Armstead Deerford — clenched his hands in impotent anger, seeing, not the fair unremembered face
before him, but the noble visage of his adopted
father.

"You may sometimes have wondered, Francis
Armstead Deerford," she cried, "why you carry
on your face the birth-mark which would cause
your detection, were you the wariest murderer that
ever lived.   It is not beautiful, that slash across
your cheek!   And I will tell you, since I am
telling you other things, how you came by it!"

She related with cruel minuteness the episode of
the mutilated portrait.   For the first time, since
she began to speak, Hilliard recoiled, lifting his
arm as if to shield himself.   He felt it like a stab
in his own heart, the pitiless ripping of the knife
across that dear pictured face.

But he still kept silence while she sketched
more hurriedly the history of her second marriage
with the man she really loved.   Then came the
curious story of the birth of her first child — the
longed-for heir, the baby boy, the son who now
stood before her an alien, and who was an alien
in his father's house from the day and hour he
was born; the pain and anguish of her own dawn-
ing knowledge of the fatal, inexplicable likeness;
the shame of it, oh, the shame of it! the bitter
hatred of the man whose loathed features by some
mysterious freak of nature were laid like a curse

upon Francis Deerford's child; the suspicions —
vague, nameless, horrible — of her husband which
enveloped her like a pall; his frenzied abhorrence
of the child; into the midst of all this, the coming of the second boy — "you, Allan." She paused
to say this with a glance at him which transformed
the cruel face into a radiant expression of motherhood. "You, who have been my heart's love,
and my life's joy and comfort since the moment
I first held you in my arms."

"Yes, mother." Hilliard thrilled, through all
his anguish, to hear the tone. It was so unlike
anything he had ever heard issue from Allan Deerford's lips. "Yes, mother," Allan said. He was
hearing all this for the first time. He had learned
— within the hour — only the simple fact that the
man calling himself Leroy Hilliard was his own
brother. "But who knows," he continued, a shade
of bitterness creeping into his voice, "who knows
if the strength of your own and my father's hatred
and despair may not have left its stamp upon me
also, and made me — what I am!"

"If there is anything in you to deplore, Allan,"
she cried fiercely, "Leroy Hilliard first, and after
him this creature whom I myself brought into the
world, have been the cause of it!"

"I was glad, yes, glad," she concluded passionately, addressing her eldest son once more, "when
your father carried you away, though I never
dreamed that I would not see you again. I did
not know that he had taken you to the man whose

living image you were then and are still. I do
not know why he did so, unless " — she paused,
then added recklessly — "unless he supposed you,
my God! to be that man's son! I did not dream
that you were living until this day. For," a deep
shuddering sob shook her from head to foot, "my
dear husband was killed in a railroad accident on
his homeward journey. I never saw him alive
again. We supposed that you had perished at
the same time, as we ascertained he had never
been to New York with you. His poor mangled
body was brought home to me, and I — my little
Paul came into the world during the first wretched
hours of my widowhood!"

She sank back, closing her eyes, as if to shut
out Hilliard's marked face. "Allan was right,"
she said after a pause, and in a calmer voice, "I
need not have told you all this. It can only be a
source of misery to you hereafter, as it has ever
been to me. But the sight of you — the sight of
you! I felt driven to speak." She seemed to be
framing these excuses more for herself than to
him. "Moreover," — here she drew herself up
with a motion of pride, — "with the blood of
Henry Armstead in my veins, and the light of
Francis Deerford's strict integrity shining like a
star before my children's eyes, I could not keep
from you, without shame to myself and to them,
the fact that you are, according to your father's
will, the heir to the bulk of his property." Again
she ceased, but her uplifted eyes spoke on; they

said plainly, "Take your belongings, and be-gone!"

Hilliard continued to stare at her mutely, feel-ing that if he opened his lips howls of rage and blasphemy would escape them. Finally, master-ing himself with a powerful effort, he spoke. The sound of his own voice was terrible in his ears.

"I recognize the truth of your story, Mrs. Deerford, except so far as it relates to the charac-ter of the man whose name I have borne since I can remember. In telling me the story, you have amply revenged yourself upon me, who am the innocent cause of your suffering. I trust it has made you happier to take away from me the father whose memory I adore — who was the noblest, bravest man that ever caressed a forsaken child, or carried a sword into battle — to give me in his place a cold-blooded monster for a father, and a mother — oh, my God! my God!" He suddenly lost all control of himself. His fury and despair broke forth in a hoarse roar resembling the cry of a wild animal, — "a mother, who, according to her own deliberately chosen words, hated her own help-less little child, and cast it from her without a pang of pity; and a brother" — he turned fero-ciously on Deerford — "a brother who is a red-handed murderer, and about whom at this moment the net of justice is drawn!"

"What does he mean, Allan?" Mrs. Deerford sprang to her feet, alarmed. She looked at Allan, who made no reply, but turned his eyes question-

ingly on Hilliard. "What do you mean?" she
repeated, seizing his arm and shaking it violently.
"Tell me! Tell me!"

"I mean," he said, urged on by a blind rage
which took no account of sex or kinship, and quite
reckless of consequences, "I mean that Allan
Deerford, your son! my brother! is an assassin!
the midnight murderer of his host and chosen
friend. Oh, he will not deny it! Ask him! I
mean that determined men whom he cannot escape — though he has no telltale birth-mark on his
cheek! — are now near this house, armed with
authority to drag him to the gallows!"

"Is this true? Oh, Allan, Allan, tell me that
it is not true!" the mother shrieked, running from
one of her sons to the other and searching their
faces with her terrified eyes. "Francis, my son —
Leroy Hilliard, I beseech you to say that it is not
true."

The coldness, the biting sarcasm, the retrospec-
tive anger, were all gone. In their stead the entreaty of anguished love, the outcry of stricken
motherhood, the fierceness of maternity at bay.
"How dare you! How dare you! Where are
those men? Oh, Leroy, you will send them away,
will you not? You will save my boy? You will!
You will!"

She sank upon the floor and embraced his
knees. "Mother! mother!" said Deerford, choking with emotion, trying to raise her in his arms.

"No, no. I will not cease to pray to him, to

supplicate him as if he were God himself. Forgive me, Leroy, forgive me all the dreadful past.
I mean — oh, Francis, my son, my son, forgive
me. See how strong you are, strong and masterful like — like *him*. You must, you shall listen
to me."

Hilliard had tried to release himself from her
clasp. He wished to escape from the rising flood
of anguish which threatened to overwhelm him.
But her long arms held him fast. Finally, a sob,
more like the convulsive gasp of a dying creature
than a human sound, tore her throat, her head fell
backward, her despairing hands relaxed their hold.

He stooped and caught her wrists again with his
trembling fingers. "Go, for God's sake! I will
do what I can. Yes, yes. I promise!"

He dropped unnerved upon a chair and buried
his face in his hands. A rush of hot tears came
to the relief of his overcharged heart.

Deerford lifted his mother in his arms as if
she had been an infant, and carried her from the
room. Hilliard never noticed their absence; and
he looked up with dazed, uncomprehending eyes
when he heard his name spoken once more. "Hilliard!" He rose, and the two brothers stood looking at each other, long and silently. "I do not
know how it might have been," Allan said at last
slowly, "had I known that you were my brother.
It is too late now. I could not, if I would, justify
myself in your eyes — that I understand, of course.
But I will at least risk saying that the night you

found me setting fire to your cotton I was mad-
dened by drink and jealousy. I wish to God you
had killed me then! And I swear to you, standing, as I believe I am, on the brink of eternity,
that I did not intend to kill Jack Ransome. He
was choking me like the drunken madman that he
was, and I used the knife to free myself. For a
long time I could not believe that he was dead.
Then the awfulness of it and the thought of the
consequences to myself, and — believe it or not, as
you like! — of my mother's grief, swept me on
into doing — what I did."

"And into laying the burden of your crime, or
the suspicion of it, at least, upon me."

A deep red dyed Allan's pallid face. "Yes,"
he said desperately, "and that! And although I
have done much in my life which calls for remorse
and atonement, *that* is the blackest crime I have
ever committed! I am not asking for mercy at
your hands; I merely mention the fact." A faint
semblance of his former reckless jauntiness crossed
his speech. "And now, having said so much, Hilliard, I desire only to add that you will not, of
course, feel yourself bound by any promise you
have made to my mother — under the circumstances. I understand, by what you have said,
that I am in danger of immediate arrest. I have
counted upon this danger, of course. I know
much that took place after I left Crouch's, and I
quite realize the bitter — pardon me, I should say
the just prejudice against me there, and therefore

what it would mean for me to be taken back there for any so-called trial — even " — he bowed, with a mocking smile — "even if Mr. Hilliard himself should offer to defend me! I am prepared to re- sist capture until my last breath. I am willing to die, if it comes to that, for — for what happened at Peleg Church. But, by God, I will die my own way!"

"I have promised," Hilliard said sullenly, "and I will keep my promise. I may not succeed. I came here, as I told you, on other business. I did not know that you were here, though I had pledged my word to search the world over until I had found you. I met in the town yonder, on my arrival this morning, the man who has followed you for weeks, spying upon your every step. He has planned your arrest. I do not know the plan. I only know that you are to be taken to-night."

He got up and walked back and forth the length of the room several times. When he spoke again, it was in a terse, business-like voice. "Deerford," he said — all recollection of their relationship had for the moment slipped his mind; he remembered only the problem confronting him. "Deerford, I am going back to St. Denis at once to see the man who holds your life in his hands. You will give me your word, not for my sake, but your own, that you will not attempt to leave this house during my absence."

"Very well." Deerford's curt tone was an echo of his own.

"You will have your horse saddled and be, your-self, ready for any emergency. I count upon get-ting back here a little after dark. If all so far has gone well, I will come in and rap twice upon the front door. We can then confer as to further arrangements. I hope to be alone, but it may fall out otherwise. The whole success or non-success of my plan, I confess, hinges upon the in-fluence I may have with Dan Roper. I think it but fair to warn you that he is very bitter against you. In any event, I will return. A single call from my hunting-whistle will mean immediate danger. You must then act as seems best to you, and — I will do my utmost to assist your escape. If escape should be impossible " —

Deerford returned his meaning look. "You may rest easy on that score," he said proudly; "I will never be taken. If all other means fail, I count on a bullet from — from — my brother's pistol."

"Very well. In the mean time, I repeat that the least movement on your part looking toward flight will precipitate matters. There are spies in your very household. You will await my re-turn."

"I will await your return," said Deerford calmly.

Hilliard took up his hat and gloves which he had laid down on entering. "One moment, Hil-liard," said Deerford; "I may not see you again. The chances seem to be pretty slim for much more

explanation between us in this world! I think
you may not have noticed what my mother said
about my father's will, which devised to his eldest
son the bulk of his property. This will, my
mother has told me, was made before the birth of
the eldest son — whom I have always supposed to
be myself. I have managed to scatter a good deal
of your inheritance," — he laughed shortly, — "but
the property is still a large one. You will, I
judge, take immediate steps to secure it" —

"I shall not touch Mr. Deerford's money,"
Hilliard interrupted curtly.

"My mother will certainly insist" —

"I shall never see or communicate with your
mother again. *Your* mother! For as there is
a God in heaven, though she had brought me into
the world a thousand times, she is not *my* mother!"

"By God!" cried Deerford, flashing into sudden fury, "if I can get out of this house and far
enough away from it to spare the two women I
love the horror of seeing me shot, I would rather
die like a dog than owe my life to you!"

"The two women you love!" There was a
sneer in Hilliard's voice as he repeated the phrase.

"Yes, the two women I love — my poor mother
and Helen Wingate."

The two faces distorted by passion were close
together; both were terrible — almost inhuman in
their frenzied emotion. Hilliard's all at once
softened; the image of the little child — blue-

eyed, golden-haired, rose-wreathed — danced with up-flung arms before him! "*Ally!*" he whispered. It was the name by which he used to call his baby brother.

Roper came running out of the stable to meet him. He reeled in his saddle and dropped like a lump of lead into the arms which were outstretched to receive him. Roper supported him into the private office of the manager of the livery. "What in the name of God is the matter with you, Hilliard?" he demanded when they were alone, and he had closed and locked the door. "Have you killed him?"

Hilliard shook his head.

"Has he given us the slip? No? Are you sick? Then what is it? I found out directly you left that you had gone to Eastwood plantation."

"I did not know he was there," Hilliard panted.

"I was a d—d fool not to speak more plainly. But I took it for granted that you knew where he was. Besides, I did n't know you were bound for Eastwood. You asked for Mrs. and Miss Wingate there. I did not know that you knew them. But you saw Deerford?"

"Yes, I saw him. Roper," — he lifted his pinched and drawn face from his breast with an effort, — "Roper, Deerford must not be arrested."

"*What!*" shouted Roper, bounding from his seat. "Are you crazy, Hilliard? Do you know what you are saying?"

"Deerford must escape. *He must escape.* I will tell you why, if you insist. But "—

"Tell me nothing," interrupted Roper savagely. He lifted the chair upon which he had been sitting and dashed it violently against the floor.

"If you attempt to arrest him, I will die with him. For he is prepared to die rather than be captured."

Roper had hardly heard the threat which fell from Hilliard's bloodless lips. He was pacing like a baffled beast about the small office. At the end of a few moments he came to where Hilliard sat and laid a hand on his shoulder.

"Roy," he said huskily, "Tom treated you like a hound-dog, and you paid him for it by dragging him from the gallows, or out of the penitentiary. I don't know what you want with Deerford, d—n him. I'd rather tear out my heart and burn it on a rail-pile than to let him go. But if you want him — if he was the devil from hell, chained and ready to be delivered up, by God, I'd knock off his chains and give him to you! Take him." He turned his burly body about, and groaned. "God-a-mighty, it comes hard! But take him. And I don't ask any questions."

"I'll. ride ahead," he said half an hour later, when the situation had been fully discussed between them. "I'll have to ride ahead and call off my men. The woods are full of 'em," he laughed, though with a wry face, "and God knows what lies I'll tell before I'm through!"

"You are a good fellow, Dan!"

"Am I, though! Not much. Don't you make the mistake of supposing I am letting that double-dyed scoundrel of a Deerford slip because I love my enemies. I don't. But I love my friends, and there's no goodness in that, that ever I heard of!"

They walked out into the stable, where Roper selected a horse for himself and one for Hilliard. "Now let us get some supper," he suggested. "We may both need all our strength before this business is concluded."

He mounted his horse about dusk. "You had better follow in an hour, or a little less," he said at parting. "The train passes the flag station at eight o'clock. I'll have things clear for you, if possible. Don't waste time when you get there. Strike across the plantation — he'll show you the way — and catch that train. Get him aboard, and tell him to put the width of the world between himself and Dan Roper as quick as he can. I don't think there will be any trouble, unless somebody else is after him, or unless my men suspicion that they are losing their game — and the reward. But I'm pretty sure I can get 'em out of the way."

He rode off at a hand gallop. "That girl is in it, somehow," he muttered. "Ding the women. They're in everything. This is the way I put it up. Hilliard has found out that she loves that villain, Deerford, and to please her, he's running

Deerford out of reach of the law. Well, she's a mighty big fool, and so is Hilliard, and so am I! But then, so is pretty near everybody else!"

It was a quarter past seven o'clock when Hilliard, for the second time, walked across the lawn at Eastwood. It was a cloudy night; the wind blowing in from the river was soft and warm; it was heavy with the scent of orange-blossoms. The windows were lighted on the lower and upper floors of the house, giving it a gala look. But everything was very still, without and within. The negroes over in the quarter were singing a plantation chorus; he could hear the words distinctly as he stepped upon the veranda and rapped lightly, twice, with his riding-whip on the great carved door. It opened, and Deerford appeared on the threshold.

"We have no time to lose," Hilliard said without preliminary. "Are you ready?"

"I will be with you in one moment." Deerford turned; as he did so, Hilliard saw that he held a pistol in each hand.

"You had best carry your arms, in case of possible trouble. But I do not think you will need them. We are riding to catch the train at Eastwood flag station."

Deerford nodded and entered the library.

"Miss Helen have left this note for you, Marse Roy." Samp's outer and visible man betrayed no curiosity as he handed an envelope to the young man whose name and features he had been discussing the whole afternoon in the servants' quarters.

Hilliard thrust the sealed envelope into his breast-pocket. He stepped out upon the veranda and stood waiting in the soft, perfumed darkness. A confused sound within drew his attention. He glanced at the library window; the shutters were wide open, and he saw, framed like a picture there, Allan Deerford clasped in his mother's arms; Mabel and Paul bent over them; the lamplight played over the blond heads and illuminated the anguished faces.

A spasm of anger tore his heart; he half lifted his whistle to sound the summons agreed upon with Roper, in case he should decide after all to let the law have its will. But he dropped the hand and walked noiselessly down the steps. When Deerford joined him, he hurried with him to the stables, giving him brief instructions as they went.

Deerford threw himself into his saddle, and led the way down one of those rose-hedged lanes which had so stirred Hilliard's sense of beauty that morning. The Cherokee roses shone on the dense background of leaves like white stars; a faint rustle of wings hinted of birds sheltered within the foliage; the clear whistle of a mockingbird now and then thrilled the night air.

Roper had been as good as his word. Nothing disturbed their rapid journey. Neither spoke after leaving the Eastwood stables until they had cleared, in a swift gallop, more than half the distance to the station.

"You will go and see my mother?" Deerford's question startled Hilliard. He stopped his horse with a jerk, laying his hand at the same time on his companion's bridle, and compelling him to stop also.

"Mr. Deerford," he said sternly, "I wish to say once for all that after I get you safely on board of the train we are riding for, all communication between your family and myself will cease forever. As for yourself, I think I need say nothing — though indeed I could say much. But we are wasting time." He flung Deerford's bridle from him, and galloped on without awaiting a reply.

They dismounted in silence at the station. "We have ten minutes," Hilliard said, coming back from his brief interview with the solitary flagman in charge. His heart was beating, and the blood was buzzing in his ears; he started at the cracking of a twig under his feet. Deerford was far the more calm and collected of the two.

"You will sail at the earliest possible moment?" Hilliard asked, with his ears strained nervously to catch any unusual sound.

"I have my passage engaged on a steamer which sails to-morrow for Liverpool direct from New Orleans. I had already secured it."

"There is the train," said Hilliard in a quick tone of relief. The great yellow eye of the locomotive rounding a curve projected its level block of light along the shining rails.

"Hilliard, this moment, as you have said, ends our acquaintance forever. If I made any protestations, you would not believe me, I know. But will you " — Deerford reached out his hand with a timidity which sat strangely upon him.

Hilliard drew back instinctively; his heart surged; he opened his lips to say, "I cannot." But they said, without his own volition, "*Ally! Ally!*" And his hand for the first and last time clasped convulsively the hand of his brother.

The train paused for one second. Deerford swung himself up the steps of a car and was instantly lost to sight in the shadow of the overhanging roof. The engine tore off with a shriek.

Hilliard stumbled blindly back across the ditch to where the two horses were fastened. Two figures detached themselves from the gloom and came forward to meet him.

"Marse Roy!" called old Jerry anxiously.

Roper said nothing for several minutes; he supported Hilliard up the bank as if he had been a woman. "I followed you," he said at length. "I thought I 'd better be somewhere around in case of trouble. This fool nigger thought I was after doing you some harm, so *he* followed me!"

XIX

HELEN

W<small>HEN</small> Helen Wingate left her lover in the hall at Eastwood, she ran lightly up the stair to her mother's room, pausing on the landing for a last look at him, as he followed Mabel into the library.

Mrs. Wingate was a sweet-faced, somewhat timid woman of about sixty. The tie between her and her only child was of an unusually strong character. Helen, quiet, reticent, and self-contained, with a tinge of brooding sadness at times in her voice and eyes, had been, during the whole of her life, not only her mother's companion, but the strong arm upon which her mother leaned. This had given her a sort of sweet imperiousness to which the older woman submitted with secret content.

"What are you doing here, madam?" cried the girl, shaking a white forefinger laughingly as she came into the room. "Did I not order you to sun yourself on the lawn for two hours at least?"

"Helen." The tone was so strange, and the eyes which looked at her were so appealing, that she stopped short, trembling and wondering.

"What is it, mother? Has anything happened?

Are you ill?" she asked, dropping on her knees beside her mother, and gazing anxiously in her face.

"Leroy Hilliard is here. I recognized him at once, as he passed me on the lawn."

"Oh, is that it!" laughed Helen, reassured. "And now that he is here, mother dear, you must make the best of him! He has come to ask you for your dearest treasure, namely my precious self. And oh, mother darling, I am so happy! — but I did not know that you had ever met him?"

"I never have. But I recognized him at once," groaned Mrs. Wingate. "Oh, Helen, Helen!"

"What do you mean, mother darling? Tell me. How can you dare to have any trouble without letting me share it?" She laid her young cheek on the thin hands she held and kissed them tenderly. "Tell me, mother. What is it?"

"Listen then, dear. I tell you because I must. I thought and hoped you might never need to know. But — I have often spoken to you of your father, Helen, the gallant Confederate officer who was wounded in battle and brought home to us to die."

"Yes, oh yes."

"I have described to you the old farmhouse where we were then living — and where you were born, and my lovely young sister. Dear, it is of that sister, whose name you bear, that I wish to tell you. She was very young and very beautiful, and about a year before you were born to be my joy and comfort, she married a Confederate officer, a brilliant and lovable man much older than herself, who was drawn to her, I think, as much by her open and undisguised affection for himself as by her beauty and innocence. My own husband was in the same brigade, and we were all very happy together, despite the time — which was one of doubt, anguish, and despair for the country. A day came when my sister Helen's husband dashed in for a few moments to press a good-by kiss upon her quivering lips. An hour later the din of battle at close quarters raged around us; in the midst of it he was brought in mortally wounded. He died with Helen's name upon his lips. That night Helen, too, died — in giving birth to you, dear. For you are my very own in love only."

"I do not — understand — mother," faltered the girl piteously.

"You are the daughter of my little sister Helen, who died in giving you birth." Mrs. Wingate spoke slowly, raising her voice a little. "And your father — the gallant officer who gave his life for the cause he cherished — was General Leroy Hilliard."

"Was — " Helen knitted her brows, still uncomprehending.

"I took you, dear little wailing orphan," continued Mrs. Wingate, relieved by Helen's apparent calmness, "and made you my own, giving you my name. I too was left a widow very soon afterward. I never dreamed that there could ever be a reason for you to know! I could not bear " —

"*Mother! Mother! Mother!*" cried Helen, clinging to her passionately. "Oh, as if you were not doubly my own, own mother! Oh, why should you grieve yourself by speaking of it!"

"Do you not see, my darling! This young man, Leroy Hilliard, is General Hilliard's son by a former marriage, and your " —

"No, no, no! Do not say it! Do not say it!" She shrank back, white with terror, and put out her hands imploringly. "Do not say it. Mother! mother!"

Mrs. Wingate encircled her with tender arms. "It is true, darling. I must say it. I did not know — doubtless my sister did — that General Hilliard had been married before. She had several letters from his sister, and he intended to take her to his old home as soon as the war should be at an end. I, at least, never heard him mention his son. It was only when in one of your letters from Texas you mentioned a Leroy Hilliard and spoke of his father's brilliant record as a soldier, that I began to suspect. I sent at once to B—— in Carolina, and learned that General Hilliard had left a son, a bright young fellow named for him, who had gone to Texas and settled there. Something in the tone of your letter determined me to call you home. But I could not then make up my mind to tell you that you were not my own " —

"Mother! mother!" the cry came again, broken by sobs.

"I returned to Kentucky upon my husband's death, taking you with me, hoping you would never know," concluded Mrs. Wingate wistfully. "But now that you do know, you will realize, dear child, that you have gained a brother" —

"Never! Never!" Helen shuddered as she sprang to her feet. "I do not wish him to know. I wish never to look on his face again. He is here in the house. I will not see him again! Let us go away at once, at once!"

She rang the bell violently. When her maid appeared, she sent an order for the horses to be harnessed to the carriage without delay and brought around to a side entrance of the park. She assisted feverishly in the necessary packing, leaving her mother to see Mabel and leave messages for Mrs. Deerford, who, it appeared, was engaged in the library and could not be disturbed. Mrs. Wingate, dimly comprehending the pain of the young creature, usually so calm and self-reliant, acquiesced in all her hurried arrangements.

In a very short time the carriage was announced. Helen had returned for a moment to her own room — the same chamber in which Aunt Pauline had so often wept and prayed over another Leroy Hilliard — and had thrown herself on her knees in an agony of despair. She arose, and stood trying to recover her self-control. "I cannot see him again — ever," she murmured at length. "But I may at least leave him a line of farewell."

She wrote a few words, constrained and formal,

to tell him of her departure, signifying her wish
not to see him again, and dissolving the tie which
for a brief time had held them together. She
signed her name to the note, slipped it into an
envelope, and left it to be delivered to Hilliard.

As she stole down the stair to the carriage, she
heard a voice in the library, which she recognized
as his. It fell upon her heart like a faint and
dying echo of lost happiness.

They drove to the station some miles below
that where a few hours later Deerford caught the
train. There, dismissing the carriage, they waited
for the train. And so it came about that when
Helen entered the car the first person upon whom
her eyes fell was Allan Deerford.

"*Helen !*" he cried, starting up bewildered.
"How came you here?" She busied herself with
the small luggage, leaving her mother to respond.

"We found ourselves obliged unexpectedly to
start at once for home," Mrs. Wingate said.
"We were unable to see Mrs. Deerford. But we
left explanations and good-bys for her with Mabel
and Paul. They will be coming back to Kentucky
soon, I fancy. And you, Allan? Are you really
off for England?"

"Yes. At last." His tone was absent. He
seated himself opposite to them, but showed no
disposition to talk. He turned his head and stared
out of the window into the opaque darkness weirdly
illuminated by the flying lights of the train; Mrs.
Wingate leaned back among the pillows in her

corner and sank at once into wearied slumber. Helen sat watching the young man's face for a long time; her own matched it in pallor and listlessness.

Finally she leaned forward. "Allan," she said in a soft whisper.

He looked up quickly; his gloomy eyes lighted. "Can I do anything for you, Miss Helen?" he asked.

"I — I wanted to ask if I could do anything for *you?* You look ill and troubled."

"No. Nothing that you would be willing to do," he returned, smiling, but rather wistfully. "I *am* ill and troubled. I am leaving my mother, and — others, who are dear to me, for a long time, perhaps forever. I sail to-morrow morning, if nothing happens to prevent, for England. Ah, Helen, if you were but going with me!"

He spoke without expectation of a reply, and turned his face again toward the window.

A shiver passed through her frame. Her eyes dilated and then closed. She sat quite still, hardly breathing, grasping the arm of the seat with her ungloved hand, her mind darting hither and thither in swift question and halting answer. Presently the whirling chaos subsided into quiet; she saw, or thought she saw, clearly. She leaned forward again.

" *Why not?* " The whisper was just audible to him above the monotonous rush of the car over the rails.

He looked at her in bewildered amazement. "*Helen!*" He seized both her hands in his, pressing them until she almost cried out with pain. "You do not mean it! You cannot mean it!"

"I will go with you to-morrow, if you wish it."

"As my wife?"

"As your wife — if you wish it." The poor girl clutched at the thought as the drowning man at the rope which floats unexpectedly into his grasp.

"*If I wish it!* Helen, you are offering me heaven — when I was all ready for hell!" The last words were spoken under his breath. He still clasped her hands, devouring her beautiful pale face with hungry eyes. At length he released them and said, in an altered tone: "You do not know what you are doing, Helen. I — I dare not allow you to take a step which you would regret afterwards — bitterly, perhaps. I am not going to England of my own free will, but because" — He bit his lips; the words were costing him more than he had foreseen. "I must tell you first why I am leaving this country forever — do you understand, Helen? *forever!* Then you can decide."

"Do not tell me," she said quickly. "I do not wish to know. I will never ask. I, too, have reasons for going, which I must tell you" — Her eyes filled with tears; the rope at which she had grasped seemed slipping away from her; the waters closing over her.

"Helen!" He seized her hands again. "It

does not matter to me why you are going, so only you go with me. I promise you, on my part, that I will never seek to know. And oh, my dear, my dear, I also promise that I will do my utmost to make you happy."

She shrank back a little, but left her hands in his. It was a strange wooing, in open view of the crowded car, with the trainmen passing back and forth, and looking curiously at them. The lights of the city were beginning to gleam in the distance, blurred by a gently falling rain. Tired-looking women were slipping wraps on their sleepy and fretful children; the smug porter was ostentatiously brushing coats and setting out traveling-bags; old travelers were still reading their papers by the light of the swaying lamps, while the less experienced ones stood nervously in the aisles, grasping umbrellas and valises. And still the two forlorn young creatures leaned toward each other, clasping hands as if for mutual safety.

They were married at an early hour the next morning in the hotel parlor. Mrs. Wingate looked on, uneasy and astonished, but powerless to interfere. The few other witnesses crowding the doors — guests and employees of the hotel — agreed that the bride was aristocratic and elegant, but too pale for beauty. The groom looked nervous, but then, all grooms look nervous!

The portly clergyman attended Mrs. Wingate and Mr. and Mrs. Deerford down the stairs to their carriage, and watched them drive off to the steamer. He was vaguely distressed by an expression on the faces of the newly married pair. "Really," he said whimsically to himself, "I think a diagnosis of every matrimonial case ought to be written out and handed to the performing clergyman to read before he undertakes it."

One of the witnesses to the marriage, a rather commonplace-looking man, had also descended the stairs. He brushed past the musing clergyman and jumped into a cab; the coachman galloped his horses after the carriage. The man stood about the wharf until the passengers were on board the Brenda, and the great steamship swung slowly down the yellow stream. Deerford, plainly visible amid the small knot of voyagers on the vessel's deck, had bared his head; his yellow curls glistened like gold in the morning sunlight; his wife stood beside him.

"Go and be d—d to you," the watcher on the wharf groaned, apostrophizing him, "with your yellow head, and your white face, and your black heart, and your bride! But if you keep your neck out of the halter ten years longer, my name's not Dan Roper!"

XX

VICTORY

HELEN'S note, which he read by the light of the flagman's lantern, while Roper and the old negro, Jerry, waited for him with the two horses, produced in Hilliard's mind only a profound feeling of thankfulness that she had left Eastwood plantation. He put aside the incoherent farewell it contained as not worth a moment's consideration, satisfied that Mrs. Wingate, removing her daughter precipitately from his reach, had also insisted, for some reason, upon such a farewell. As if the width of the world could separate him from Helen! As if Helen could really wish to put him out of her life! Unless — unless she had heard the story of his birth and his banishment, and had been repelled by it; unless she had learned, through Mrs. Deerford, of his denunciation of Allan, and held him to blame for lack of brotherly feeling; unless she thought him hard and cruel to his — mother! unless, unless —

As he galloped on, now ahead of his companions, now far behind them, feverishly anxious to be alone, the rain beating his wan face, his square jaws set, his black brows drawn together, he might have been the ghost of that Hilliard who thirty years before had sped over these lonely roads by night!

"He is hard hit by something outside of Deerford's deviltry, poor fellow!" sighed Roper, forgetting that he was not alone.

"Dat he is, marster," said Jerry, who rode at his elbow, leading Deerford's spirited horse. "I knows de signs. Marse Roy is hamstrenk!"

Jerry was sent on to Eastwood with a single word, already agreed upon, by way of a message, to Deerford's mother. Roper accompanied Hilliard to St. Denis. The latter had hardly reached his room in the village hotel when the deputy-sheriff appeared in the doorway. He carried a traveling-bag. "I'm off, Roy," he said. "Good-by."

Hilliard looked at him, surprised.

"I'm going down to the city. Another train passes here about half past eleven. I want to see *him* off." He grinned ruefully. "There might be trouble yet, you know," he added.

"Thank you, Dan." Hilliard grasped his hand. "I wish I could tell you how grateful I am" —

"Shucks!" said Roper roughly. "Tom ain't much account. But I think he's worth that! to say nothing of you!"

The next day Hilliard remained in St. Denis, although he was possessed by an overpowering desire to be once more at "home" — among those dear ones whose love and tenderness were now dearer to him than ever before. About noon he started out with the intention of calling upon Milgrove, with the confessed hope of hearing something which might cast a new light upon Mrs. Deerford's monstrous revelation — or give it the lie. He found, easily enough, the office he sought. It was upon one of the long shaded roadways — for they could hardly be called streets — of the little old town. The small detached wooden building, whose steep roof and broad eaves were green with moss, looked with one eye, as it were, upon the old brick court-house in its triangular square; the other opened into the stately garden of a large brick mansion. From the doorway one could see the sluggish Bayou Teche creeping along between its sloping banks. A sign above the door read, "Ralston & Milgrove." There seemed to be no one within, although the door stood open, and the wind blowing up from the bayou fluttered the leaves of a law-book open on a table. Hilliard hailed a negro lad at work in the garden. "Is Mr. Milgrove in?" he asked.

"Mist' Milgrove has jest druv home, sah," the lad replied, "but de jedge is in de library."

Hilliard turned to go. A window was opened in the dwelling-house, and an elderly gentleman stepped out upon the veranda. "Did you wish to see me?" he asked, advancing, newspaper in hand. "Oh, Mr. Hilliard! I heard of your arrival yesterday from my partner, Milgrove. How do you do?

I should have recognized you anywhere. I knew
your father long before you were born. Come in.
Come in."

Hilliard winced, but he followed Judge Ralston
into his library and sat down. Ralston, now an
old man, was still hale and hearty. The sight of
Hilliard brought to him, as it had to Milgrove,
a swarm of pleasant recollections. He chatted on
exuberantly, not observing his visitor's embarrassment; recalling what he was pleased to character-
ize the "good old times," when Leroy Hilliard
was one of his own friends and neighbors. Suddenly he paused, embarrassed in his turn. "By
Jove," he reflected. "I certainly am falling into
my dotage. I had forgotten that it was I who
brought the suit for the divorce! The lad evidently knows it, too."

But Hilliard had merely been nerving himself
to speak. Something in the old man's tone or
manner, or both, inspired confidence. Begging in
advance an assurance of secrecy, he laid before
the astonished lawyer the extraordinary facts of
his life, as he had received them from Mrs. Deerford the day before. He heard in return the
history of her earlier years before and during her
first marriage, and afterward, up to the time she
had left Eastwood plantation with her second
husband; all this in a much more connected and
coherent manner than the excited and unhappy
woman herself had been able to give it. Any lingering hope that the part of it which related to

himself might be a dream of her imagination was dispelled. Ralston remembered the rejoicings at Eastwood over the heir's birth; he himself had drawn up Francis Deerford's will. He had remarked, perhaps before the mother noticed it, the curious likeness the boy bore to Leroy Hilliard; he had observed the scarlet mark upon the infant's cheek. He confessed that he had also observed Francis Deerford's increasing dislike of his first-born, and the wife's growing anxiety. All these things had long ago faded from his memory, and were revived only by the young man's story.

"Lilla Armstead was a very strange girl," he concluded. "I knew her from her infancy. She was self-willed, and she had a fierce, overbearing temper. Perhaps Henry Armstead — why, God bless my soul, boy, he was your grandfather, and the best soul that ever lived! — perhaps he was responsible for much of her waywardness, for he spoiled her systematically. She and Hilliard hated each other like young tiger-cats. I saw that soon enough, but she certainly adored Deerford. I never could understand how you came by your looks! But I now remember hinting to Deerford that he ought to leave this State. He said nothing to me, but I could see what was passing in his mind. So. It has turned out strangely enough. I took it for granted, when Milgrove mentioned your arrival, — as he did, — that your fa — that Hilliard had married again, and that you were the son of that marriage. But how came Hilliard to have charge of you?"

"I do not know. Mrs. Deerford herself does not know," Hilliard replied, sick at heart. "I may learn something of my earlier life when I get back to Carolina. I remember nothing."

"And the property? Deerford's, I mean? The greater part of it was to come to you unconditionally, in the event of his death, upon your coming of age."

"I shall not touch it, Judge Ralston; not a penny of it!"

"Tut-tut! Don't be quixotic, boy. It would serve Lilla right if she had to give up every cent she has. Unfeeling mother! Well, well. They tell me, by the way, that there is another son, who is a sort of a scamp. I believe he is at Eastwood now!"

"I — I met him yesterday. In fact, strangely enough, I knew him in Texas, though I was at that time unaware of the relationship."

The spoken word, *relationship*, jarred disagreeably upon him; mind, reason, and heart refused to accept the hideous fact; he continued to think and speak of this family, so painfully thrust upon him, as strangers. He led the talk away from them. This was easy enough; Ralston was soon launched upon a full tide of reminiscences, and in the prolonged talk which followed, the listener learned much that then and afterward threw light on the strange events of his life.

The old judge parted with him almost affectionately. He had cherished a secret fondness for the dashing young fellow whose reputation he had so scored during the progress of the suit entitled *Lilla Hilliard vs. Leroy Hilliard.* This living presentment of him — a Deerford though he really might be — awoke pleasant sensations in his old breast.

Hilliard posted the letter he had addressed to Helen at her home in Kentucky. It contained little more than the notification that on that day two weeks hence he would present himself there to claim her as his promised bride. The words were masterful, but perfect love and perfect confidence pervaded them.

The same afternoon he started on his homeward journey.

He reached B—— at nightfall. Leaving his luggage at the railway station, he walked along the familiar streets of the town, toward the old house in the suburbs.

Nothing was changed since he had been here last; or indeed since he first remembered the long straggling street. The little corner shop where he had bought his marbles, when a boy, hunched its protruding show-window on the sidewalk as of old; the stubby one-legged proprietor within sat tilted against the counter in a split-bottomed chair, spelling out the newspaper precisely as he used to do. He was hard bestead to keep from going in! And there was the open lot sacred to the circus; the ploughed ring in the middle looked as if it might have been turned up yesterday. A little farther on, the brick sidewalk curved around the big-bellied chestnut, whose burrs were always "rocked" down before the nuts within had a chance to ripen; he stopped and touched the rough bark with his hand, prolonging the delicious sensation of home-coming. But at the front gate his heart began to beat painfully. The old garden, sombre and silent under a starlit sky, was full of shadowy figures that seemed stealing forth to meet him. Foremost among them, the majestic soldierly form in gray uniform, with the beautiful grave face of his fa —

Ah! he had no right here! That father was his no longer! He had been robbed of kindred, name, and home. Why had he come here! He had walked up the graveled way to the house, and set one foot on the lower step. Now he turned to flee. "I cannot, I dare not enter the old house to whose shelter I have no right," he thought despairingly.

"Roy! Are you there? *Roy!*" The door was flung wide open, and Mrs. Blackmore stood on the threshold, the hall-light illuminating her crown of silvery hair. "No, Jessie," to some one within. "No, I am *not* mistaken! I heard his step! I would know it among a thousand! I know he is here. Or he is dead and his spirit has come to warn me. My Roy! My boy!"

The sob in the dear voice was too much. He rushed up the steps and clasped her in his arms, shouting aloud in the excess of his relief.

There was a tremendous clatter of voices and of flying feet about the old halls and on the old stairways; a chorus of surprised and joyous greetings, and a confused tumultuous presentation of very young gentlemen in kilts and very young ladies in bibs, and of unknown brothers-in-law. For the annual celebration of Mrs. Blackmore's birthday had brought together all her daughters, with their husbands and their children. Roy found himself handed about as the crowning glory of the occasion. After the stress and strain of the past few days, the gates of paradise had suddenly opened to him!

But later in the evening Mrs. Blackmore took him into the old boudoir and closed the door. "Roy," she said, laying her hands on his shoulders and looking anxiously into his face, "what have they been doing to you out there? What has happened? What trouble or suffering or illness have you been concealing from me?"

"Aunt Amanda," — he overlaid her hands with his and returned her troubled look with a searching gaze, — "did my fa — did General Hilliard leave any papers or messages for me? Or is there anything you know concerning me which I have never heard?"

She gave a slight start, but replied promptly: "Yes, Roy. I have some papers in my possession. But your father wished you to see them only under certain conditions."

"If those conditions refer to my knowledge of

his adoption of me, I think I may claim them now," he said, steadying his voice.

She drew his head down and kissed him, asking no questions. Then turning to a small cabinet, she unlocked a drawer and took out a bulky envelope, and placed it in his hand. "I will come to you when you have read it," she said; and she left the room.

He seated himself in the very chair which Leroy Hilliard had occupied that night when little Francis, pattering over the floor, had crept to his elbow to ask, "Is *you* my fazzer — now?" He looked up at the portrait of the red-lipped lady whom as a child he had believed to be his mother. He smiled; by her costume, she must have flourished at least a century ago!

The envelope he held in his hand was unsealed. It was addressed "*To Leroy Hilliard, Junior.*" And across the top, in the bold handwriting of General Hilliard, he read, "*For my son.*"

The yellowed pages which he unfolded contained a brief account of the writer's earlier life, his marriage with Miss Armstead, and their separation. The young man could read into this account much which the writer had left unsaid. A minute relation followed of Francis Deerford's sudden and almost mysterious appearance with the child — himself. As he read on, he seemed to remember it all — the wild-eyed madman struggling in the soldier's muscular grasp, the travel-stained child playing with the tasseled sword, the grave-faced doctor bending over him!

The conversation between Colonel Hilliard and Dr. Greaves, the physician, — recorded with old-fashioned fidelity, — came in the nature of a revelation to the second Hilliard, as it had come to the first, explaining what had hitherto seemed so inexplicable. "The birth-mark or scar across the boy's left cheek remains unaccounted for," Colonel Hilliard wrote. The reader supplied even this link in the strange chain.

With the decision of the writer to keep the child, for the time at least, the story, written in camp, closed. A letter in the same envelope, dated nearly four years later, was addressed to young Roy personally. In this Colonel, now become General Hilliard, stated that, sorely against his own inclination, he had made a persistent effort to discover the whereabouts of Mr. and Mrs. Deerford. He had only been able to learn from friends in Louisiana that they had sold Eastwood just before the beginning of the war, and removed to Kentucky. They added that the family was understood to have gone abroad since, for an indefinite stay. He therefore felt justified in concluding that they desired to leave the child permanently in his hands. He had taken the necessary steps for a legal adoption, and the name the child bore was now his by right. A will, of which his sister, Mrs. Blackmore, possessed a copy, secured to this son of his adoption the property belonging to his name and station.

He commended to his son, as he grew to manhood, in the event of his own death, the care of his, the general's, young wife, and of the child whose birth was then hourly expected.

"You have become very dear to me, my son," he concluded, in a burst of affection. "I cannot believe that you could be more to me were you my own in nature as you are in love. I trust that your eyes may never fall upon the lines which I am writing — at midnight in the solitude of my tent, and with the lights of the enemy's camp-fires gleaming in the distant darkness. But if the time should come when you must know what you will now have learned, you will pardon me if the course I have taken shall have proved to be a mistaken one; and you will remember — whatever may chance, whatever love or fortune or happiness may come to you from your natural protectors — that I am — I say it jealously, I confess — your father,

LEROY HILLIARD."

The young man had hardly read the last words through a blur of downfalling tears, when Mrs. Blackmore's arms were around his neck. "Did — do you know, Aunt Amanda?" he faltered.

"Why, yes, dear! My brother never kept anything from me in his life. I knew from the beginning. But no one else except dear old Doctor Greaves ever knew. We were wrong, perhaps, in not making more strenuous effort to find your people; for, however Mr. Deerford felt, your mother must have grieved over parting from you. If she is living, she must still be grieving for you."

"Mrs. Deerford is living. I have seen her" —

"Ah! I feared it! She will take you from me, Roy!" Mrs. Blackmore clasped him in her arms as if he had been still the baby boy she had tended.

He smiled bitterly. "You will judge how much she wishes to take me into her life when I tell you of our meeting," he said. "But my fa — but General Hilliard's wife?"

"Roy! never dare to speak of your father as General Hilliard again! His poor little wife died less than twenty-four hours after he was buried. The shock killed her. Her still-born infant was buried on her breast. I had one letter from her sister who was with her at the time, giving me the sad details. But she had long been gone when I visited the spot after the war was over. And I have never heard of or from her since. You were with me on that sad journey, Roy. But tell me" —

"About Mrs. Deerford. It is not a pleasant story, Aunt Amanda." He slid into his familiar place on the rug at her feet and laid his arms on her lap. The gray dawn was breaking before he finished speaking. "And so I came home," he concluded, looking up into the sweet kind face.

"Of course," she said cheerily, "where else? No," she mused, with a long sigh of relief, "no, they can never take you away from me now, my son, my boy!"

He went to bed in a state of complete and

happy exhaustion, and slept profoundly for many
hours. He found her sitting by his bedside when
he awoke. "I wanted to say to you, first of all,
Roy," she began at once when he opened his eyes
and looked about, but half remembering where he
was. "I wanted to say, that a man who has loved
two women — his mother and another — cannot be
wholly bad."

In a subsequent conversation — they naturally
had many in the attempt to unravel the tangled
skein — Mrs. Blackmore, referring to his astonishing likeness to Leroy Hilliard and to the physician's explanation of the physiological fact, said:
"These are subtle questions, too subtle for an old
woman like myself to solve — into whose education
the problems of heredity and surroundings did not
enter. But I know something about maternity,
and this is the way I have reasoned out certain
things: My poor brother's influence upon Lilla's
life was powerful enough, as Doctor Greaves observed, and as we bear witness, to mould the outward features of yourself, her first-born child.
At the same time, from all that you have learned
from her own lips, and from Mr. Ralston, she
must have been very happy during those first
years of her married life with Francis Deerford,
and especially during the time when prenatal in-
fluences were shaping your spiritual nature. In
consequence of this, you were born with a lovely
and harmonious disposition " —

"Oh," he protested, flushing crimson, "you

do not know how unworthy I am of such praise. But if there is any good in me at all, it is because of the tender training and unfailing love with which I have been surrounded since my own father and mother cast me out!'"

"Your environment has had something to do with it; yes, I admit that. But not overmuch. On the other hand, it would seem that the months before poor Allan came into the world were filled with unrest and misery for his mother; it was a time when all that was worst in her nature was aroused; when she began to hate you—really, I do not blame her much, Roy!—as the cause of her suffering; when the doubt and suspicion of her husband drove her to a madness which revenged itself in cruelty upon you. Is it any wonder that Allan should be just what he is! It is in this way that monsters are made."

"What a wise old philosopher you are, Aunt Amanda," laughed Hilliard.

It was a pleasant thing to him to hear his own laugh resounding once more through the old house. His naturally robust and buoyant nature had reasserted itself after a season of apathy during which even the thought of his approaching meeting with Helen could hardly rouse him.

"It all seems like a dream," he remarked, walking about the garden after Mrs. Blackmore, who had entered upon the serious business of transplanting violets, training rose-vines, and poking seeds into fat flower-beds, "everything that has passed since I left this blessed old Garden of Eden four years ago!"

"Not everything," objected Mrs. Blackmore, shaking her pretty white head. "Not David French. How I love that dear little David! Not Red Parsons, nor Abner, nor Amen! Not Billy Crouch, nor Lorena! Not Helen" —

"Oh, no, not Helen," he interjected fervently.

"Above all, not Margaret Ransome! I would not have Margaret Ransome a dream for the world. How I long to see her!"

"Well, you shall see her, and all of them. For you are going back with Helen and me, you know. And we will be in time to see the blue-bonnets bloom on Mesquit Creek."

They were now alone in the old house — the "girls" with their husbands, and the regiments of white-capped nurses and children, having all returned to their respective homes. He had Mrs. Blackmore to himself; he followed her about from morning to night, as he had been used to when a boy, pouring into her never-wearying ears Helen's praises, Helen's beauty, Helen's goodness, his love for Helen, his dreams of a future with Helen!

He was in no wise surprised or disappointed that his note to Helen from St. Denis had remained unanswered. "It means only that she respects her mother's wishes. But even her mother cannot keep us apart. She is looking for me. She will come home with me. I read *that* in her beautiful eyes, at Eastwood! Oh, I understand!" he said to himself rapturously.

The day set for his departure came quickly enough. The arrangements for his journey were all made, and he sat, a little before noon, in the library with Mrs. Blackmore.

> " When from my window-pane
>   I gaze on night again,
> I still am lonely, my love, mine only,"

he sang softly and idly.

Old Robert entered, bringing the mail, and handed him a letter post-marked "Crouch's Well." It was from Amos Bagley. He read it aloud.

"Why the dickens don't you come home?" Amos began without ceremony. "I *ought* to tell you that your place is going to rack and ruin, for that might fetch you. But to tell the truth, it goes mighty well without you. First, because of old Manuel, who has got more horse-sense than any interloper I ever saw [*interloper*, in the vernacular of Crouch's, meant everybody not American!]. And second, because the doublets are running things. It's nip and tuck betwixt 'em to see which will do the most. One day it's Red with his troop of boys, clearing up your west field. Next day it's Green and his platoon of girls, planting your east field. The neighborhood, generally, *bets on the girls*.

"Crouch's has got back into harness. No Deerford that ever lived will ever be able to pull it out of traces again — not until all this generation is dead, anyhow. (You ought to heard little David preach the Sunday after you left. He give us h—ll.) Roper's brother has got back. It seems he mighty nigh had Deerford by the scruff of his neck, but Deerford give him the slip and got off to Australia, or somewhere. The boys run Roper's brother about it a good deal, but he keeps his mouth tight shut.

"Billy sets on the fence and chaws the air, as usual, about the president and the post-office. Margaret Ransome is prettier than ever.

Amos.

"P. S. I forgot to tell you that your water-tank is all O K again. Croft and the boys fixed it up again. There was a barbycue there, and everybody made speeches, from Uncle Joe Wyatt down to your humble servant.

"N. B. Why in thunderation don't you come home?"

Hilliard thoughts leaped westward. "You ought to see the blue-bonnets around that water-tank, Aunt Amanda!" he said. "And the wild verbena, and the cold-lilies, and the standing cypress, red as fire, and the yellow tendrils of the love-vine on the shinn-oak! You ought to see that bit of prairie of mine in the spring! It is like Jacob's coat of many colors. It would make you open your eyes. You've got to see it this spring — with Helen and me."

Dan Roper kept his mouth tight shut at Crouch's as to his recent pursuit of Deerford and its failure. But he lost no time, after his arrival in the Settlement, in seeking the Reverend David French. He found him stopping over Sunday at Hilliard's place. "I thought I'd come to you, parson," he said, concluding a concise but clear account of his meeting and parting with Hilliard, and the circumstances attending Deerford's flight; until the moment he had lost sight of the Brenda dropping down the river. "I don't know where Roy Hilliard's at. He said he was going over to Carolina to see his folks. But wherever he is, he's in a peck of trouble. And I'm pretty sure that girl has got something to do with it."

French glanced at the marriage-notice in the paper Roper had given him, and read the half column under the heading, "A Romantic Marriage," which described the early morning ceremony at the hotel, and dilated on the extraordinary beauty of both bride and groom. An extended account of the well-known families, Deerford and Wingate, was given. "Mr. and Mrs. Allan Deerford," the reporter added gracefully, "set sail, a few moments after launching on the sea of matrimony, for Europe in the steamship Brenda. May both voyages prove successful!"

French laid down the paper, and looked over at Roper, coloring a little. "Mr. Roper," he said, "can — can you lend me enough money to take me there and back?"

"I brought it on purpose." Roper dived promptly down into his trousers pocket and brought up a roll of bills. "I knew you'd go,

and I never heard of a preacher having any money.
You can catch to-day's stage from Skipton, if
you 'll hurry."

When they rounded the corner of Mrs. Ransome's field on their way over, French caught a
glimpse of Margaret standing on the gallery, slim
and graceful against a background of vines. She
saw him and waved her hand. He had a momentary impulse to stop and tell her. "But no," he
thought. "She will suffer — for him — soon
enough!"

When Robert ushered him, several days later,
into the library where Mrs. Blackmore and Hilliard were sitting, he was surprised and delighted
by the open joyousness in the latter's face. Hilliard still held in his hand Amos Bagley's letter,
which he had just finished reading. "Why,
David!" he shouted. "This is really too good to
be true! Aunt Amanda, here he is! The bless-
edest mortal alive! Have you dropped from the
skies, man!"

"I need not have come," thought David, leaning
back in his chair, with a sigh of relief. "He
could not have loved her after all! How good it
is to see him like this!"

Mrs. Blackmore had bustled away to order
breakfast for this welcome guest.

"You arrive just in time, David," cried Hilliard exuberantly. "Like a *Deus ex machina*. I
am leaving to-night for Kentucky to see Helen.
I shall take you with me."

"To see " — French gasped for breath.

"Helen. My bride to be. I expect to bring her away with me, David. You shall tie the knot, old fellow. To think of your happening along like this! How came you here, anyhow, parson? Oh, don't tell me. I look upon your coming as a special dispensation of providence in favor of Helen and me. We will all go back to Crouch's together — for Aunt Amanda is going, too — and we shall reach Mesquit Creek in time to see the blue-bonnets in blossom, eh, David?"

The boyish gayety, the open, unaffected, confident joyousness of the man almost stunned David. He had to moisten his dry lips with his tongue before he could speak.

"Roy," he began, "Roy, you do not know " —

"Know what? David! you are in trouble! What a selfish brute I am not to have noticed it. What is it? Has anything happened to Margaret Ransome?"

"No, no. Listen, Hilliard. I beseech you to prepare yourself for ill news. The morning Deerford sailed for England he married — Miss Wingate."

"That is not true," said Hilliard, with unexpected calm. "If any one but you had said it, David, I would cram the lie down his throat."

"It *is* true, Roy. Dan Roper witnessed the ceremony, and he saw the bride and groom, with Mrs. Wingate, go aboard the Brenda."

"Oh! *Roper!* " laughed Hilliard. "Roper

does not know Miss Wingate. He told me himself that he had never seen her. He means no harm. He is simply mistaken, that is all. As for Deerford, I am not surprised at anything he — The story is too absurd, David! Why, I *know* Helen."

David groaned. He felt like a bungler who had undertaken to put a pin through a butterfly, and only succeeded in jabbing the point in a little way. He took the newspaper from his pocket and handed it to his friend, pointing without another word to the marked notice of the marriage.

A frightful pallor overspread Hilliard's face as he read; his head dropped to his breast; his nerveless hands fell on the table before him. David got up and laid a hand silently on his shoulder.

"Oh, yes," Hilliard said, with sullen apathy, as if in answer to some spoken word. "Oh, yes. I know that you, too, have suffered. You know what it is to love a woman who does not return your love. But at least you have not been duped and betrayed! At least Margaret Ransome is incapable of treachery!"

"I will not weary you with words now," French said gently. "This is indeed a hard blow. But you will not succumb. My very soul aches for you, but I know you well enough " —

"You do not know me at all, Mr. French," exclaimed Hilliard, jumping to his feet, and speaking in a loud, harsh voice. "You do not even know who I am! Shall I tell you? It will be only one humiliation the more. Only one more drop of poison added to the deadly draught I have drained since I saw you last! I am own brother to Allan Deerford — that liar, gambler, murderer — and husband of my promised wife! No, I am not mad," he continued, again answering French's unspoken thought. "I wish I was! I am sane — sound in mind and body — and a Deerford!" He laughed mirthlessly, striding furiously about the room. Then, pausing, he faced the astounded French and related once more the story of his life, as he now knew it, with all its hideous and painful details. The words burst like a raging stream from his lips. When he came to his interview with Helen Wingate at Eastwood — oh, the joy of it! the gladness and glory of it! — he faltered; but his voice gathered strength and bitterness again, as he went on to describe the scene in the library at Eastwood, with the woman who called herself his mother — *his mother!* — and the night-ride with Deerford to the railway station. "I dragged him out of the clutches of justice. May the devil himself repay me for it! May God blast Allan Deerford's soul forever!"

"Stop!" said the minister sternly, seizing his wrist. "You shall not blaspheme. You shall not take the name of God upon your lips in such a fashion!"

"And why not? Has He been so tender with me that I should be sparing of his name! Has He not ground me to dust beneath his feet! Has

He not robbed me of father, mother, brother, sister, wife! Has He not even branded me with the mark of Cain, while Cain, the beloved murderer, dwells abroad in pleasant places?" He drew his finger savagely along the scarlet birth-mark on his cheek. "What would you do with such a God, you?"

David's pity and tenderness were too great for words. He realized the utter uselessness of any present attempt at remonstrance or consolation; the creature before him was too mortally stricken. But for his own soul's sake, he murmured: —

"*Though He slay me, yet will I trust in Him.*"

"Roy!" Mrs. Blackmore's voice sounded in the hall. She entered, fluttering with pleasant excitement over Mr. French's unexpected arrival. "The breakfast will soon be ready."

Hilliard led her to a seat and stood behind her. "David, will you excuse me for a few moments?" he asked. He stooped and kissed Mrs. Blackmore's forehead. "She is the dearest woman in the world — this mother of mine!" he cried playfully. "I leave her in your care when — while I am gone, David!"

He walked rapidly across the hall, and along the great double parlors, and entered the little morning-room beyond.

When he had closed the door, he looked around. But he saw nothing except the thing he sought — a loaded pistol lying upon the mantel. He seized it and instantly placed the muzzle against his tem-

ple, his finger on the trigger. A few seconds
only passed while the conflict raged in his soul;
they seemed like centuries! — light and darkness,
evil and good, death and life, courage and despair,
alternate advance and repulse, struggle, skirmish,
battle-royal! Finally, his own voice coming from
somewhere far away: "*Though — He — slay —
me — yet — will — I — trust — in — Him!*"

He laid the pistol on the table. The fireless
room was cold, but heavy drops of sweat stood on
his forehead.

"Roy!" The knob turned, and David on the
outside threw himself violently against the door.
Hilliard unlocked and opened it. "You were
right, my friend, my brother," he said humbly.
"I *was* about to play the coward — and a small,
mean coward at that!"

"Forgive me, Roy. I feared — I ran after
you," panted the clergyman, still trembling with
apprehension.

"And you prayed while you ran, David, eh?
Well, your prayers saved me. Oh, you need not
lay hands on the pistol! The temptation has been
a sore one, but it is overpast, and now, by God's
help, I mean to live out my days as becomes a
man."

"Thank God!" cried French solemnly.

"You have come to me in the time of my great-
est need, David French. May Heaven help me
to prove myself hereafter worthy of your saving
hand!"

That night they lingered until long after midnight over the cheerful fire in the library talking together, or thinking in unison. When they separated for the night, Hilliard repeated: "Yes, we will go back together — you, and Aunt Amanda, and I — to Mesquit Creek. In time to see the blue-bonnets bloom."

And only David could have detected the sob in his throat.

The Brenda, about the time that David French greeted Hilliard in Mrs. Blackmore's library, was nearing her journey's end. The weather, after a day or two of storm, was perfect. The gently rolling billows under the keel of the tranquil ship were as blue as the expanse of sky above, broken only by the white fluttering of sea-gulls. A flood of cold sunshine brightened the deck where Helen Deerford reclined in her steamer-chair. Deerford sat beside her. Mrs. Wingate had retired to her stateroom for her noonday rest.

There had been a long silence between the husband and wife; indeed, they talked but little at any time. Allan had been devoted and tender to a degree which Helen could hardly have believed possible; she felt soothed and grateful for his quiet and unobtrusive attention, but each seemed to dwell, for the moment at least, in a world apart from the other.

"That is a pretty ring, Helen," he said idly. He was looking at her slim right hand which rested on her knee; he touched the pearl with the tip of his finger as he spoke. "Where did you get it?"

It was the ring Hilliard had slipped on her left hand in the summer-house at Eastwood. "Since Leroy Hilliard is my brother," she had said to herself, transferring it to her right hand, "I may keep it."

"Leroy Hilliard gave it to me," she replied, looking bravely into his eyes, her cheek flushing imperceptibly. "Do you mind my wearing it?"

"Did he? Oh, no. Keep it, my dear." He looked out over the wide glassy sea, with his elbow on his knee and his chin propped upon his palm. "Helen, there is something I want to tell you," he began slowly. She made a movement of distress. "It is something which I have never known myself until lately. Leroy Hilliard is my brother."

"Your"—

"My own brother. You may well look startled, dear. When I think of what I might have been saved if I had only known it!"

He told her as much of Hilliard's story — and in his own way — as he cared for her to know. It had made a profound impression upon him — how lasting he could not himself conjecture. He cynically doubted its long duration. But he was still under the influence of the spell which the hitherto unknown elder brother had thrown over him, and his voice trembled with emotion as he repeated, "What might I not have been saved had I known! What might *he* not have been saved!"

He made no reference to his own career in Crouch's Settlement, but Helen could not avoid the suspicion that his flight had something to do with some misdemeanor there. This, however, was an afterthought. At the moment, a sense of suffocation oppressed her. She heard herself saying a word or two in answer to her husband's revelation. They must have been kind and gentle words, for he took her hand and kissed it gratefully.

He left her at a summons from Mrs. Wingate. She sat up and stared after his retreating form until it disappeared from her view. Then she drew Hilliard's pearl from her finger. "Since he is not my brother," she whispered with dry lips, "I may not keep it." She leaned over the railing and dropped it into the sea. It showed for a second, a white speck in the air, then the blue waters closed over it.